Study Guide to Accompany

Introduction to Business Statistics

A COMPUTER INTEGRATED, DATA ANALYSIS APPROACH

FOURTH EDITION

Alan H. Kvanli
C. Stephen Guynes
Robert J. Pavur
UNIVERSITY OF NORTH TEXAS

Prepared by
Wilke D. English
UNIVERSITY OF MARY HARDIN-BAYLOR

West Publishing Company   MINNEAPOLIS/ST. PAUL   ■   NEW YORK   ■   LOS ANGELES   ■   SAN FRANCISCO

WEST'S COMMITMENT TO THE ENVIRONMENT

In 1906, West Publishing Company began recycling materials left over from the production of books. This began a tradition of efficient and responsible use of resources. Today, up to 95% of our legal books and 70% of our college texts and school texts are printed on recycled, acid-free stock. West also recycles nearly 22 million pounds of scrap paper annually—the equivalent of 181,717 trees. Since the 1960s, West has devised ways to capture and recycle waste inks, solvents, oils, and vapors created in the printing process. We also recycle plastics of all kinds, wood, glass, corrugated cardboard, and batteries, and have eliminated the use of Styrofoam book packaging. We at West are proud of the longevity and the scope of our commitment to the environment.

Production, Prepress, Printing and Binding by West Publishing Company.

COPYRIGHT © 1995 by   WEST PUBLISHING CO.
                     610 Opperman Drive
                     P.O. Box 64526
                     St. Paul, MN 55164–0526

All rights reserved
Printed in the United States of America
02 01 00 99 98 97 96 95   8 7 6 5 4 3 2 1 0

ISBN 0–314–05405–7

Table of Contents

Chapter 1	A First Look at Statistics and Data Collection	1
Chapter 2	Data Presentation Using Descriptive Graphs	9
Chapter 3	Data Summary Using Descriptive Measures	19
Chapter 4	Probability Concepts	33
Chapter 5	Discrete Probability Distributions	45
Chapter 6	Continuous Probability Distributions	55
Chapter 7	Statistical Inference and Sampling	75
Chapter 8	Hypothesis Testing for Population Mean and Variance	97
Chapter 9	Inference Procedures for Two Populations	115
Chapter 10	Estimation and Testing for Population Proportions	129
Chapter 11	Analysis of Variance	145
Chapter 12	Quality Improvement	165
Chapter 13	Applications of the Chi-Square Statistic	179
Chapter 14	Correlation and Simple Linear Regression	193
Chapter 15	Multiple Linear Regression	215
Chapter 16	Time Series Analysis and Index Numbers	245
Chapter 17	Quantitative Business Forecasting	271
Chapter 18	Decision Making Under Uncertainty	297
Chapter 19	Nonparametric Statistics	317

UNIVERSITY OF MARY HARDIN-BAYLOR

To the Student,

This book was written for you...to help you in your study of statistics.

It was written in close collaboration with Dr. Kvanli, the principal author of the main text. The book is designed to guide your study efforts in the text, and to provide you with additional practice opportunities.

Like many study guides, the page format allows you to cover the answer while making an 'unaided' attempt to work the problem. It is recommended that you first attempt the problems with the answers covered, using the answers as a check rather than a crutch.

If you have questions, suggestions, comments or corrections, please do not hesitate to drop me a line!

Best Wishes!

Wilke English
Wilke English
Professor of Marketing and Business Statistics
The University of Mary Hardin-Baylor
Belton, Texas 76513

CHAPTER 1

A First Look at Statistics and Data Collection

CHAPTER OBJECTIVES

The purpose of this chapter is to establish the frame of reference for the study of statistics. It introduces key terms as well as types of data and methods of data collection. By the end of the chapter you should be able to answer the following questions:

1. What is "statistics" and why is the study of statistics important to the business manager?

2. What is descriptive statistics? What is inferential statistics?

3. What is a census? A population? A sample?

4. What are the types of data? (discrete/continuous)

5. What are the strengths of data? (nominal, ordinal, interval, ratio)

6. What distinquishes qualitative data from quantitative data?

7. When should one use primary versus secondary data?

8. When should one use random vs. convenience samples?

9. What should one keep in mind when designing and coding a questionnaire?

2

§ 1.0

What Is This Thing Called Statistics?

1. The typical evening news program will expose a body to an amazing barrage of statistics. Give an example of statistics you might hear in the area of sports? economics? weather? government?

---

§ 1.1

size, complexity of operation

Most definitely TRUE! If only to prevent others from misleading you.

Uses of Statistics in Business

1. The modern business faces a greater degree of uncertainty as a result of increases in _____ and _____.

2. Even if you are not a professional statistician, even if you never personally perform statistical analyses, you will still be exposed to statistics as a user and consumer of statistical analysis. True/False

---

§ 1.2

collecting, describing, analyzing, interpreting

descriptive

inferential

population

Some Basic Definitions

1. Statistics is the science of _____, _____, _____, and _____ numerical data.

2. When statistics are collected which simply describe the data set under consideration, but do not attempt to make inferences or generalizations to a larger realm, this is called _____ statistics.

3. When statistical data is used to make inferences or generalizations regarding a larger group, this is called _____ statistics.

4. This larger group (which represents the entire set of objects which are of interest) is referred to as the _____.

5. That portion of the population selected for study is referred to as the _____.	sample
6. When we use a relatively small sample to make inferences about a much larger population, we are operating under the assumption that our sample is _____ of the population.	representative
7. When a sample is drawn so that each available elementary unit of the population (i.e., each person in the population) has the same probability (chance) of being selected, this is a _____ _____ sample.	simple random sample
8. The analysis and manipulation of statistical data has become much easier, and hence much more popular because of the tremendous developments that have been made in electronic computers. Numerous statistical programs have been written to perform various types of analysis. For what do these popular software acronyms stand? SAS? SPSS? SASS?	SAS: Statistical Analysis System SPSS: Statistical Package for the Social Sciences SASS: what you gave your Mom when you were in high school

Types of Numerical Data

Types of Numerical Data	§ 1.3
1. A data set in which there are gaps between values is called _____ data.	discrete
2. A data set in which the numbers can take upon any possible value, with no gaps between numbers is called _____ data.	continuous
3. The counting integers would be an example of (discrete/continuous) data.	discrete
4. Time would represent (discrete/continuous) data.	continuous
5. Yet as reported on the radio, time is (discrete/continuous) data.	discrete 6:14 AM, not 6:14.38592436713429, etc.

4

§ 1.4	Level of Measurement for Numerical Data
nominal, ordinal interval, ratio	1. What are the four types of numerical data?
nominal	2. The weakest form of data is _____ data.
nominal	3. In _____ data, the values are really not numbers at all, but are simply labels, used to designate different categories or classifications.
ordinal	4. In _____ data, the values can be ranked, but we do not know the magnitude of the difference between the various ranks.
interval	5. A data set which has constant differences between the values, but does not have a true zero point is called _____ data.
fixed zero point	6. In order to form meaningful ratios you need a _____ _____ _____.
interval stupid!	7. Most statistical routines require that the data be at least _____ data. Failure to insist upon data of the proper level can result in a _____ mistake, such as trying to determine the average for a set of football jerseys.
Fahrenheit	8. The example (the only true example) which ever seems to be provided for interval data is the _____ temperature scale.
ordinal	9. Frequently, ranking scales (i.e., give a 1 to your first preference, a 2 to your second preference, a 3 to your third preference) are treated as interval data. This is done by assuming that there is the same difference between each value in the ranking. Although this assumption is made quite often in business research, it is questionable. Technically a ranking scale is _____ data.
§ 1.5	Sources of Data

1. Primary data is data that involves simple counting numbers (1, 2, 3) the kind that are used in the elementary or primary grades. True or False.

False

2. Secondary data is data that involves more complex numbers (2.34, $\pi = 3.14$, etc.), the kind that are used in high schools or secondary schools. True or False.

False

3. A set of data (i.e., survey results) that you have personally collected is called a set of _____ data.

primary

4. A set of data (i.e., survey results) that was previously collected by someone else is called a set of _____ data.

secondary

5. Which is the correct phrasing of the following sentence?
Secondary data *is* usually cheaper than primary data.
Secondary data *are* usually cheaper than primary data.
(PS For the above, true or false?)

Correct sentence is "data are". The word 'data' is a plural. The singular of data is datum. Sounds awkward, but that's life. True

6. The U.S. government is an excellent source of many sources of secondary data such as the *Statistical Abstract of the United States* and the *Census of the Population*. True or False.

very true

7. The best way to make use of the vast amount of secondary data is to become personally knowledgeable by spending hour upon hour in the library. True or False.

False. Make friends with the librarians and tell them what you want. This is an area where you need a real pro.

8. A convenience sample is a sample of customers taken in front of a convenience store (7-11, Circle K, etc.) True or False.

False

9. You can get a good 'random' sample by going to a big shopping mall and selecting customers 'at random'. True or False.

False

10. To have a true 'random' sample, every available member of the population must have a _____ probability of selection.

known

11. In a simple random sample, each available member of the

6

known	population is assumed to have an _____ probability of selection.
True. For most consumer surveys it is hard to come up with a list which enumerates all of the persons in the population being sampled.	12. True or False: To truly select a random sample you need: a. a list which enumerates all of the units in the population b. a probability mechanism (such as a random number table) for selecting from that list
True, results from a truly random sample can be generalized; results from a convenience sample cannot.	13. A convenience sample is any sample which violates either of those two assumptions. Thus, from a truly technical standpoint, most surveys in business are not true random samples. True or False.
True	14. The main advantage of the random sample is that the results of that sampling effort can be statistically generalized to the population which comprised the sampling frame. True or False.
True	15. To draw names out of a hat could be an example of a probability mechanism if the names were well stirred. True or False.
True. Don't try to 'help' the table. Random number tables are carefully constructed to produce the proper proportions of high and low number...over time.	16. To use a Random Number Table, simply start anywhere in the table and pick numbers consecutively. Do not skip around and try to 'balance' your selection by deliberately picking some high numbers and some low numbers. Instead pick them consecutively and let the table take care of the randomness. True or False.
§ 1.6	Business Research Questions in Practice 1. The study of statistics is a study of numerical answers to questions. By answering questions numerically we can state results in a consistent, objective, reproducible manner. True or False.
True	
Select two groups, young and old and have them taste-test the various colas. (But also survey for other emotions and feelings regarding colas.)	2. 'Conventional Wisdom' says that Pepsi is 'supposed' to appeal to younger consumers, Coke is 'supposed' to appeal to older consumers. Suggest an experiment to statistically test this marketing hypothesis.

3. Some management consultants argue that incentive programs such as sales contests, actually hurt morale more than they improve sales performance. Suggest an experiment to statistically test this management hypothesis.	Survey employees before and after the contest...monitor them over an extended period.
4. Many credit cards will offer very low rates to attract customers. But are the new customers worth the loss of income which would have been received at the higher rate. Suggest an experiment to statistically test this financial hypothesis.	Use (at least) two mailings with one group getting the low rate, another group getting the regular rate. Monitor for profitability over an extended period.
5. Is the collection of income tax by the IRS worth the trouble it takes to perform the collection? Suggest an experiment to statistically test this accounting hypothesis.	Carefully survey a group of citizens for their 'total' cost of compliance.
6. Is electronic mail a good idea for employees? Do they actually save time and effort through the use of E-mail, or do they waste time 'flaming' anonymous messages through the system, reading screens of useless communication, and otherwise wasting valuable time? Suggest an experiment to statistically test this information systems hypothesis.	Probably the best approach would be to survey firms that have already installed E-mail systems...go to school on their experience.

Designing and Coding a Questionnaire

§ 1.7

1. Questionnaire design can be a critical area of survey research. Poorly written questions will produce bad data, no matter how carefully the statistical analysis is conducted. True or False.

True
GIGO: Garbage In-Garbage Out

2. The five steps of questionnaire design suggested by the text are:

1. decide what type of questions
2. write questions
3. decide quesionnaire length
4. pretest and revise
5. ensure good response rate

3. An open-ended question is a question that does not end with a questionmark, or any other kind of punctuation. True or False.

False

4. The biggest problem with closed-ended questions is that they can force respondents to choose from a set of responses, none of which really capture their true sentiments. True or False.

True

8

easy to code easy to statistically analyze	5. The biggest advantage of closed-ended questions is that they are _____ __ _____.
difficult, perhaps impossible, to code, thus cannot be statistically analyzed	6. The biggest disadvantage of open-ended questions is that they are _____ __ _____.
Likert	7. A question that features a five point scale ranging from Strongly Disagree to Strongly Agree is usually referred to as a _____ scale.
ordinal...non-metric data, tech. unsuited for most stat. analyses	8. Technically speaking, a Likert scale produces what kind of data?
True Serious researchers want to find what people are thinking and they are careful to write questions that do not sway the results.	9. When you see a 'leading' question (i.e., Do you agree with other intelligent Americans that somthing should be done to stop the wasteful practices of Congress that are bankrupting the country?), that is usually a good sign that the questionnaire is being used for political grandstanding and not serious research. True or False
False. The longer the questionnaire, the lower the response rate. Non-response bias is a major problem with survey research.	10. Questionnaire length is seldom of major importance. Once respondents have started to answer a questionnaire, they will almost always finish, no matter how long the questionnaire may be. True or False.
True	11. Most questionnaires start with non-threatening questions at the beginning and save questions relating to sensitive areas until the end. True or False.
False. No matter how many questionnaires you have written, you still need to pretest.	12. Good researchers who have written questions previously can skip the pretest stage. True or False.
convenience (Assuming that pretest group is roughly similar to final population under study.)	13. While the final questionnaire may be administered using a very careful designed and painstakingly executed <u>random</u> sample, the pretest often uses a _____ sample.
Pre: contact them before Post: follow-up cards and calls Pay: $ or gifts for participating Play: make it fun, short, easy Personal: send results, stress importance of survey	14. There are a number of things that researchers can do to increase the response rate, such as:

CHAPTER 2

Data Presentation Using Descriptive Graphs

CHAPTER OBJECTIVES

Graphical presentation has always been one of the best ways to transmit statistical information. A statistical graph allows you to summarize and describe a set of values from a sample or population. Because of the ease with which many microcomputers can create and print graphs this usage is bound to grow. Though often simple in appearance, pitfalls can await the unwary. By the end of the chapter you should be able to answer the following questions:

1. What is a frequency distribution, and how would you construct a frequency distribution from a set of data?

2. Define, and be able to construct (when appropriate) the following graphs:
   a. Histogram
   b. Frequency Polygon
   c. Ogive
   d. Bar Charts
   e. Pie Charts
   f. Stem-and-Leaf Diagrams

3. What are some of the ways in which a seemingly accurate graph can be drawn in a misleading and deceptive manner?

DESCRIPTIVE GRAPHS

§ 2.0

A Look Back/Introduction

True

1. A picture is worth a 1000 words. True or False

True...probably more so for numbers than words!

2. A graph is worth a 1000 numbers. True or False

False! Micro-computers make it easy to construct graphs, which increases our need to understand their construction and to recognize possibly misleading representations.

3. Because the popular personal computers can crunch numbers so easily, we do not need to worry about the topic of graphs any more...there is no need for graphing. True or False

---

§ 2.1

Frequency Distributions

1. To simply be presented with a data set of perhaps several hundred items is quite overwhelming. One way to get a "handle" on such a set of numbers is to break the numbers down into classes, and then count how many of the items fall into each class. This breakdown is referred to as a

frequency distribution

_____ _____ .

5 - 15

2. When breaking the data into classes, it is generally recommended to use between _____ and _____ classes. Actually there is a formula for computing the 'optimal' number of classes. Known as Sturges' Rule, the formula is: $(1 + 3.22(\log_{10} n))$ (n = the number of observations). Frankly, it is more trouble than it is worth. Because different possibilities can be tested so easily using a personal computer, it is easier to simply try different numbers of classes and class sizes to see which one looks best.

highest
lowest
number of classes

3. Once you have decided how many classes to have, the class width is simply the _____ value in the data, minus the _____ value in the data, divided by the _____ of _____ . Or, more simply, the range, divided by the number of classes. Usually an attempt is made to use "nice", -"round" numbers (5, 10, 50, 100)

4. You also might want to calculate the percentage of the total data set that falls within each class. This is referred to as the _____ _____.

relative frequency

5. The center of each class is the class _____.

midpoint

6. In choosing a class width, you should choose a "nice", "clean" number. That is, a round number with which it is easy to work. For example, what would be the class widths for these situations:
Highest = 358, Lowest = 134, Number of classes = 8
or
Highest = $62,000 Lowest = $3,500 Number of classes = 7

224/8 = 28.0, use 30

58,500/7 = 8357.1428
use 8000? Be careful about rounding down! You will run out of classes. I would go from 0-70,000 in units of 10,000.

7. A set of data which has been arranged in ascending (or descending) order is called an _____ _____. Data in its original, unsorted, and unaltered state is referred to as _____ data.

ordered array

raw

Sorting is another situation in which a computer can be very helpful. To sort a large number of items (i.e., several thousand) is no easy task. Actually, this difficulty of manipulation was one of the reasons for the development of frequency distributions. You did not have to handle all of the items individually, simply sort them into piles (classes), and then count how many were in each pile.

8. The class midpoint is often used as if it were the average of the items in that class. In that way, the class midpoint is used to _____ all of the values in the class.

represent

9. A data set will sometimes have a few values which are quite different from the bulk of the data (i.e., a small town where everyone makes under $20,000, and a millionaire moves there to retire). A value like this which is markedly different from the others is called an _____. These are often handled by using _____ _____ classes.

outliers
open ended classes

False. The descriptions and the midpoints will be different. 2.4

First sort the numbers. There is no 'right' or wrong' number of classes, but the following breakdown seems appropriate:

10-19: 12,15,18
20-29: 20,24,29
30-39: 31,32,35,37,38
40-49: 42,47,48,49
50-59: 52,55
or FD = 3,3,5,4,2

Let's use the same breakdown for the second set.

10-19: 11,13,14,16,18,19
20-29: 21,28,29
30-39: 36
40-49: 44,47
50-59: 51,54,55,56,57
or FD = 6,3,1,2,5

---

§ 2.2

frequency distribution shape

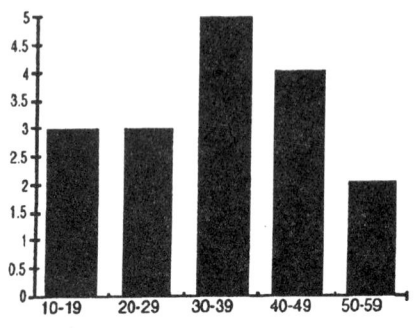

---

10. When constructing frequency distributions, discrete data is handled exactly like continuous data. True or False

11. Develop a frequency distribution for the following data set: 47, 35, 55, 15, 18, 49, 37, 24, 52, 20, 32, 48, 42, 31, 12, 29, 38.

(After you have constructed the frequency distribution, notice how much better "feel" you have for the data set. Just looking at the raw data, you probably had no feeling whatsoever about the data, but now you do. Speaking of how you feel, after you constructed the frequency distribution, did you feel better? I was afraid you would say that.)

For comparison, now try this data set: 36, 51, 19, 44, 21, 55, 18, 28, 16, 54, 14, 56, 11, 29, 57, 13, 47.

Like the first set, this set consists of 17 numbers, all falling between 10 and 60. At initial inspection, the two sets probably appeared to be essentially the same...but compare the frequency distributions. It can now be seen that the two data sets are dramatically different.

Histograms

1. A histogram is a graph of a _____ _____. It shows the _____ of the data.

2. Construct the histogram for the first set of data from problem 11, section 2.2.

ps. To a real purist...I cheated. A histogram should not have any gaps between the bars. Quite frankly, I tried graphing it both ways and I like it better with the gaps. Besides, both data sets featured discrete integers exclusively, so you could argue that the discrete format (with the gaps) is appropriate.

3. Construct the histogram for the second set of data from problem 11, section 2.2.

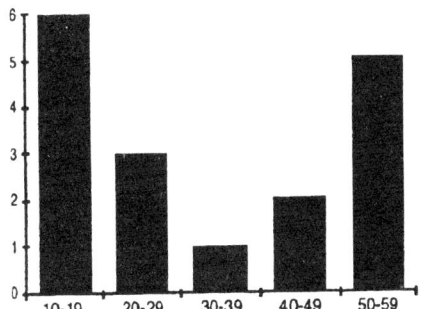

4. The height of each box in the histogram is representative of the _____ of that class.

5. For continuous data, the edges of the boxes should be _____. There should be a gap between the boxes if the data are _____.

6. Construct the relative frequencies histogram for the first set of data from problem 11, section 2.2.

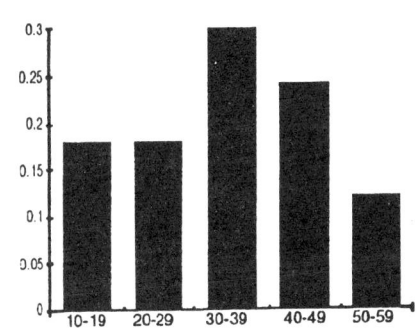

7. Construct the relative frequencies histogram for the second set of data from problem 11, section 2.2.

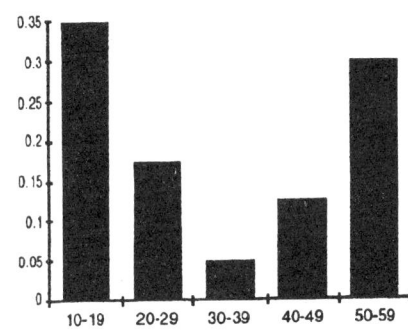

14

shape

Stem	Leaf (unit = 1)
1	1 3 4 6 8 9
2	1 8 9
3	6
4	4 7
5	1 4 5 6 7

§ 2.3

frequency polygon

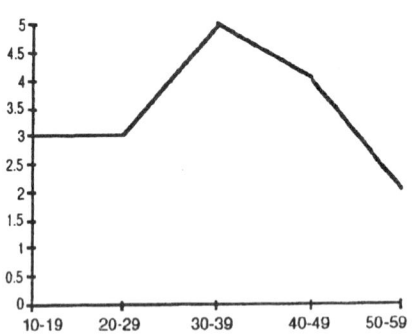

You may be tempted to draw it like this, but the freq. poly should start and end on the X axis.

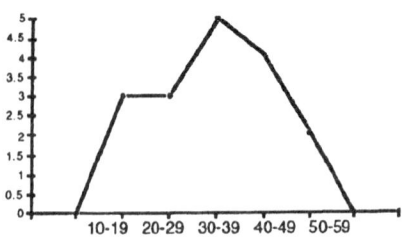

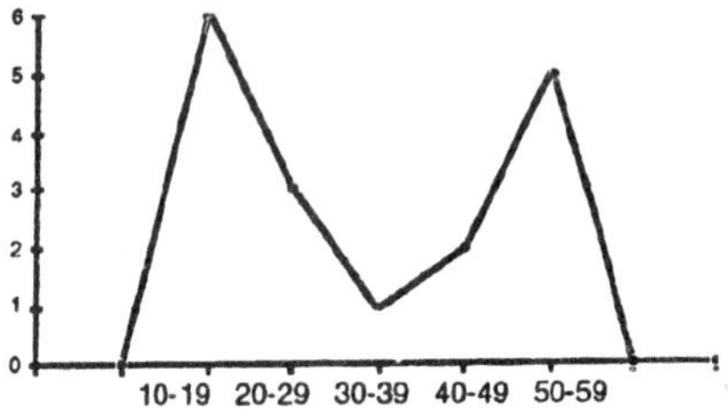

8. (As just seen), a histogram constructed from the relative frequencies will have the same _____ as a histogram constructed from the original frequency distribution.

9. Give the Stem-and-Leaf diagram for that second data set: 36, 51, 19, 44, 21, 55, 18, 28, 16, 54, 14, 56, 11, 29, 57, 13, 47.

Frequency Polygons

1. A line graph which connects the midpoints of each bar of the histogram is called a _____ _____.

2. Construct the frequency polygon for the first set of data from problem 11, section 2.2.

3. Construct the frequency polygon for the second set of data from problem 11. section 2.2.

* Interesting comparisons can sometimes be made by superimposing one graph over the other one, as shown at right.

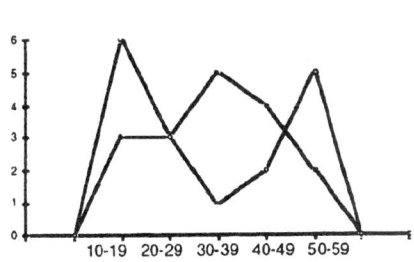

Cumulative Frequencies (Ogives)

§ 2.4

1. A line graph of the cumulative frequencies is called an _____.

ogive

2. The word "ogive" is pronounced which way:
   a. oh-give, short "i", give rhymes with live?
   b. oh-give, hard "g", rhymes with dive?
   c. oh-jive, "j" as in jive, rhymes with dive?

c. oh-jive

3. Construct an ogive for the first data set from problem 11, section 2.2.

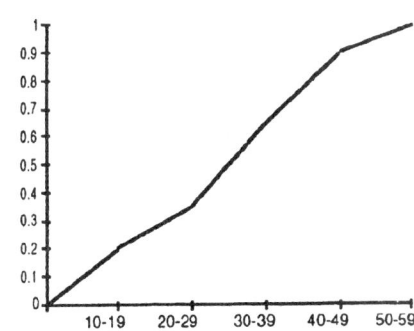

16

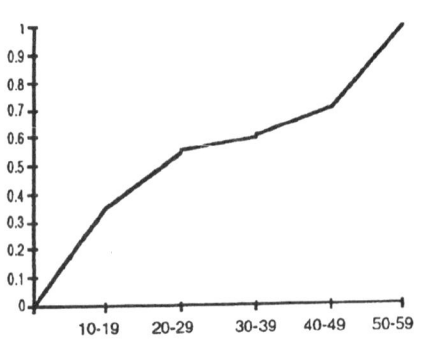

4. Construct an ogive for the second data set from problem 11, section 2.2.

100%

4. Percentagewise, an ogive always ends at _____ percent.

---

§ 2.5

nominal

True

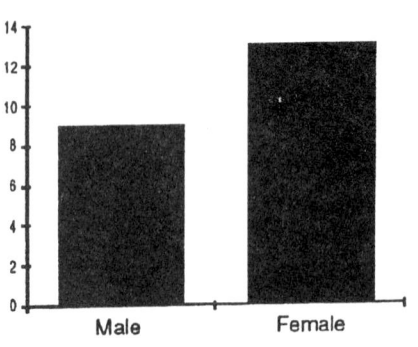

Bar Charts

1. A bar chart looks like a histogram, the difference is that bar charts are designed for use with a data set that is _____ on at least one axis.

2. Because a bar chart is concerned with nominal data, there should always be space between the bars. True or False

3. At a recent meeting there were 13 women and 9 men. Construct a bar chart for this situation.

Pie Charts

§ 2.6

1. A pie chart represents the total universe (100%) as a circle, or _____. The relative shares of the different components are indicated by the size of the respective pieces of the pie.

pie

2. A bar chart is used by problem drinkers to chart how many times they fall off the wagon. Likewise, a pie chart is used by problem eaters to check how often they go to the refrigerator for a piece of pie. True or False.

False on both counts.

3. Construct a pie chart for the data presented in problem three, section 2.6 (13 females, 9 males).

(for those doing this problem with pencils and protractors)
the males represent 9/22 = 40.909% = 41%
        41% of 360 degrees = 148 degrees
the females represent 13/22 = 59.09% = 59%
        59% of 360 degrees = 212 degrees

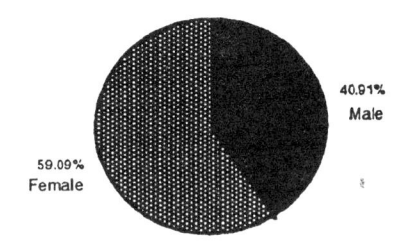

Deceptive Graphs in Statistics

§ 2.7

1. A graph is designed, not so much to convey the numerical data, but to convey a visual impression that summarizes the nature of the data. By drawing the graph in a different manner it is possible to change the visual impression while still presenting the same numbers. True or False

True! The visual impression can be changed without changing the numbers.

2. Using pictorial representations of three dimensional figures can be dangerous. While length may change proportionately, area (length x width) goes up by _____, and volume (length x width x depth) goes up by _____.

squares
cubes

3. Be suspicious of graphs without titles, scales that are not clearly labeled, or sources- not clearly identified. True or False

True! Always consider WHO is presenting the information, and WHY. This will give you a tip as to possible biases.

zero

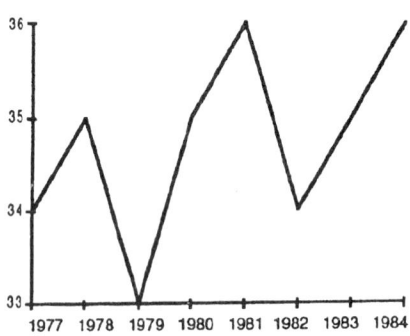

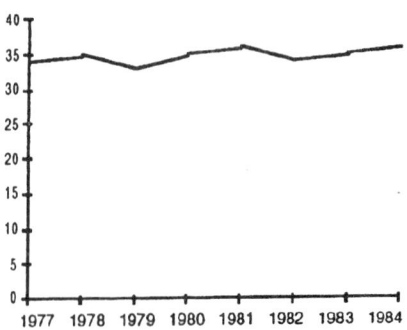

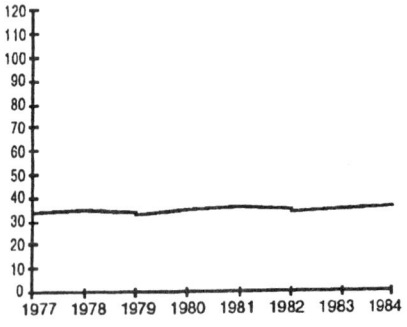

4. One way to convey a different visual impression while still presenting the same numbers is to make a break in the vertical axis so that the scale does not start at _____. This will tend to make fluctuations in the data look more significant.

Consider these numbers:
1977 34
1978 35
1979 33
1980 35
1981 36
1982 34
1983 35
1984 36

Look at the graphs at the left. Both graphs present exactly the same numbers, but if you were to simply glance at them, you might think that there were two different companies, one of them showing wild fluctuations, and the other showing great stability.

When you do not start the Y axis at zero, it is proper to at least alert the viewer by making a squiggle in the axis.
That was not done on these graphs in order to dramatize the effect of changing the axis...without warning!

5. Another way to convey a different visual impression is to change the scale of the axes. In this last graph, the same numbers have been made to look even more stable by changing the scale of the Y-axis.

CHAPTER 3

Data Summary Using Descriptive Measures

CHAPTER OBJECTIVES

The last chapter examined techniques for visually describing a set of data. The purpose of this chapter is to introduce techniques for mathematically describing a set of data. By the end of the chapter you should be able to define and use the following measures:

1. Measures of Central Tendency:
   Mean, Median, Mode, and Midrange.

2. Measures of Dispersion:
   Range, Average Deviation, Standard Deviation, Variance, and Coefficient of Variation.

3. Measures of Position:
   Percentiles, Quartiles, and Z scores.

4. Measures of Shape:
   Skewness and Kurtosis.

5. Techniques for handling frequency distributions (grouped data), and special coding techniques.

6. Construction of box plots.

DESCRIPTIVE MEASURES

§ 3.0 A Look Back/Introduction

1. The last chapter discussed the use of graphs to describe a set of data __visually__. This chapter discusses the use of certain summary statistics which can be used to describe a set of data __mathematically__.

2. A descriptive measure which is obtained from a sample of items from the population is called a sample __statistic__. If that same descriptive measure would have been obtained from the entire population, it would be called a population __parameter__.

§ 3.1 Various Types of Descriptive Measures

1. Measures of __central tendency__ answer the questions of, "where is the middle of the data?", and "what single value best summarizes the data set?"

2. Measures of __variation or dispersion__ answer the question of, "what is the spread or distribution of the data?".

3. Measures of __position__ answer the question of, "where does one value lie relative to other values?".

4. Measures of __shape__ answer the questions of, "is the data symmetric?", or is it normally distributed?".

§ 3.2 Measures of Central Tendency
§ 3.2-1 The Arithmetic Mean

1. What most folks call the average is technically referred to as the __arithmetic__ __mean__, or more simply as the __mean__.

2. If the mean is computed using all of the values in the population, it is called (X-bar, mu), and the formula divides the sum of the items divided by (n, N).	mu (μ) N
3. If the mean in question has been computed from a sample of values from the population, it is referred to as (x bar, mu), and the formula represents the sum of the items divided by (n, N).	X-bar ($\bar{x}$) n
4. For the first data set from problem 11, S 2.2, find the arithmetic mean. (To save you the trouble of going back, here are the numbers: 47, 35, 55, 15, 18, 49, 37, 24, 52, 20, 32, 48, 42, 31, 12, 29, 38.)	34.35
5. For the second data set (problem 11, S 2.2) find the arithmetic mean. (Once again: 36, 51, 19, 44, 21, 55, 18, 28, 16, 54, 14, 56, 11, 29, 57, 13, 47.)	33.47

<u>The Median</u>	§ 3.2-2
1. The median is the middle value of an _____ array of numbers.	ordered
2. An outlier will have less effect upon the median than upon the mean. True or False	True. With the median, each value has only one vote. Government statistics use the median almost exclusively.
3. Find the median for the first data set in problem 11, section 2.2.	35
4. Find the median for the second data set (#11 S 2.2)	29

<u>The Midrange</u>	§ 3.2-3
1. The midrange is simply the average of the two end values, the _____ and the _____.	smallest, largest (or minimum, maximum)

21

22

33.5

34.0

| | 2. Find the midrange for the first data set, problem 11, section 2.2. |
| | 3. Find the midrange for the second data set. |

---

§ 3.2-4

frequently

No mode for either group. (sorry about that!)

The Mode

1. The mode is the most _____ occurring value.

2. Find the mode for the two sets of data from problem 11, section 2.2.

---

§ 3.3

spread, variation

Measures of Variation

1. § 3.2 discussed measures of central tendency, this section discusses measures of variation. Variation concerns the _____ or _____ in the data. Variation tells whether a set of data is bunched tightly, loosely, or not at all!

---

§ 3.3-1

largest - smallest

(55-12) = 43

(57-11) = 46

The Range

1. The Range is simply the difference between the _____ and the _____ value in the data set.

2. Compute the range for the first data set from problem 11, section 2.2.

3. Compute the range for the second data set from problem 11, section 2.2.

The Variance and the Standard Deviation

§ 3.3-2

1. The most widely used measure of variation is the _____ along with the square root of the variance, the _____ _____.

variance
standard deviation

2. The total of the deviations from the mean will equal _____, with the positive distance cancelling the negative distance.

zero

The average deviation solved this problem by taking the _____ _____ for each difference.

absolute value

The standard deviation solves this problem by taking the _____ of each difference.

square

3. The variance of a population is the sum of the squares of the deviations from mu, the population mean, divided by _____. Write this formula.

N, $\dfrac{\Sigma(X-\mu)^2}{N}$

4. The values for the population variance and standard deviation are designated by the Greek letter _____, written _____.

sigma,
σ, σ^2

5. On the other hand, the variance of a data set which has been obtained from a sample, is the sum of the squares of the deviations from Xbar, the sample mean, divided by _____. Write this formula.

n-1, $\dfrac{\Sigma(X-\bar{X})^2}{(n-1)}$

6. The values for the sample variance and standard deviation are designated by the English alphabet letter _____, written (obviously) _____.

s
s^2, and s

7. Compute the standard deviation and variance for the first data set from problem 11, section 2.2. Use formula for population.

SD = 13.01,
VAR = 169.29

8. Compute the standard deviation and variance for the second data set from problem 11, section 2.2. Use formula for population.

SD = 16.83,
VAR = 283.31

24

$$s^2 = \frac{\Sigma X^2 - \frac{(\Sigma X)^2}{n}}{n}$$

9. The text presents another formula for computing the variance. Although this formula may look more difficult, it is actually much more amenable to hand calculation. Write this formula and use it to recompute the variance for the first data set from problem 11, section 2.2. (If you don't get the same value (allowing for rounding) you did something wrong.)

---

§ 3.3-3

relative

The Coefficient of Variation

1. The coefficient of variation provides a means for investigating the _____ amount of variation. This is useful for comparisons between two sets of data.

standard deviation
mean

2. The coefficient of variation examines the size of the _____ relative to the size of the _____.

.3787 = .38

3. Compute the coefficient of variation for the first data set from problem 11, section 2.2.

.5028 = .50

4. Compute the coefficient of variation for the second data set from problem 11, section 2.2.

sure
standard deviation
mean

5. Can the coefficient of variation be greater than 100? (Which would imply that the _____ _____ is greater than the _____.)

---

§ 3.4

relative

Measures of Position

1. Many times an absolute score tells very little. We need a _____ measure which compares scores to each other.

---

§ 3.4-1

100

Percentiles

1. A percentile, ('kinda' like whole-integer percentages) divides the data into _____ parts.

2. At the 30th percentile, that means that _____ of the elements in the data set lie below, and _____ of the elements in the data set lie above. | 30%
70%

3. For the first data set from problem 11, section 2.2, what values lie below the 10th percentile? Above the 90th percentile? | 12, 15
52, 55

4. The 50th percentile is equivalent to which measure of central tendency? | the median

---

Quartiles | § 3.4-2

1. Whereas percentiles had divided the universe into _____ parts, quartiles divide the universe into _____ parts. | 100
4

2. For the first data set from problem 11, section 2.2, what values lie below the first quartile? Above the third quartile? | 12, 15, 18, 20
48, 49, 52, 55

3. The 2nd quartile is equivalent to the _____ percentile, which is equivalent to the _____ (measure of central tendency). | 50th
median

Z Scores | § 3.4-3

1. Z scores tell _____ _____ standard deviations lie between some observation and the mean. | how many

2. Give the formula for Z, assuming that the mean and the standard deviation have come from the population. | $Z = \dfrac{x - \mu}{\sigma}$

3. Give the formula for Z, assuming that the mean and the standard deviation have come from a sample. | $Z = \dfrac{x - \bar{x}}{s}$

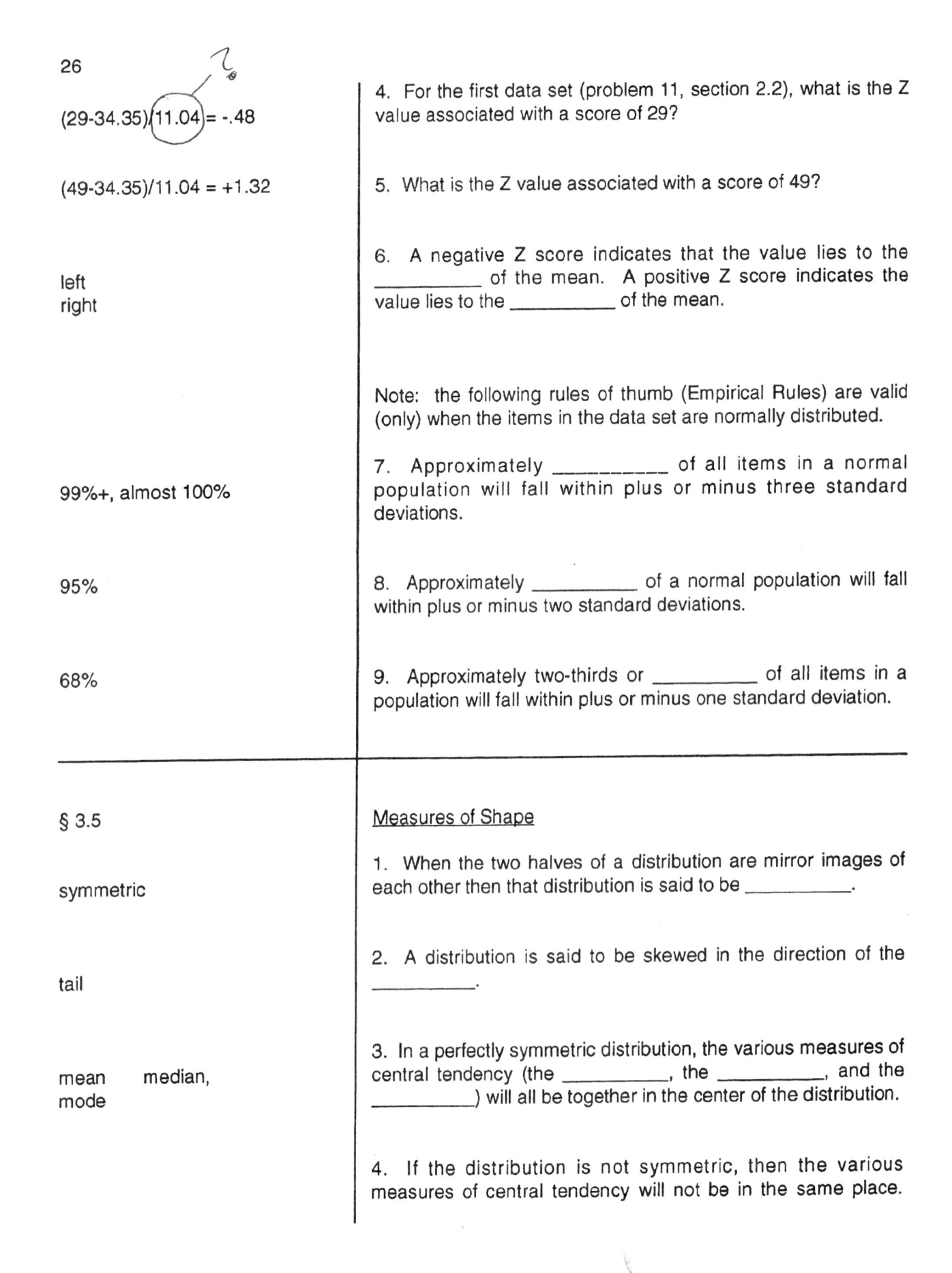

26

(29-34.35)/11.04 = -.48

(49-34.35)/11.04 = +1.32

left
right

99%+, almost 100%

95%

68%

§ 3.5

symmetric

tail

mean   median,
mode

---

4. For the first data set (problem 11, section 2.2), what is the Z value associated with a score of 29?

5. What is the Z value associated with a score of 49?

6. A negative Z score indicates that the value lies to the _____ of the mean. A positive Z score indicates the value lies to the _____ of the mean.

Note: the following rules of thumb (Empirical Rules) are valid (only) when the items in the data set are normally distributed.

7. Approximately _____ of all items in a normal population will fall within plus or minus three standard deviations.

8. Approximately _____ of a normal population will fall within plus or minus two standard deviations.

9. Approximately two-thirds or _____ of all items in a population will fall within plus or minus one standard deviation.

Measures of Shape

1. When the two halves of a distribution are mirror images of each other then that distribution is said to be _____.

2. A distribution is said to be skewed in the direction of the _____.

3. In a perfectly symmetric distribution, the various measures of central tendency (the _____, the _____, and the _____) will all be together in the center of the distribution.

4. If the distribution is not symmetric, then the various measures of central tendency will not be in the same place.

The highest point on the distribution curve will be the _____. The measure of central tendency which will be the farthest out in the tail will be the _____. And the _____ will be in the middle.	mode mean median
5. Compute the Pearsonian coefficient of skewness for the first data set for problem 11, section 2.2.	-.176
6. Compute the Pearsonian coefficient of skewness for the second data set for problem 11, section 2.2.	+.86
7. Based upon the relative proportions of rich people to poor people, how would you estimate the distribution of income would be skewed? (right, left, or symmetric)	right
8. In an income distribution, which measure of central tendency would you anticipate having the highest value? The lowest?	mean, mode
9. Kurtosis is a statistical measure which is concerned with the _____ of a distribution. A normal curve has a nice, pleasant bell shape, and is not overly flat nor overly sharply peaked.	peakedness
10. In summary, the most popular measure of central tendency is the _____, and the most popular measure of dispersion is the _____ _____. The mean and standard deviation are the most popular because they represent the two parameters of the normal curve.	mean standard deviation

---

Interpreting the Mean and the Standard Deviation — § 3.6

1. Using the mean and the standard deviation, a curve can be broken into areas of various percentages. There are two different formulas for handling this type of problem. The selection of the proper formula revolves around the existence (assumption) of _____.   —   normality

28

empirical

2. If the data is known to be normal (or if normality is a reasonable assumption) then the _____ Rule can be used to delineate areas under the curve.

95%

100%

3. The Empirical Rule will predict the following results: Roughly _____ percent of the items will lie within plus or minus two standard deviations.
Virtually_____ percent of the items will be within plus or minus three standard deviations of the mean.

Chebyshev's Inequality

4. If the shape of the distribution is not normal (or if normality is not a reasonable assumption) then _____ _____ can be used to delineate areas under the curve.

$(1 - (1/k^2))$

5. Chebyshev's Inequality specifies that at least _____ (give formula) percent of the items will lie within plus or minus "k" standard deviations.

75%

89%

6. Chebyshev's Inequality gives the following results: At least _____ percent of the items will lie within plus or minus two standard deviations of the mean. At least _____ percent of the items will lie within plus or minus three standard deviations of the mean.

either 95%(ER) or 75%(CI)
within 12.27 - 56.43
and 2.35 - 64.56

7. For the data sets from problem 11, section 2.2, use the Empirical Rule and Chebyshev's Inequality to find the limits for plus or minus two standard deviations.

normality

conservative

8. The existence (assumption) of _____ enables the Empirical Rule to make a much stronger statement. Because it does not make this assumption, Chebyshev's Inequality is statistically more (liberal/conservative)

---

§ 3.7

Grouped Data

midpoint

1. The formulas for grouped data (frequency distributions) will produce only approximations of the true value. They are approximations because the class _____ is used as the average (as representative) of all of the values in that class.

2. For the first data set from problem 11, section 2.2, estimate the arithmetic mean using the formula for grouped data. (Use 15,25,35,45,55 as class midpoints.)

34.41 (vs. true value of 34.35)

3. Estimate the arithmetic mean for the second data set using the formula for grouped data.

33.24 (vs. 33.47)

4. For the first data set, estimate the variance and standard deviation using the grouped data formulas.

169.38, 12.98
(vs. 169.29, 13.01)

5. For the second data set, estimate the variance and standard deviation using the grouped data formulas.

302.94, 17.41
(vs. 283.31, 16.83)

6. For the first data set, estimate the median using the formulas for grouped data.

37.0 (vs. 35)

7. For the second data set, estimate the median using the formulas for grouped data.

28.3 (vs. 29)

8. If you were given your choice, that is, if you had a frequency distribution as well as all of the original data. You should use the _____ _____, because the formulas for grouped data are only _____.

original data
approximations

Exploratory Data Analysis

§.3.8

1. Two popular means of constructing pictures that summarize a data set are _____ ___ _____ diagrams and _____ plots.

stem and leaf
box

2. Stem-and-leaf diagrams are like _____, but in a sense they are better than _____ in that there is no loss of information.

histograms
histograms

30

original data	3. No loss of information means that you can reconstruct the _____ ____ from the stem and leaf diagram.
quartile	4. Box plots are graphical representations of the _____ measures of position.
left	5. If the median bar is located in the right half of the box, then the data is skewed _____.
symmetric	6. If the median bar is located in the center of the box, then the data is _____
Skewed right (the tail is longer to the right), but the bulk of the data set is to the left of the mean... there are more 'poor' folk than there are rich folks.	7. If you had income data collected from a random sample of households in a typical small southern town, in what direction would you expect the data to be skewed?
The data would probably be skewed in a similar manner, that is the distribution would look the same.	8. If you had income data collected from a random sample of households in a typical large northestern city, in what direction would you expect the data to be skewed?
We would anticipate that the mean of the northeastern city would be higher than the mean of the southern town.	9. Although the shape of the distributions would be similar (there are more poor households than rich households) what would you predict about the means of the two sample groups?

Data Coding

It would mean that the researcher was stupid. You cannot perform statistical manipulations such as finding the average (the mean) on nominal data.	1. Great care must be taken in the coding of nominal data. (i.e., French = 1, German = 2, Swiss = 3, Italian = 4). What would it mean if it a survey was taken of two towns in the Alps and the average nationality (using the coding scheme just presented) for one town was 2.3 and the average nationality of the other town was 2.8?
	6. What would it mean if the survey in one town produced an

average nationality of 1.0, and the survey in the other town produced an average nationality of 4.0?

It means either:
a. the population of first town is all (100%) French and the second town is all (100%) Italian, or
b. it was a very biased sampling design which produced all French and all Italian subjects for the surveys.

CHAPTER 4

Probability Concepts

CHAPTER OBJECTIVES

This chapter presents methods for dealing with events involving uncertainty. Uncertainty is a very real part of the business environment. Any type of forecast involves elements of risk and uncertainty. By the end of the chapter you should be able to answer the following questions:

1. What is meant by the term "probability"? How would each of these techniques be used to generate a probability?
   a. classical approach
   b. relative frequency
   c. subjective probability

2. How are multiple events handled? What is meant by the term "joint" probability? How do you compute probabilities using the additive rule? The multiplication rule?

3. What is a Venn diagram? How are they used to compute probabilities?

4. How do you count the possible number of outcomes using permutations and combinations?

PROBABILITY CONCEPTS

§ 4.0 A Look Back/Introduction

probability
probability

1. In statistics, uncertainty is represented by the concept of _____. Rather than being absolutely certain that some event will occur, we give the _____ (or likelihood) that it will occur.

False, very false. There is nothing more uncertain than the business environment. If you don't believe me, go try your "luck" in the stock market

2. Since business deals with hard, cold, cash...you know, the "bottom line", "results not excuses", and all of that, there is no need for probability...the study of the uncertain. True or False

---

§ 4.1 Events and Probability

experiment

1. In probability, an activity that results in an uncertain outcome is referred to as an _____. (That is certainly the way my chemistry "experiments" were...highly uncertain events ...even though my instructor surely did not plan it that way!)

event

2. One of the possible outcomes of an experiment is referred to as an _____.

head, tail

3. Suppose that you flip a coin, what would be the two events of this experiment?

head, head
head, tail
tail, head
tail, tail

4. Suppose that you flip two coins, what would be the four sets of events of this experiment?

.25
(.25+.25) = .50

5. From the above problem, what is the probability of getting a head and a tail (in that order)? What is the probability of a head and a tail (in any order)?

6. No matter how they are obtained, all probabilities must be between _____ and _____. | zero - one (0.0 - 1.0)

7. When a probability has been obtained from someone's opinion, from their guess, it is referred to as a _____ probability. | subjective

8. Because they are based upon guesses, subjective probabilities cannot be used in subsequent mathematical calculations. | False, they can be used like any probability (although caution is advised...they are still guesses.)

Contingency Tables

§ 4.2

An investigation was made of the relationship between the purchase of a personal computer, and the level of education of the purchaser. One hundred persons were surveyed, resulting in the following contingency table:

Personal Computer Purchases

	Buy	No Buy	
HS or less	20	40	60
More than HS	30	10	40
	50	50	100

1. The probability of a single event (as computed using the values around the margin of the table), such as the probability of someone buying a computer, is known as a _____ probability. | marginal

2. What is the probability of a person having more than a high school education? | .40

3. What is the probability that someone will buy a computer? | .50

35

36

joint

20

and

or

90

1.00

given

P(A|B)

(30/40) = .75

---

4. When the event of interest involves two events (ie. the probability of HS and computer) it is referred to as a _____ probability.

5. What is the probability of selecting a person who is both HS or less, and is buying a computer?

6. When statisticians talk about A "intersect" B, they are asking for the probability of A _____ B.

7. When statisticians talk about A "union" B, they are asking for the probability of A _____ B.

8. What is the probability of a person who is either below high school or buying a computer?

9. What is the probability of someone either buying a computer or not buying a computer?

10. In a conditional probability, you are asked to find the probability of one event _____ the occurrence of some other event.

11. Notationally, the probability of A given B (ie, the probability of a win, given the star quarterback is injured) is designated _____.

12. Referring back to the contingency table which was presented at the beginning of Section 5.3, what is the probability of a computer purchase given that the person has above high school education? (Notice how the extra information (knowing their education) has changed the probability from what it would have been...in other words, the difference between P(Buy) = .50, and the P(Buy|GTHS) = .75.)

13. When the probability of one event is changed by the outcome of some other event, these events are said to be _____ events. Mathematically, that is to say that the P(A) (equals/not equals) the P(A|B).	dependent not equals
14. When the probability of one event is not changed by the outcome of some other event, these events are said to be _____ events. Mathematically, that is to say that the P(A) (equals/not equals) the P(A|B).	independent equals
15. When two events cannot occur simultaneously (ie, buy and not buy) the events are said to be _____ _____.	mutually exclusive
16. When two events are said to be "not mutually exclusive", that says that the two events (could/must) occur simultaneously.	could (i.e.,. male & blond) can occur together, but do not have to

Mathematical Rules of Probability with Applications	§ 4.3 and § 4.4
1. The pictorial representation of probabilities by little circles is called the _____ diagram.	Venn
2. The Venn diagram was developed by Antonio Venn, who went on to even greater fame as the inventor of the Venetian blind. True or False	False
3. No Venn diagram can have more than two circles.	False
4. If events A and B are mutually exclusive, then the probability of A and B (P(A and B)) is _____; and the probability of A or B (P(A or B)) is _____.	P(A and B) = zero by definition. P(A or B) = P(A) + P(B)
5. At a certain gathering, 30% were freshmen, and 20% were sophomores. What is the probability of someone being a freshman and a sophomore? What is the probability of someone being a freshman or a sophomore?	zero (.30 + .20) = .50

38

P(A and B) = P(A) x P(B)
P(A or B) = P(A)+P(B) - (P(A)xP(B))
or = 1-(P(A')xP(B'))

6. If events A and B are independent, then the probability of A and B (P(A and B)) is _____; the probability of A or B (P(A or B)) is _____.

(.30 x .40) = .12
(.30+.40 - (.30x.40))=.58
or 1-(.70x.60) = .58

7. At that certain gathering, (problem 5) 40% of the persons were male. What is the probability of someone being a freshman and a male? What is the probability of someone being a freshman or a male?

8. The above problem had assumed independence, that is, the probability of being a freshman was independent of being a male. When the probabilities are dependent hen these formulas do not apply. Thus the formula for dependent events:

$$P(A|B) = \frac{P(A \text{ and } B)}{P(B)}$$

False

In this case P(A and B) = P(A) x P(B). True or False

Note: That is true only for independent events, in fact that is the definition of independent events:

$$P(A|B) = \frac{P(A \text{ and } B)}{P(B)} = \frac{P(A) \times P(B)}{P(B)} = P(A)$$

There is a formula for computing the dependent probability of P(A and B) (multiplicative rule), but for now let's just look at the problem and take the intersection of (A and B) from the problem.

P(S|HS)=$\frac{P(S \& HS)}{P(HS)}$=$\frac{20}{60}$= .33

9. For the problem involving the computers, what is the probability of a sale given that the person has less than high school? Illustrate with the formula.

P(C|NS)=$\frac{P(C \& NS)}{P(NS)}$=$\frac{10}{50}$= .20

10. For the problem involving the computers, what is the probability of a college person given no sale? Show how this answer fits the formula.

P(A and B) = P(A)xP(B)

11. When events A and B are independent, then the probability of (A and B) is _____.

12. However, the formula from above is really just a special case of the multiplicative rule of probability, (which can handle both independent and dependent events). Give the formula for the multiplicative rule.	P(A and B) = P(A|B) x P(B) = P(B|A) x P(A)
13. Many times, items are drawn without replacement. When items are drawn without replacement this becomes a situation involving (dependent/independent) events, and the probability of the event on the second draw (changes/is constant).	dependent changes
14. When items are drawn with replacement, this is a situation involving (dependent/independent) events, and the probability of the event on the second draw (changes/is constant).	independent is constant

---

Tree Diagrams	§ 4.5
1. Actually, any type of probability problem or counting problem can be worked with a tree diagram (if you had enough paper and enough time to draw all of the branches). T F	True
2. In Bayesian or posterior analysis, the probabilities are revised on the basis of subsequent knowledge. T F We do the same thing (subjectively as opposed to objectively) all the time. For instance, suppose that the probability of the NBA Chicago Bulls winning is 60%. Now someone tells you that Michael Jordan is sick and won't play. Would you revise the probability of a Chicago win?	True Yes, revise probability down
3. Revised forecasts occur with dependent/independent events?	dependent - the probability of Chicago winning is dependent upon Michael Jordon playing. George Foreman might also be sick that weekend, but the Bulls are independent of Foreman.
4. In a certain factory there are two machines, a new machine which supplies 70% of the parts, and an older machine that supplies the rest. The probability of a bad part given the new machine is 1%, while the probability of a bad part given the old machine is 10%. A customer receives a bad part, what is the probability that it came from the old machine?	Bayes' theorem, revised prob. P(old machine | bad part) = .81 (.030/.037) = .81 (revised probability is almost triple the original value of .30)

Bayes' theorem, revised prob

P(kids | broken glass) = 76.9%

(.30/.039) = .769

	5. In a certain home, the mother washes 90% of the dishes and breaks a dish only one day out of a hundred. The remainder of the time the kids wash the dishes and they will break a dish three times out of every times that they wash. (Dad is so clumsy that Mom won't let him touch the dishes at all...in fact, she makes him eat from a paper plate.) Grandmother has come for a surprise visit (she has her own key and she find evidence of broken glass in the kitchen. What is the probability that the kids were washing dishes that day?

§ 4.6-1

Applying the Concepts, Independent Events

P(rain in next 24) =
1 - P(no rain next 24) =
1 - (.60x.40x.70)= .832

1. If the weatherman lists the probability of rain as 40% this morning, 60% this afternoon, and 30% tonight, what is the probability of rain in the next 24 hours?

a.(.50x.50) = .25
b.(.50x.50)+(.50x.50)=.25
c.(.50x.50) = .25
d.(.50+.25) = .75 or,
   1-none = 1-.25=.75

2. A fair coin tossed twice: Find the probability of:
a. no heads
b. exactly one head
c. two heads
d. at least one

a.(.50x.50x.50)= .125
b.(HTT)or(THT)or(TTH)=.375
c.(HHT)or(HTH)or(THH)=.375
d.(HHH)=(.50x.50x.50)=.125
e.(one)+(two)+(three)=.875...or
   1-none = 1-.125 = .875

3. Three coins are tossed: What is the probability of:
a. no heads
b. exactly one head
c. two heads
d. three heads
e. at least one

Sorry, peddler, no sale to that idea.
(2/3)x(2/3)x(2/3) = .296

4. A salesman has discovered that he makes a sale on average of once every three sales calls. So he says, "I will be sure to make three calls every day, that way I can be guaranteed of a sale every day." Is that true? What is the probability of day with no sales?

12, since
P(none out of 11)=.01156
P(none out of 12)=.00771

5. For the salesman in problem 4 (an average of one sale in three tries), how many calls would he have to make to be 99% sure of at least one sale?

6. You are going to flip a coin 10 times. What is the probability of getting 10 consecutive heads?

$(1/2)$ to the tenth power = $(1/1024)$ = .00097

7. You have now thrown 9 consecutive heads, what is the probability of getting one more head to complete your string of 10 heads?

.50

(This is a problem that often baffles students. They feel that after 9 heads, surely the next toss must be a tail, or at least the probability of a tail should be higher than 50/50. However, the coin tosses are independent events. A coin has no memory, and the coin still has just two sides, so, p = .50.)

recap,
P(10 heads) = .00097
P(10 heads | 9 heads) = .50

8. Three kids are eating open-faced jelly (grape!) sandwiches. They all drop their sandwiches. What is the probability that at least one sandwich will land jelly-side-down, ruining Mom's new white carpet?

P(at least one) = 1 - P(none)
= 1 - (.5 x .5 x .5)
= 1 - (.125) = .875
(The odds don't look good, Mom)

(Actually this problem is an illustration of Bigelow's Law, which states: "The probability of an open-faced sandwich landing face down is proportional to the cost of the carpet".)

Applying the Concepts, Dependent Events

§ 4.6-2

1. An urn contains 4 balls, 2 white and 2 black.
   a. On the first draw, what is the probability of a white ball?
   b. If the sampling is done without replacement, give the probability of a white ball on the second draw?

   .50

   either .33 or .67

   c. Two balls are drawn: What is the probability of two white balls?

   (.50 x .33) = .16

   d. Two balls are drawn: Give the probability of one white ball and one black ball (in any order)?

   (WB or BW) =
   (.50 x .67) + (.50 x .67) = .67

2. A poker hand (five cards) is drawn (without replacement) What is the probability of drawing:

   $\frac{13}{52} \times \frac{12}{51} \times \frac{11}{50} \times \frac{10}{49} \times \frac{9}{48}$ = .0004

   a. 5 hearts?

   b. 5 Aces

   zero, can't do it, only four aces

42

$\frac{1}{52} \times \frac{1}{51} \times \frac{1}{50} \times \frac{1}{49} \times \frac{1}{48} = 3.2 \times 10^{-9}$

c. The Ace, King, Queen, Jack, and 10...all of spades.
 1. In that order

$\frac{5}{52} \times \frac{4}{51} \times \frac{3}{50} \times \frac{2}{49} \times \frac{1}{48} = 3.0 \times 10^{-7}$

 2. In any order

3. There are 5 names on slips of paper in a proverbial hat: Three men and two women.

a. 2/5 = .40
b. either (1/4) or (2/4)
   overall (.6x.5 + .4x.25)
   = (.30+.10) = .40
c. (2/5)(1/4) = .10
d. MW or WM =
   (.6x.5)+(.5x.75)=.60

a. On the first draw, what is the probability of drawing a woman's name?
b. If the slip is not replaced, what is the probability of a woman's name on the second draw?
c. What is the probability of drawing both women's names if two slips are drawn?
d. What is the probability of ending up with one man and one woman if two slips of paper are drawn?

---

§ 4.7

Counting Rules

multiplying

1. In the "filling slots" method of computing the number of possibilities, you find the total number of possibilities by simply _____ the number of each individual situation times each other.

produced more permutations
10x10x10x10x10x10=1,000,000
26x26x26x10x10x10=17,576,000
(and most have gone to allowing letters and/or digits in every position...even more plates)

2. Why did the various states change from license plates with 6 digits to plates with 3 letters and 3 digits?

the social security
2L,6D = 676,000,000
9D = 1,000,000,000

3. The military changed from ID numbers with 2 letters and 6 digits to the 9 digit social security number. Which option provided more combinations?

2 x 6 = 12

4. How many ways can you throw one coin and one die? (dice)

5. At Rosie's Diner you have your choice of: 1 of 4 salads, 1 or 3 meats, 1 of 5 vegetables, and 1 of 3 deserts. How many possible meals can you have? How many meals can you eat?

$4 \times 3 \times 5 \times 3 = 180$
Most patrons are lucky to keep down one a week.

6. When you are trying to compute the number of sets of "k" objects which can be selected from a larger set of "n" items and the order of selection counts, this is called a _____. Give the formula.

permutation
$$\frac{n!}{(n-r)!}$$

7. The notation 5! stands for _____, and is computed as _____. (Actually the notation 5!, stands for FIVE!!! and indicates that the author is really serious about that problem!)

five factorial
$5 \times 4 \times 3 \times 2 \times 1 = 120$

8. There are 8 teams in the Mediocre Athletic Conference. Assuming no ties, how many different orders of finish are possible?

Allowing for ties, how many different orders of finish are possible?

permutation 8 draw 8
$= \frac{n!}{(n-r)!} = \frac{8!}{(8-8)!} = 40320$

Beats me! I worked on this one for a few hours and the number of different arrangements was becoming absolutely mind-boggling. Many probability problems are this way, change one word and the problems can go from trivial to impossible.

9. A monkey is typing 3 letter "words" on a typewriter. How many different "words" can the monkey form if:
a. no letter can be repeated in a given word
b. a letter can be repeated in a given word

a. perm 26 draw 3 = 15,600
b. $26 \times 26 \times 26 = 17,576$

10. Three (different) prizes are going to be awarded to a group of seven people. How many different sets of three can be selected?

permutation 7 draw 3
$$\frac{7!}{(7-3)!} = \frac{7!}{4!} = 210$$

11. When sets are selected and the order of selection does not count it is referred to as a _____.
Give the formula.

combination
$$_nC_r = \frac{n!}{r!(n-r)!}$$

12. Using a standard deck of cards, how many different hands are possible in Black Jack. (with replacement)

comb 52 draw 2 = 1326

44

comb 7 draw 3 $_3C_7 = \binom{7}{3} = \frac{7!}{3!\,4!} = 35$	13. Three (equal) prizes are going to be awarded to a group of seven people. How many different sets of three can be selected?

§ 4.8

Simple Random Samples

same

1. A random sample is a sample in which each available unit has a known probability of selection. A simple random sample is one in which each unit has the _____ probability of selection.

False, a random sample, and sampling "at random" are horses of entirely different colors.

2. To pick a random sample, all you need is a list, and then just jump around, picking numbers "at random". True or False

random number
random number

3. To actually pick a random sample, you need some type of probability mechanism such as a _____ _____ table, or a _____ _____ generator.

CHAPTER 5

Discrete Probability Distributions

CHAPTER OBJECTIVES

The preceding chapter introduced the concept of probability as well as the basic rules for computing the probability of various events. This chapter introduces the concept of probability distributions, that is, mathematical distributions which "automatically" compute the probability of various events. By the end of the chapter you should be able to answer the following questions:

1. What is meant by the term "probability distribution"?

2. What is the formula for the mean and variance of a discrete random variable?

3. When, and how is the discrete uniform distribution used?

4. When, and how, is the binomial distribution used?

5. When, and how, is the hypergeometric distribution used?

6. When, and how, is the Poisson distribution used?

§ 5.0

chance or likelihood

discrete

continuous

A Look Back/Introduction

1. The previous chapter introduced the concept of probability, a method for statistically measuring the _____ of something happening.

2. A variable which can only assume certain interval values (i.e., 1,2,3 etc.) is called a _____ variable.

3. A variable which can assume any imaginable value is called a _____ variable.

---

§ 5.1

random variable

discrete random variable

1,2,3,4,5,6

1,2,3,4,5,6,8,9,10,12,
15,16,18,20,24,25,30,36

probability distribution

Random Variables

1. A variable which takes its value from the result of a random (probability) event, is called a _____ _____.

2. A variable which takes its value from the result of a discrete probability event is called a _____ _____ _____.

3. What are the values of the discrete random variable for the throw of a single die of a pair of dice?

4. What are the values of the discrete random variable for the product of the throw of a pair of dice?

5. The list of all of the possible values of a random variable (X), and the corresponding probabilities of each of those values is known as a _____ _____.

6. Give the probability distribution for problem three, the throw of a single die. Also, multiply each value (x_i) times its probability (p_i). Get the sum of the (x_i) times (p_i). What is that value and what does it represent?

x_i	p_i	($x_i p_i$)
1	= 1/6	1/6
2	= 1/6	2/6
3	= 1/6	3/6
4	= 1/6	4/6
5	= 1/6	5/6
6	= 1/6	6/6
		21/6 = 3.5 $\Sigma(p_i x_i)$

Figured in this manner, it is called the Expected Value. This value is also the arithmetic mean,

7. Give the probability distribution for problem four, the product of a pair of dice. Once again, multiply each value (x_i) times its probability (p_i). Get the sum of the (x_i) times (p_i). What is that value and what does it represent? Compare that value to the value computed in problem six.

x_i	p_i	($x_i p_i$)
1	= 1/36	1/36
2	= 2/36	4/36
3	= 2/36	6/36
4	= 3/36	12/36
5	= 2/36	10/36
6	= 4/36	24/36
8	= 2/36	16/36
9	= 1/36	9/36
10	= 2/36	20/36
12	= 4/36	48/36
15	= 2/36	30/36
16	= 1/36	16/36
18	= 2/36	36/36
20	= 2/36	40/36
24	= 2/36	48/36
25	= 1/36	25/36
30	= 2/36	60/36
36	= 1/36	36/36
sum		441/36 = 12.25

Expected Value equals the average or arithmetic mean.
From #6: $(3.5)^2 = 12.25$

Probability Distributions for Discrete Random Variables

§ 5.2

1. There are three methods for describing the probabilities associated with a discrete random variable (X), they are:

list each Xi and Pi,
graph,
use a math. function

48

prob. mass function

2. The function that assigns a probability to each value of X is called a _____ _____ _____ (PMF).

zero - one (0.00 - 1.00)

one (1.00)

3. There are two requirements for a Probability Mass Function. One, the probability for each individual event in the distribution have a probability between _____ and _____. Two, the total of all of these individual events add up to exactly _____.

---

§ 5.3

Mean and Variance for a Discrete Random Variable

sum of the values times their probabilities

1. The mean of a discrete random variable (also known as the expected value) is the _____ of the _____ times their _____.

21/6 = 3.5

2. Compute the mean for the probability distribution developed in problem six (the throw of one die).

mean
probability

3. The variance for a discrete random variable (formula 6.4, the more intuitive one) is the sum of the squared difference between each value minus the _____, weighted by the _____ of each value.

2.917

4. Find the variance of the probability distribution developed in problem three (the throw of one die).

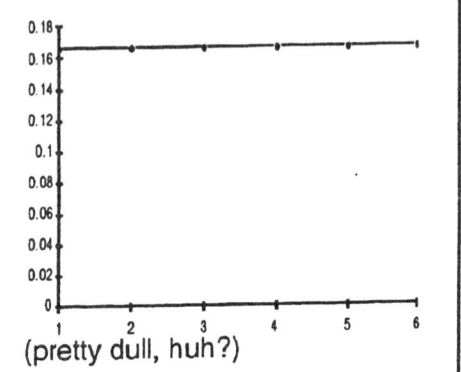

5. Sketch the graph of the probability distribution for the problem above (the throw of one die).

[graph: flat line at ~0.167 across x = 1 to 6, y-axis 0 to 0.18]

(pretty dull, huh?)

6. Compute the mean for the probability distribution developed in problem four (the product of two dice).	12.25
7. Compute the variance for the problem above (the product of two dice).	79.965
8. Sketch the diagram for the probability distribution of the product of two dice.	*(graph showing probability distribution from 1 to 34 with peaks, y-axis 0 to 0.12)*

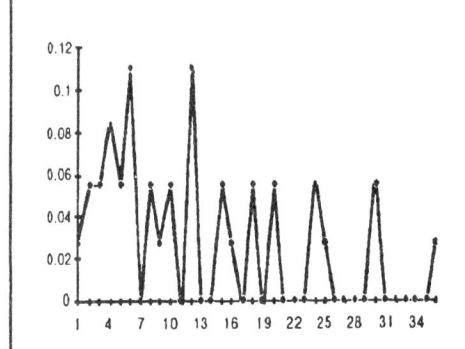

The Binomial Distribution

§ 5.4

1. The binomial distribution is designed to handle problems which can have only _____ outcomes, usually referred to as success or failure.	two
2. The binomial is used for finding the probability of obtaining a specified number of successes in _____ trials, when the probability of each success is defined as _____, or b(r, n, p).	n p
3. The probability of each success is (dependent/ independent) of the other trials.	independent
4. Use the binomial distribution for finding the probability of 4 heads in 7 tosses of a fair coin.	.2734

50

.6779

5. The Stinging Scorpions football team is rated as a 20% chance of winning any given football game. What is the probability that they will win at least 2 games (assume an 11 game season)? (Hint: turn the problem around: Prob(at least 2 wins) = 1 - (zero + one))

left
right
normal

6. The shape of the binomial distribution is skewed _____ if p is greater than .50 with small n. The binomial is skewed _____ if p is less than .50 with small n. Most importantly, the binomial is roughly _____ if p is near .50, or if n is large.

n times p

7. The mean of the binomial is equal to _____ times _____.

7 x .5 = 3.5

8. Compute the mean for problem four (7 tosses of a fair coin).

n x p x q
where (q = 1-p)

9. The variance of the binomial is equal to _____ times _____ times _____.

7 x .5 x .5 = 1.75

10. Compute the variance for problem four (7 tosses of a fair coin).

---

§ 5.5

The Hypergeometric Distribution

dependent

1. The binomial distribution was used with independent trials (constant probability, with replacement sampling). In contrast, the hypergeometric is used with _____ events (changing probability, without replacement sampling).

2. Suppose a friend has piled all of his socks (loose and unsorted) into a drawer. He has 8 black socks, 6 white, and 7 red (one of the red socks has been lost). Without looking, he reaches into the drawer and picks a pair of socks. What is the probability that he has picked a pair of black socks? Hint: This

means he needs to draw 2 of the 8 black socks, zero of the 6 white socks and zero of the 7 red socks. The numerator uses the combination formula to compute the total number of ways this "success" can happen. Then the denominator uses the combination formula to express the total number of ways that you can draw 2 socks out of the total of 21 socks.

$$\frac{_8C_2 \times {_6C_0} \times {_7C_0}}{_{21}C_2} = \frac{28}{210} = .133$$

3. Now suppose that he has a couple of friends over, and each of them also draws a pair of socks from the drawer. What is the probability that there will be one black pair, one white pair, and one red pair?

$$\frac{_8C_2 \times {_6C_2} \times {_7C_2}}{_{21}C_2} = \frac{8820}{54264} = .162$$

4. The hypergeometric is often used to work problems involving cards. Suppose a player is dealt a poker hand of five cards. What is the probability of getting 2 spades and 3 hearts?

$$\frac{_{13}C_2 \times {_{13}C_3} \times {_{13}C_0} \times {_{13}C_0}}{_{52}C_5}$$

$$= \frac{22308}{2598960} = .0086$$

5. In a certain lottery there are 5 prizes to be won out of 100 total tickets. A person buys two draws, what is the probability that they will win twice?
Exactly one time?
At least one time?

Twice = 20/9900 = .00202
Once = 950/9900 = .09595
At Least = 1 + 2 = .09797

The Poisson Distribution

§ 5.6

1. The Poisson distribution estimates the probability of a specified number of success when we would normally expect an average of _____ successes within this time period.

μ

2. The mean and the variance of the Poisson distribution are both equal to _____.

μ the avg # of occurrences
(μ also designated as λ in some texts)

3. In 7 tosses of a fair coin, we would expect an average of 3.5 heads. Use the Poisson distribution to compute the probability of 4 heads in 7 flips of a fair coin. Compare this answer with the answer computed using the binomial.

Poisson (4,3.5) = .1888
 compare
Binomial (4,7,3.5) = .2734

52

Poisson(3,3.5) = .2185 compare Binomial(3,7,.5) = .2734 also compare Poisson(4,3.5) = .1888	4. The binomial segment of the previous problem (4 heads in 7 tosses) could have been turned around to say that 4 heads in 7 is the same as 3 tails in 7. Being equivalent, it would produce exactly the same answer. But let us see what the Poisson of 3 given an average of 3.5 would be. Which answer is correct? (The binomial is the correct answer. The binomial is an exact distribution, it gives the same value you would get if you actually enumerated all of the possibilities. The Poisson is an approximation and will not generate the exact probabilities.)
Poisson(7,1.2) = .0002	5. The football team at Dullsville High, the Fighting Potatoes, wins an average of 1.2 games a year. What is the probability of them winning 7 games next year?

§ 5.7	The Poisson Approximation to the Binomial
$n \times p$ r, μ (or np)	1. The notation for the binomial is b(r, n, p), that is, "r" successes in "n" trials, when each "r" success has a probability of "p". The mean of the binomial is equal to _____ times _____. This means that a binomial of b(r, n, p) can be converted to a Poisson f (_____, _____).
large small	2. This conversion of binomial problems into Poisson problems is especially useful when "n" is very _____, and "p" is very _____.
Poisson(0,10) = .000045 or, in other words, there is a .999955 (a 99.99% chance) that at least one part will malfunction during the launch.	3. Suppose that a rocket ship has one million different parts and each part has been tested to insure reliability of only 1 failure in 100,000 parts. What would be the probability of a totally successful launch? Hint: Convert Binomial(0, 1,000,000, p=.00001) to a Poisson (0, 10)
Poisson(0,6) = .002479	4. A machine makes 75,000 parts an hour. The probability of a defective part is 1/100,000. In an 8 hour production day, what is the probability of an entire day with no bad parts? Hint: Convert Binomial(0, 600,000, p=.00001) to a Poisson (0, 6)

5. If 2 people in every 1000 in the United States are 6'5" or taller, what is the probability that coach Smith will have a center for his basketball team who is 6'5" or taller if there are 600 eligible persons?
Hint: At least one = 1.0 - none
= 1.0 - b(0, 600, p=.002)
convert to Poisson
= 1.0 - Poisson(0, 1.2)

1 - Poisson(0,1.2)
1 - .3012
= .6988, about a 70% chance of getting a center 6'5" or taller

6. Simeon Poisson went on to even greater fame as the developer of arsenic <u>poison</u> which he discovered while incarcerated at the Bastille prison. True or False

False

Probability Distribution Practice and Review

§ 5.8

1. What is the probability of getting 7 heads in 10 tosses of a fair coin?
Hint: If you can't find the value in the table, remember that the binomial(7, 10, p=.5) is equivalent to the binomial of (3, 10, p=.5).

b(3, 10, p=.5) = .1172

2. Rework problem one (7 heads in 10 tosses) as a Poisson problem. (For curiosity, also work it as the Poisson of 3 heads in 10 tosses.)

Poisson(3, 10, p=.5) = .1404
Poisson(7, 10, p=.5) = .1044

3. Suppose that there are 20 tokens in a box, half of them red and half of them white...in that manner rework problem one as a without replacement problem...that is, find the probability of getting 7 of the 10 red, and 3 of the 10 white.

$$\frac{{}_{10}C_7 \times {}_{10}C_3}{{}_{20}C_{10}} = .0779$$

4. In Ragongagongagoon there is an 80% probability of rain each day during the month of June. A big tennis tournament is scheduled, but they need 4 days of sunshine in the 6 days allotted for the tournament. What is the probability that they will get 4 sunny days out of 6?

b(4, 6, p=.20) = .0154

5. Rework problem four as a Poisson problem. (Work the problem as both the Poisson of 4 sunny days out of 6, as well as the Poisson of 2 rainy days out of 6.)

Poisson(4, 1.2) = .026
Poisson(2, 4.8) = .095

$$\frac{{}_5C_4 \times {}_{21}C_2}{{}_{26}C_6}$$

6. Assume a finite population of 26 days in June (30 day month, minus 4 sabbath days (Wednesday in Ragongagongagoon)) Work as a hypergeometric and find the probability of getting 4 sunny days and 2 rainy days, out of 26, when we would expect 5 sunny and 21 rainy days.

binomial(4, 6, p=.20) = .0154
+binomial(5, 6, p=.20) = .0015
+binomial(6, 6, p=.20) = .0001
                                    .0170

7. Actually, as astute students instantly realized, the tennis officials at Ragongagongagoon could have successfully completed their tournament with either 4, 5, or 6 sunny days (or at least 4). Find the probability of a successful tournament.

Poisson(4, 1.2) = .0260
+Poisson(5, 1.2) = .0062
+Poisson(6, 1.2) = .0012
                             .0334

8. Rework problem seven as a Poisson problem (do not bother to turn the problem around (4 sunny = 2 rainy, etc.)).

CHAPTER 6

Continuous Probability Distributions

CHAPTER OBJECTIVES

The previous chapter had presented four discrete probability distributions: the discrete uniform, the binomial, the Poisson, and the hypergeometric.

This chapter presents three continuous distributions: the normal, the uniform, and the exponential. By the end of the chapter you should be able to answer the following questions:

1. Distinguish between a discrete distribution and a continuous distribution.

2. For each of these three distributions: the normal, the uniform, and the exponential, sketch the distribution, and describe the situations for which each distribution is most appropriate.

3. Be able to work problems involving each of these three continuous distributions.

56

§ 6.0

A Look Back/Introduction

1. When values of the random variable can occur only at finite intervals, that distribution is said to be a _____ distribution.

discrete

2. In the last chapter, three distributions were presented. Two of those distributions could handle independent events (with replacement sampling), they were the _____, and the _____.

binomial,
Poisson

3. The third distribution presented in the last chapter could handle dependent events (changing probabilities, without replacement sampling), that distribution was the _____.

hypergeometric

4. When the values of the random variable can occur at any point along the interval, that distribution is said to be a _____ distribution.

continuous

5. Continuous distributions have no use in business, because all business dealings ultimately boil down to dollars and cents, a discrete phenomenon. True or False

False. $ and ¢ are discrete, however, many important business phenomena are continuous.

---

§ 6.1

Continuous Random Variables

1. One way to determine whether a distribution is discrete or continuous is by the presence/absence of gaps in the possible values of the random variable. If there are gaps at which no value can occur, the distribution is _____. If there are no gaps at which a value can occur, the distribution is _____.

discrete
continuous

2. This chapter deals with three continuous probability distributions, each possessing a markedly different shape. In reality, no data set will ever fit any of these distributions perfectly, yet they can serve as good working models if your data approximates one of the distributions. True or False

True, usually we must assume that the chosen distribution is close enough to the data to serve as an appropriate and accurate model.

3. Once a curve has been selected, a probability can be determined by finding the _____ under the curve. The task of finding this area usually involves the use of calculus to find the integral over the area, however, our task has been simplified by tables. | area

---

Normal Random Variables | § 6.2

1. A symmetrical, bell-shaped distribution with most of the items grouped in a bulge around the mean, and with progressively smaller numbers of items as you get farther from the mean is a _____ distribution. | normal

2. All normal curves have the same shape, therefore to describe the distribution we need just two parameters, the _____, which tells where the distribution is centered, and the _____ _____ which tells how wide the curve is. | mean
standard deviation

3. In specifying these two parameters, we use different symbols depending upon whether the values have come from the population, or from a sample: The mean of the population is designated _____. The mean of a sample is designated _____. The standard deviation of the population is designated _____. The standard deviation of a sample is _____. | μ
$\bar{x}$
σ
s

4. The square of the standard deviation (σ^2) is called the _____. | variance

---

Determining a Probability for a Normal Variable | § 6.3

1. In using the normal distribution to determine probabilities, we use the area under certain section of the curve to compute the probability, with the entire area under the curve equal to a value of _____. | 1.00

58

50%	2. The normal curve is symmetric with _____ % of the curve on either side of the mean.
zero	3. The probability of obtaining any specific point on the curve is _____, since a point has no area, by definition.
zero one	4. The standard normal curve is a special curve with a mean equal to _____, and a standard deviation equal to _____. The curve is scaled according to what is known as "Z values".

---

§ 6.4 — Finding Areas Under a Normal Curve

number of standard deviations

1. A "Z value" or "Z score" tells the _____ of _____ _____ which lie between an item and the mean.

$Z = \dfrac{X - \mu}{\sigma}$

2. Give the formula for computing the value of Z.

standardizing
standard

3. The process of converting raw, absolute scores into their corresponding Z values is called _____, and the resulting Z values are sometimes referred to as _____ scores.

The best way to gain familiarity with the working of the normal curve is to work a number of problems. The problems are easy to work once you get the hang of it, but for each problem you should sketch a picture of the distribution and shade in the area in question.

4. The rationale for the use of the standard normal curve, is that areas of equivalent shape (as defined by their Z values) have equivalent areas...regardless of the nature of the distribution.

$Z = \dfrac{108-100}{4} = 2.00$

p = .4772

For instance, consider a distribution of IQ scores, which are normally distributed with a mean of 100, and a standard deviation of 4. What percent of the population would lie between 100 and 108?

Now consider a distribution of ages, which are normally distributed with a mean of 30 and a standard deviation of 10. What percent of the population would lie between 30 and 50?

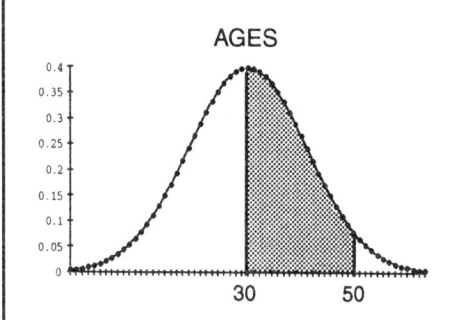

AGES

$$Z = \frac{50 - 30}{10} = 2.00$$

p = .4772

In both cases we have covered a distance of two standard deviations (Z = 2.00) and the probability in both cases is equal to approximately 48%.

5. Consider a population, normally distributed with a mean of 100 and a standard deviation of 4, what percentage lies between 100 and 106?

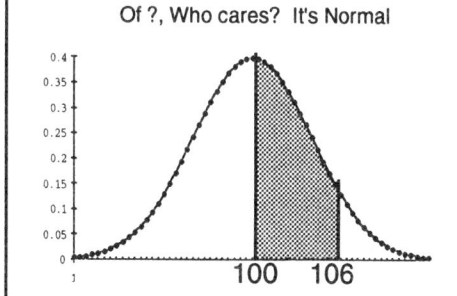

Of ?, Who cares? It's Normal

$$Z = \frac{106-100}{4} = 1.5$$

p = .4332

6. Given a normally distributed population with $\mu = 60$ and $\sigma = 3$, what percentage lies between 56 and 60?

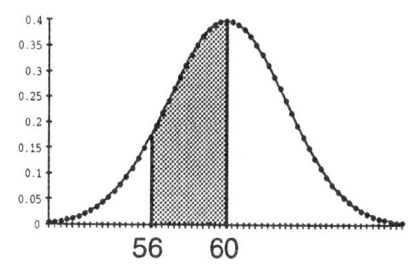

$$Z = \frac{56-60}{3} = -1.33$$

p = .4082

60

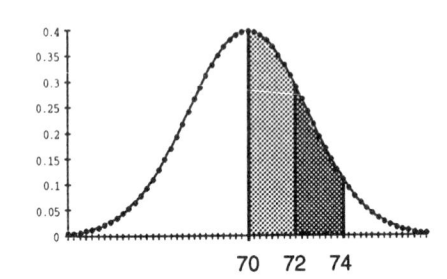

$Z = \dfrac{72-70}{2}$ $Z = \dfrac{74-70}{2}$

$Z = 1.0$ $Z = 2.0$

$p = .3413$ $p = .4772$
$p \cong .34$ $p \cong .48$

$(.48 - .34) = .14$

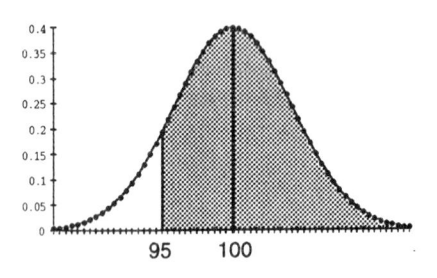

7. Given a normally distributed population with a mean equal to 70 and a standard deviation equal to 2, what percentage lies between 72 and 74?

Note: All distances must be measured from the mean, therefore this problem must be worked in two parts.

GT 95 = .8413 ≅ 84%

LT 95 = .1587 ≅ 16%
Simply the other "half"
of the picture above,
1.0 - .84 = .16

LT 100 = 50% by definition

8. Assuming a normal distribution, if the mean = 100 and the standard deviation = 5, what percent of the population is:

Greater than 95?

Less than 95?

Less than 100?

Less than 100?

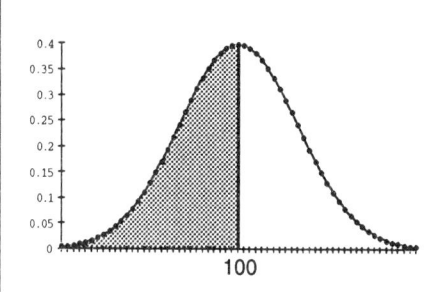

(Pretty easy, huh? Hardly justifies a picture.)

Less than 105?

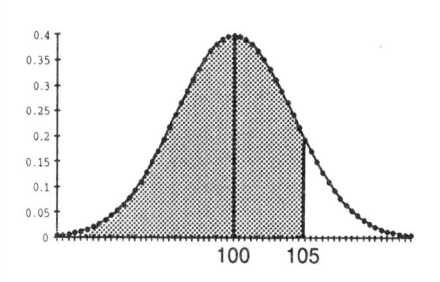

LT 105 = .8413 ≅ 84%

9. Assuming a normally distributed population, if the mean = 40 and the standard deviation = 2, what percent would lie:

Between 41 and 43?

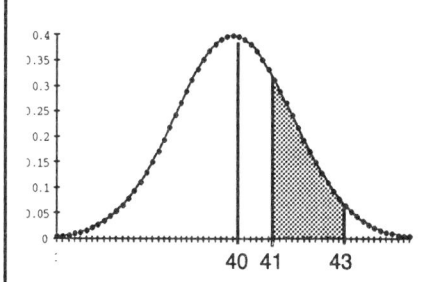

41 to 43
(.4332−.1914)= .2418 ≅ 24%

62

Problem 9. continued. Assuming a normally distributed population, if the mean = 40 and the standard deviation = 2, what percent would lie:

Between 39 and 44?

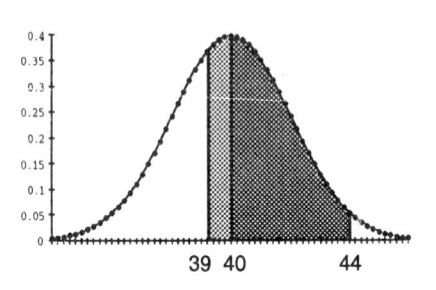

39 to 44
(.1914+.4772)= .6686 ≅ 67%

---

§ 6.5

Applications Where the Area Under the Normal Curve is Given

Light Bulb Burn-Out

1. If the burnout time for lightbulbs is normally distributed with an average life of 500 hours with a standard deviation of 70 hours, after how many hours will 90% of the the bulbs be burnt out?

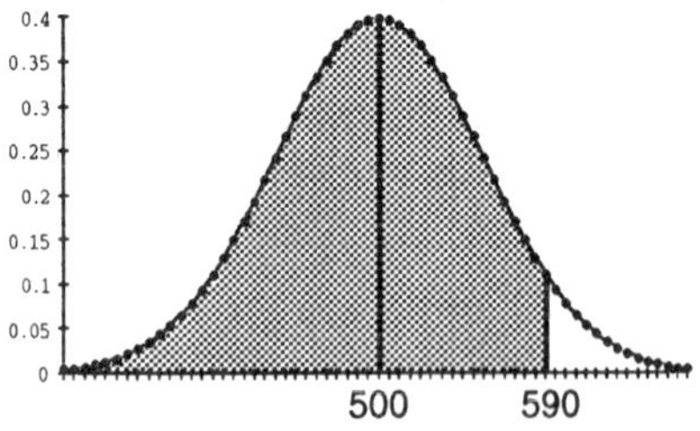

90% relates to a Z of 1.28
1.28 x 70 = 89.6
500+89.6 = 589.6 ≅ 590

half burnt out in 500 hours (by definition)

After how many hours will half of the bulbs be burnt out?

The Standard Normal Curve

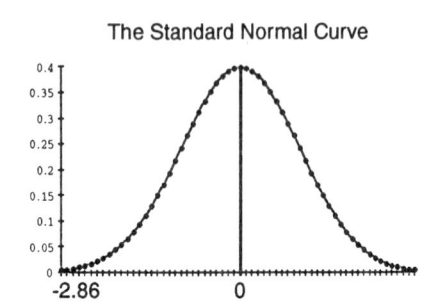

2. While his counselor had his back turned a student took a quick peek at his confidential records. On an IQ test he had taken, he had a standardized score of -2.86. Do you think that he could figure out where he ranked among students? Why?

No. Z of -2.86 puts him in the lowest .2% of the pop.

3. For a given football team, the starting running backs, (there are three of them) have an average gain (each) of 60 yards per game with a standard deviation of 30 yards. Assuming a normal distribution, what is the probability that a given back will rush for over 100 yards? What is the probability that none will rush for over 100 yards? What is the probability that all three will rush for over 100 yards?

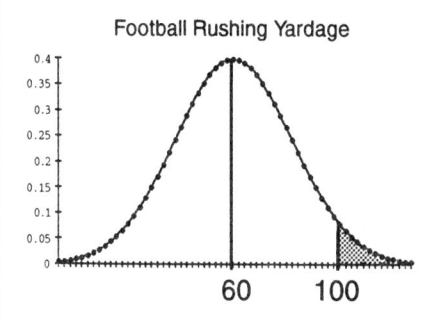

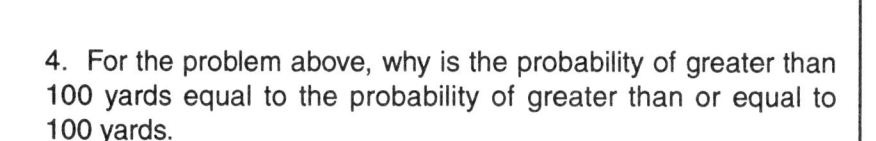

any given back = .0917 ≅ 9%
none = (.91x.91x.91) = .7535
three = (.09x.09x.09) = .0007

4. For the problem above, why is the probability of greater than 100 yards equal to the probability of greater than or equal to 100 yards.

A point (i.e., x = 100) has no area

5. Steve Slick is a senior at Alcatraz High School. Steve scored 1500 on his SAT test. If the mean is 1000 and the standard deviation is 200, Steve ranks in what percentile?

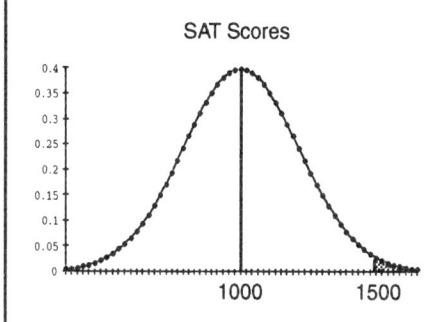

Z = 2.5
p = .9938, in top 1%

6. In the above problem, what assumption did you make? If Steve had scored 1700, in what percentile would Steve rank?

assume normality
if score=1700, assume cheating, maximum SAT is 1600

7. The unit sales of a given product have averaged 50,000/yr with a standard deviation of 7000 units. What is the probability of selling exactly 60,000 units this year?

prob of exactly 60,000 = zero, by definition, point has no area

Sales Chart

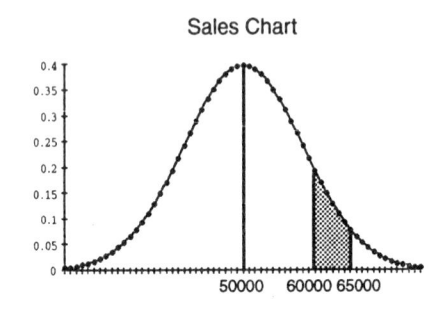

p(60,000-65,000) =
(.4838-.4236) = .0602 ≅ 6%

What is the probability of selling between 60,000 and 65,000 units? (assume normal distribution)

Battery Life-Times

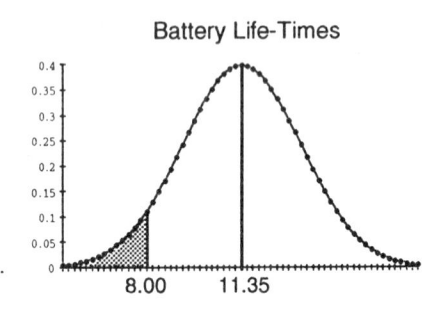

LT 8 hours = 13.4%

8. If dry cell batteries have an average life span of 11.35 hours and a standard deviation of 3.03 hours, what is the probability that a battery selected at random will have a life less than 8 hours? (assume normal distribution)

Battery Life-Times

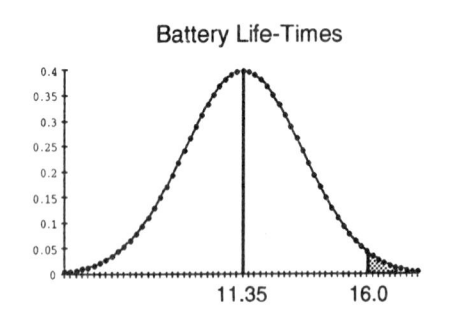

GT 16 hours = 6.3%

What is the probability of a battery life greater than 16 hours?

9. The average car runs 75,000 before needing major transmission repair (standard deviation = 12,000...normal distribution). After how many miles will 85% of the cars need (or have needed) major transmission work?

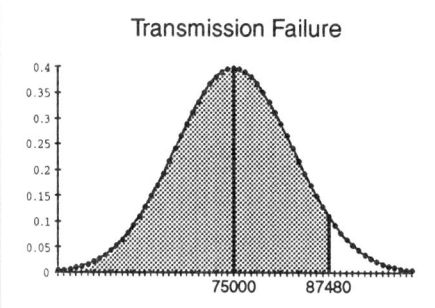

Transmission Failure

Z = 1.04,
in miles = 12,480
answer = 87,480

10. For a normally distributed population with a mean of 75 and a standard deviation of 7, what percentage of the population would be:

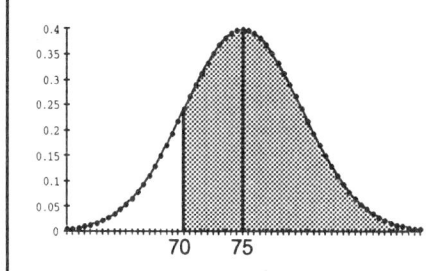

Greater than 70?

GT 70 = 76.11%

Less than 70?

LT 70, simply subtract from above LT 70 = 23.89%

Less than 90?

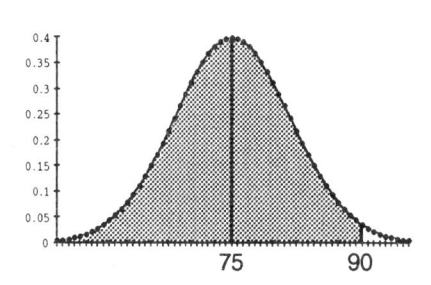

LT 90 = 98.38%

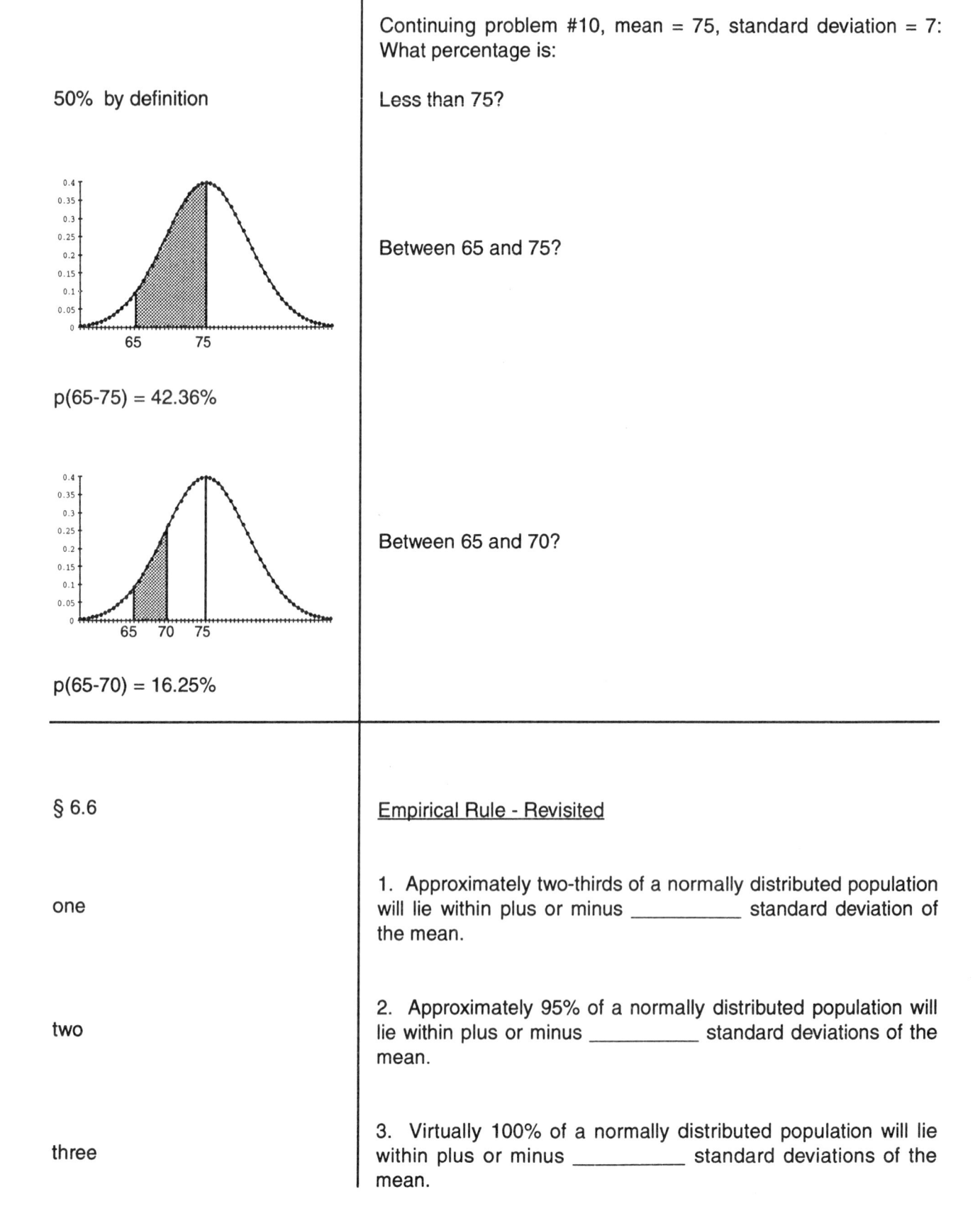

Continuing problem #10, mean = 75, standard deviation = 7:
What percentage is:

50% by definition

Less than 75?

Between 65 and 75?

p(65-75) = 42.36%

Between 65 and 70?

p(65-70) = 16.25%

---

§ 6.6

Empirical Rule - Revisited

one

1. Approximately two-thirds of a normally distributed population will lie within plus or minus _____ standard deviation of the mean.

two

2. Approximately 95% of a normally distributed population will lie within plus or minus _____ standard deviations of the mean.

three

3. Virtually 100% of a normally distributed population will lie within plus or minus _____ standard deviations of the mean.

4. A Z score tells the _____ of standard deviations between an observation and the mean.	number

---

The Normal Approximation to the Binomial — § 6.8

1. The Poisson distribution provided a convenient approximation to the binomial, especially in situations where "n" was very _____, and "p" was very _____, but multiplied together, they produced a value of "np" that was quite manageable.

   large, small

2. The normal approximation to the binomial (on the other hand) is not as appropriate for small values of "p", rather it is more appropriate when "p" is near _____, and "n" will be fairly _____.

   .50
   large

3. Suppose you were interested in determining the probability of 4 heads in 10 tosses of a fair coin. This would be the binomial(4, 10, p=.5). If this problem were worked as a normal approximation to a binomial, why could you not find the probability of x = 4.0, for a normal curve which had a mean of 5.0?

   A Point Has No Area

4. The difficulty encountered in problem three (above) is corrected by making an adjustment for continuity. This involves adding and subtracting _____ from the desired number (or range).

   Adjustment for Continuity

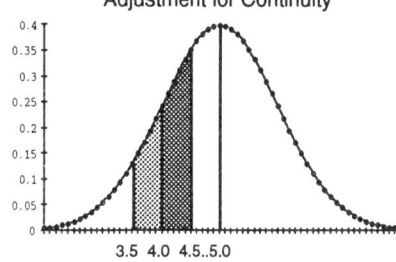

Normal Approximation to Binomial

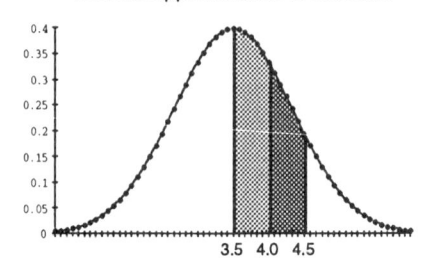

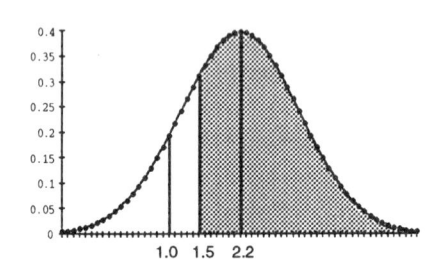

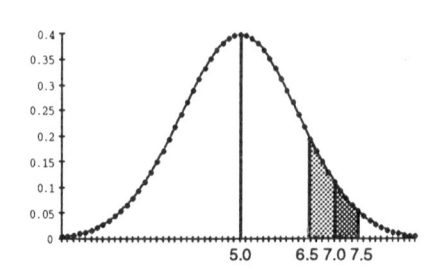

(graph showing shaded region between 3.5, 4.0, 4.5)

normal approximation
Z = .76   p = .2764

5. Rework problem 4, S 5.4 as a normal approximation to the binomial. (Previous problem had been to find the probability of 4 heads in 7 tosses of a fair coin, binomial answer = .2734.)

(Note: Actually n is a bit small to get a consistently good approximation, but let's use this problem for practice anyway (the same thing could be said about problem 6 and 8 as well).)

Normal Approximation to Binomial

(graph showing shaded region at 1.0, 1.5, 2.2)

normal approximation
Z = .527   p = .7019

6. Rework problem 5, S 5.4 as a normal approximation to the binomial. (Previous problem had been to find the probability of one minus the probability of either zero or one loss, in 11 games when the probability of a loss is 20%, binomial answer = .6779.)

Normal Approximation to Binomial

(graph showing shaded region at 5.0, 6.5, 7.0, 7.5)

normal approximation
Z = .948   Z = 1.58
p = .3289   p = .4394
       p = .1105

7. Rework problem 1, S 5.8 as a normal approximation to the binomial. (Previous problem had been to find the probability of 7 heads in 10 tosses of a fair coin, the binomial answer had been .1172.)

8. Rework problem 4, S 5.8 as a normal approximation to the binomial. (Previous problem had been to find the probability of four sunny days out of six when the probability of a sunny day was .20, binomial answer = .0154.)

Normal Approximation to Binomial

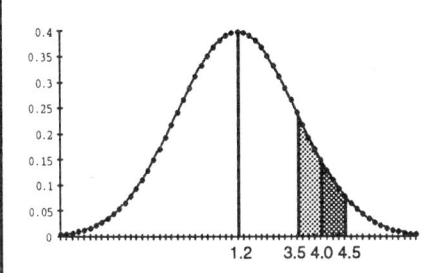

Normal Approximation
Z = 1.32   Z = 2.34
p = .4066   p = .4896
    p = .084

9. Problem 4, S 5.8 has now been worked a variety of ways, with a variety of answers, to wit:
Binomial = .0154
Poisson = .026 or .095
Hypergeometric = .0045
Normal Approximation = .083
One is reminded of the saying: "Man with one watch sure of the time, man with two watches never sure." Of all of these different answers, which one is correct?

But then to say that any four decimal probability is "correct" with respect a weather prediction has to be the height of chutzpah.

binomial
The binomial is an exact probability, not an approximation.

The Uniform Distribution

§ 6.9-1

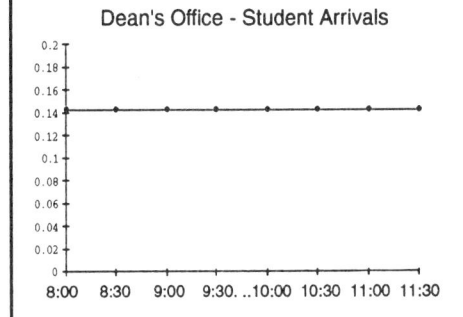

1. Student arrivals in the Dean's office are uniformly distributed at the rate of 12 per hour between 8:00 AM and 11:30 AM (when the dean and staff break for lunch).

Given this information:

Dean's Office - Student Arrivals

70

.1428	a. What is the probability of students arriving between 8:00 and 8:30?
.2856	b. What is the probability of student arrivals between 9:00 and 10:00?
	(continuing with problem 1, a uniform distribution between 8:00 and 11:30)
.023	c. What is the probability of student arrivals between 10:25 and 10:30?
.0047	d. What is the probability of student arrivals between 10:29 and 10:30?
zero, a point has no area	e. What is the probability of a student arrival at precisely 9:30?

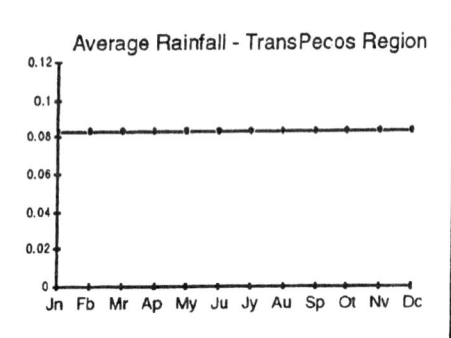

Average Rainfall - TransPecos Region

2. Consider this situation, rainfall in the Trans-Pecos region averages .94 inches per month. For the following problems assume a uniform distribution throughout the year (let each month = 30 days, the year = 360 days).

.083	a. What is the probability of rain in January?
.25	b. What is the probability of rain during the summer? (June, July and August)
.25	c. What is the probability of rain during the winter? (December, January and February)
.0027	d. What is the probability of rain during a given day?

e. Find the probability of rain during a given hour. | .00012

f. What is the probability of rain during any given minute? In other words, should you ever find yourself in the rain in El Paso, you can say: "Statistically, it should not be raining on me at this minute!" | .0000019

The rainfall does not follow a uniform distribution.
Actual rainfall is as follows:

Jan	.39
Feb	.63
Mar	.12
Apr	.36
May	1.07
Jun	1.88
Jly	1.94
Aug	3.04
Spt	.95
Oct	.07
Nov	.09
Dec	.75

Actual Rainfall - TransPecos Region

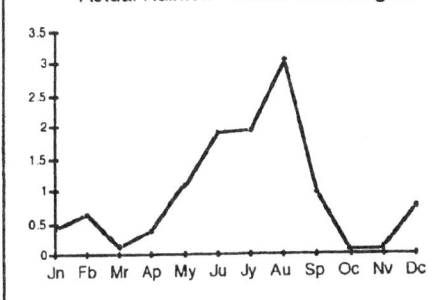

a. Does this appear to be a uniform distribution? | not really

b. Based upon these actual amounts, what is the probability of rain during the summer? (June, July, August) | .6076

c. Based upon these actual amounts, what is the probability of rain during the winter? (December, January, February) | .1567

72

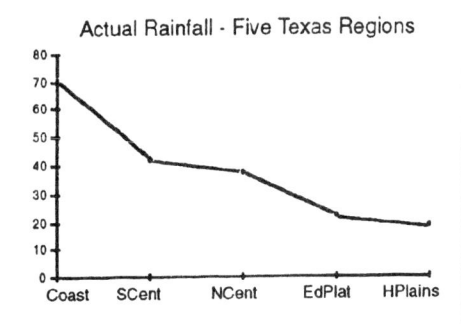

[Graph: Actual Rainfall - Five Texas Regions, showing decreasing values from Coast to HPlains]

in a word, no

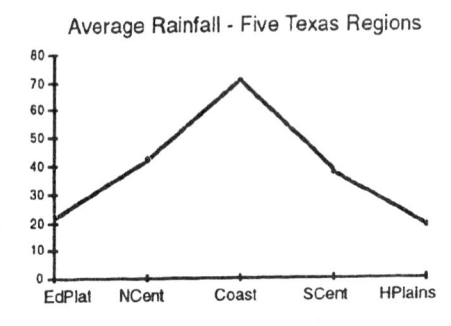

[Graph: Average Rainfall - Five Texas Regions, rearranged: EdPlat, NCent, Coast, SCent, HPlains - bell-shaped]

No, the X axis (regions) is nominal data, it must be at least interval. Problem 2 also suffered from the same problem.

3. Now consider this situation, the yearly rainfall from five Texas regions:
Coast   70.47
SCntrl   41.97
NCntrl   37.54
EdPlteau 21.68
HPlains 20.26

Average 38.38

a. Does this distribution appear to be uniform?

b. Now suppose that a sharp student notices that with a little rearranging, the distribution might look approximately normal, as shown.

Would it be appropriate to rearrange the data in this manner and then treat the situation as a normal distribution?

---

§ 6.9-2

time between arrivals

queue
(pronounced "Q")

The Exponential Distribution

1. The exponential distribution is related to the Poisson distribution. If the Poisson gives the average number of arrivals over a given time period, then the exponential tells the _____ between _____.

2. In statistics, a waiting line is a _____.

3. Students arrive at the Dean's office at the rate of 12 per hour. This situation could be expressed as an exponential distribution with a mean time between arrivals equal to _____ minutes.

5

4. For the above problem where students are arriving at the rate of 12 per hour, what is the probability of 20 or more in an hour?

.202

5. What is the probability of 5 or fewer in an hour?

1 - .67 = .33

6. If Problem three (12 students per hour) is actually a continuation of Problem 1 S 6.5, (students arriving 12 per hour) what conflict have we created?

Problem 1, S 6.5 specified that the arrivals were _uniformly_ distributed.

The exponential demands a Poisson distribution.

CHAPTER 7

Statistical Inference and Sampling

CHAPTER OBJECTIVES

The previous chapter introduced several continuous probability distributions, including the very important normal distribution. In this chapter, the use of the normal distribution will be extended to problems involving statistical estimation and statistical inference, that is, the estimation of population characteristics on the basis of sample information. By the end of the chapter you should be able to:

1. Define and distinguish between sample statistics and population parameters.

2. Discuss the Central Limit Theorem and illustrate its use in statistical inference.

3. Construct confidence intervals using both the normal distribution and the Student t distribution.

4. Describe different aspects of sampling and sampling techniques such as: sampling error, finite population correction factor, systematic sampling, stratified sampling, and cluster sampling.

STATISTICAL INFERENCE AND SAMPLING

§ 7.0

A Look Back/Introduction

1. The previous chapters have investigated the concept of probability. Chapter Five discussed discrete probability distributions such as _____. Chapter Six discussed continuous probability distributions such as _____.

discrete uniform, binomial, Poisson, and hypergeometric, normal, uniform, and exponential

2. Because so many natural and business phenomena fit a 'bell-shaped' distribution, the _____ distribution is probably the most widely applicable distribution.

normal

3. However, the normal distribution has an even greater range of applications in statistics. Perhaps its most important use comes in the area of statistical inference. Statistical inference is the technique by which we infer certain characteristics about the population on the basis of a _____.

sample

4. Characteristics of the population such as the population mean or the population standard deviation are referred to as population _____.

parameters

5. Characteristics of the sample such as the sample mean or the sample standard deviation are referred to as sample _____.

statistics

6. So that we may distinguish between them, the various parameters and statistics are designated with different symbols:
    a. The population mean is designated _____.
    b. The sample mean is designated _____.
    c. The population standard deviation is _____.
    d. The sample standard deviation is _____.

μ
$\bar{x}$
σ
s

---

§ 7.1

Random Sampling - Distribution of the Sample Mean

1. In a random sample, each available elementary unit has a known probability of selection. The most common variation of this type of sampling is the simple random sample in which each unit has the _____ probability of selection.

    same, or equal

2. The only way to insure a truly random sample is with some type of probability mechanism. If a list is present and can be numbered then a _____ _____ table can prove helpful. If a computer is available, many computers have built in routines called _____ _____ generators which can provide a random number.

    random number

    random number

3. If you select only a portion of the items in the population, that is called a _____.

    sample

4. If you select all of the items in the population, that is called a _____.

    census

5. The idea behind sampling is that certain characteristics of the population can be _____ or _____ on the basis of a small sample of items from that population. In doing that we are assuming that our sample of items is representative of the items in the population.

    inferred, estimated

6. If you have a population and you wish to estimate the mean of that population on the basis of a sample, then ($\overline{X}$, the mean of the sample) will be your estimate of _____, (the mean of the population). It is assumed that the sample mean will be (close to, exactly equal to, quite different from) the true population mean.

    μ

    close to

7. The Central Limit Theorem provides us a means for describing the shape of the sampling distribution, that is, the shape of the distributions of the values of $\overline{x}$. The Central Limit Theorem says that if you have a population with a mean of μ, and a standard deviation of σ then the distribution of sample means taken from that population will be _____ distributed with a mean equal to _____, and a standard deviation equal to _____.

    normally
    μ
    $\sigma/\sqrt{n}$

normal

normal

normal

$\mu = 100, \quad \sigma = 10$

Distribution of Population Values

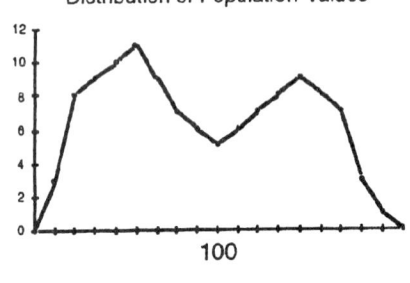

$\mu = 100, \quad \sigma = 10$

Distribution of Values in Sample

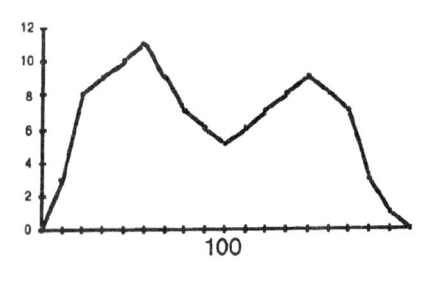

Distribution of X-BAR Values

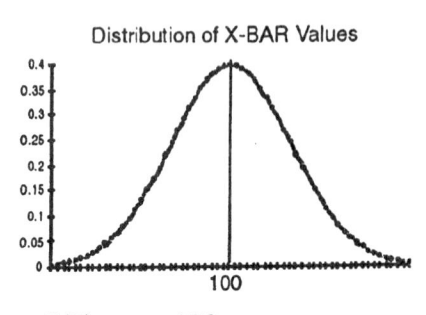

$E(\bar{x}) = \mu = 100$
$\sigma_{\bar{x}} = \sigma_x/\sqrt{n} = 10/\sqrt{100} = 1$

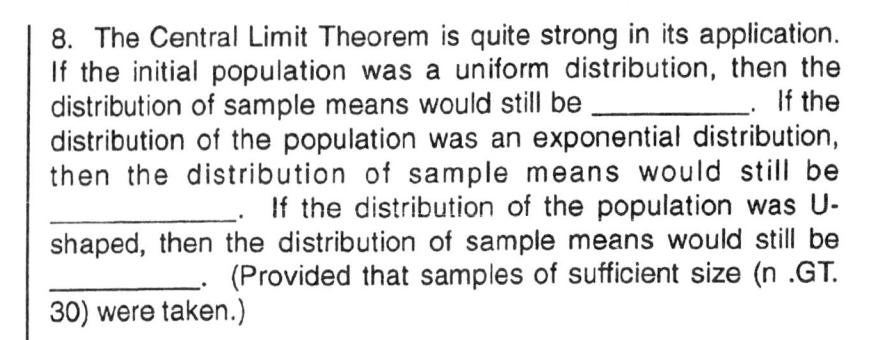

8. The Central Limit Theorem is quite strong in its application. If the initial population was a uniform distribution, then the distribution of sample means would still be _____. If the distribution of the population was an exponential distribution, then the distribution of sample means would still be _____. If the distribution of the population was U-shaped, then the distribution of sample means would still be _____. (Provided that samples of sufficient size (n .GT. 30) were taken.)

9. Suppose that you had a population which looked like the picture to the left: it has a mean of 100 and a standard deviation of 10, and it is definitely "not-normal"

Now suppose that you draw a sample of 100 of the items from that population, what would you expect the distribution of that sample to be like, that is, how would it be distributed?

Did I trick you? The Central Limit Theorem is concerned with the distribution of a set of X-BAR values, not with the distribution of the individual items in the population. A sample should approximate the population from whence it comes.

Now suppose that you took a series of samples of 100 items from that population and you made a distribution of the $\bar{X}$ values from that series of samples.

Describe that distribution, its shape, its mean, and its standard deviation.

10. This distribution of x̄ values, shows how close we would expect our sample estimate (x̄) to be, relative to the true mean (μ).

In the last chapter we gave the "Empirical Rule", that plus or minus two standard deviations should encompass about 95% of the items in a normally distributed population. Since the Central Limit Theorem specifies that the distribution of x̄ values is normal, that Empirical Rule also applies to sampling situations, the only change is that the computational expression for the standard deviation has changed to $\sigma_{\bar{x}} = \sigma_x / \sqrt{n}$ (it is still a standard deviation, only its computational formula has changed).

In light of all of this, approximately 95% of all of the sample averages (x̄) should fall within what range?

Distribution of Sample Means

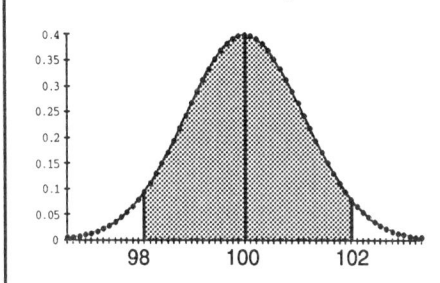

95% within 98 - 102

11. Because the standard deviation of the sample means ($\sigma_{\bar{x}}$) measures the amount by which we would expect our sample estimate to differ from the true mean, it provides us with a measure of the error of our estimate of the mean. For this reason the term ($\sigma_{\bar{x}}$) is often referred to as the _____ _____.

standard error

Sampling from a Finite Population

§ 7.2

1. When the sample is taken from a finite population, in such a manner that the sample begins to be a sizeable proportion of the population itself, the standard error (the standard deviation of the sample means) needs to be adjusted. The term that provides this adjustment is the _____ _____ _____ factor, or FPC.

finite population correction

2. The rule of thumb for determining when the sample has become a "sizeable" proportion of the population is that the finite population correction factor should be used any time that the sample represents over _____ % of the universe.

5%

80

$$\sqrt{\frac{N-n}{N-1}}$$

population
sample

Yes 100/300 = .33
.33 greater than .05

(1) $\sqrt{\frac{200}{299}}$ = .8178(1.0)=.8178

FPC = $\sqrt{\frac{100-100}{100-1}}$ = 0

std error = (1.0)(0) = 0
Which says (very logically) that if you have no sample (we have a census) you have no sampling error.

---

§ 7.3

point

zero, point has no area

---

3. Give the formula for the finite population correction factor.

where N = _____ size
and   n = _____ size

Note: if the universe standard deviation is used: s.e.= $\frac{\sigma}{\sqrt{n}} \sqrt{\frac{N-n}{N-1}}$

if the sample standard deviation is used: est s.e. = $\frac{s}{\sqrt{n}} \sqrt{\frac{N-n}{N}}$

4. For the recent problem (problem 9, § 7.1) suppose that the total size of the population had actually been only 300 items. If our sample was 100, should the finite population correction factor be used? Yes or No, and why.

5. For the above problem, sample size equal to 100 and population size equal to 300, what would be the value of the standard error after the finite population correction factor was applied?

6. What would be the standard error if the sample size were 100 and the population size were 100?

Confidence Intervals

1. You have a population. The mean of that population is unknown, so you wish to develop an estimate of that mean using a sample. You will use the average of the sample ($\bar{X}$) as your best single estimate of the value of (μ). In this case, ($\bar{X}$) is referred to as a _____ estimate.

2. Since ($\bar{X}$) is a single point, the probability of it being "correct", that is, being exactly equal to the true mean is _____.

3. Although a point has no area, and hence it has a zero probability of being correct, we can construct an interval which will have a specified probability of being correct. This interval within which we believe that true mean to be is called a _____ _____.

confidence interval

4. The Empirical Rule specified that approximately 95% of the items would fall within plus or minus two standard deviations (that is a Z value of two). Actually the "correct" value of Z for a 95% confidence interval is Z = _____. The correct value of Z for a 99% confidence interval is Z = _____.

Z = 1.96
Z = 2.58

5. Suppose you are trying to estimate the mean of a population with known standard deviation of 20. A sample of 100 items is selected which produces a sample average of 42. What is the 95% confidence interval for the estimate of the true mean?

Confidence Interval for est. of μ

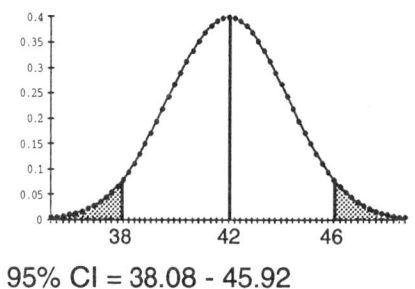

95% CI = 38.08 - 45.92
      =   38 - 46

6. Given a population with standard deviation equal to 12. A sample of 144 items produces a sample average of 120. Find the 99% confidence interval for the estimate of the true mean.

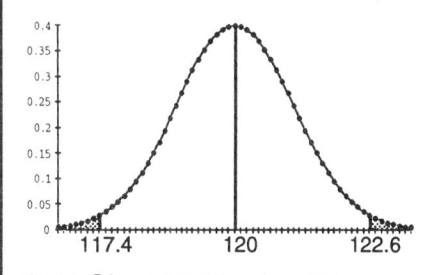

Confidence Interval for est. of μ

99% CI = 117.42 - 122.58

82

One-Tail Upper Bound

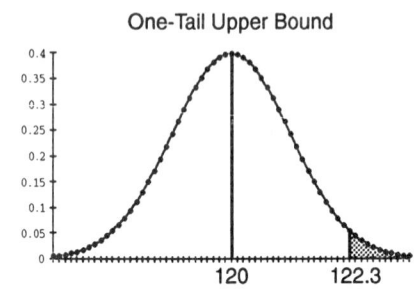

99% UB = 122.33

7. For the problem above (standard deviation = 12, sample size = 144, and sample mean = 42) find the 99% upper bound for the estimate of the true mean.

95% Confidence Interval

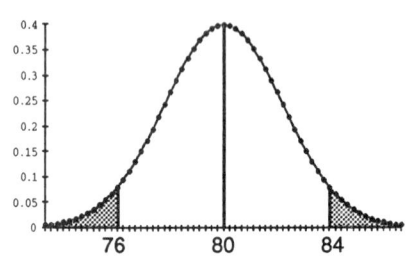

95% CI = 76.08 - 83.92
     =   76 - 84

8. Given a population with mean = 80 and standard deviation = 10, if samples of size n = 25 are taken, 95% of those sample averages should lie within what range?

99% One-Tail Upper Bound

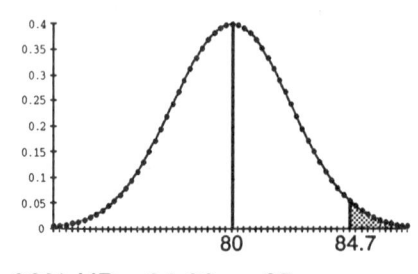

99% UB = 84.66 = 85

9. For the problem above (mean = 80, standard deviation = 10, n = 25) 99% of the sample averages should be less than what value?

10. Given a population with a standard deviation of twenty. A sample of 400 is taken to estimate the mean. The sample average is 300. What is the 95% confidence interval for the estimate of the true mean?

95% Confidence Interval

95% CI = 298.04 - 301.96
      =   298 - 302

11. For the previous problem (standard deviation = 20, n = 400, and X-bar = 300) what would be the 90% confidence interval for the estimate of the true mean?

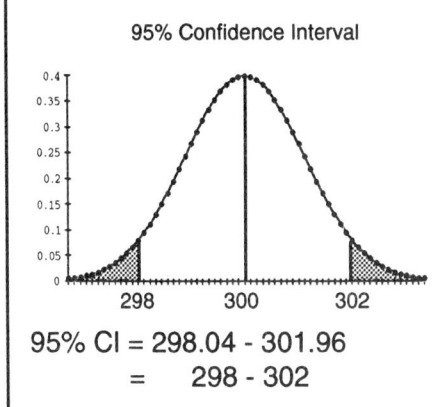

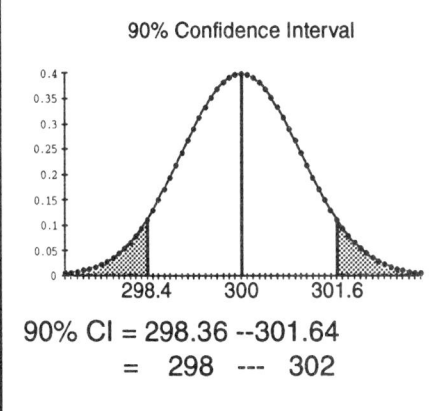

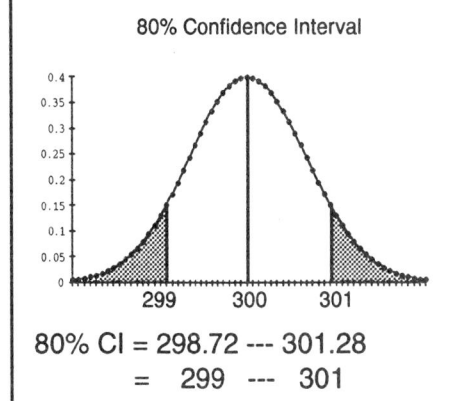

90% Confidence Interval

90% CI = 298.36 --301.64
      =   298 --- 302

12. For the previous problem (standard deviation = 20, n = 400, and X-bar = 300) what would be the 80% confidence interval for the estimate of the true mean?

80% Confidence Interval

80% CI = 298.72 --- 301.28
      =   299 --- 301

84

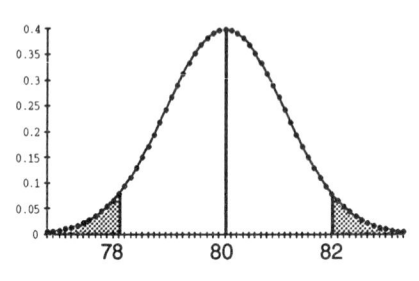

95% Confidence Interval

95% CI = 78.06 - 81.94
    =   78 - 82

13. You have taken a sample of 200 items from a population with a known standard deviation of 14. The sample average is 80. Find the 95% confidence interval for the estimate of the true mean.

Tire Mileage 99% Confidence Interval

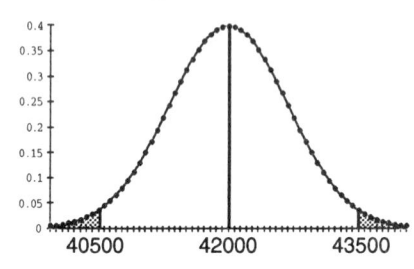

99% CI = 40452 --- 43542
       = 40500 --- 43500

14. A tire company tests 100 tires and finds an average life of 42000 miles. If the population has a known standard deviation of 6000 miles, what is the 99% confidence interval for the estimate of the true mean?

Sample Mean (n=100) Less Than 40,000

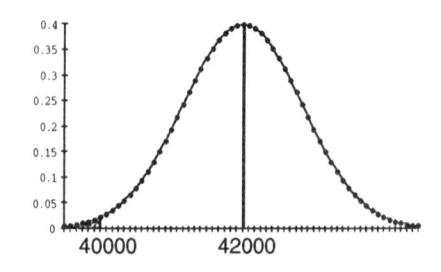

Mean less than 40000
Z = 3.33, p = .00043

15. For the tire problem above (X-bar = 42000, standard deviation = 6000, n = 100) what are the chances that the true mean is less than 40000?

Or, equivalently, if the true mean were 42,000, what is the probability of getting a sample mean based on a sample of a 100, standard deviation = 6000, that is less than 40000?

16. For the tire problem (last two problems) what is the probability that an individual tire would not last 40000 miles? (assume that true mean is 42000)

Individual Tire (n=1) Less Than 40,000

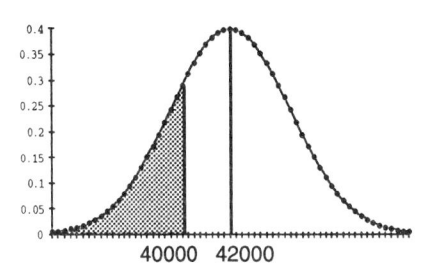

Individual tire
Z = .33, p = .3707

17. Given: a sample of 225, which produces a sample average of 450. If the standard deviation is 30, what is the cut-off for the 99% upper bound for the estimate of the true mean?

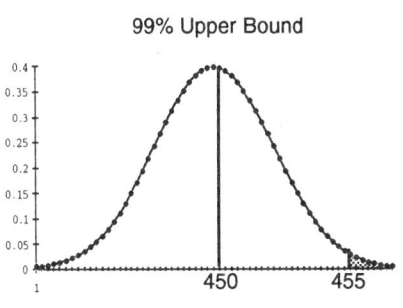

99% Upper Bound

99% UB = 455.14 = 455

18. For the problem above (n = 225, x̄ = 450, and standard deviation = 30) what would be the 90% lower bound for the estimate of the true mean?

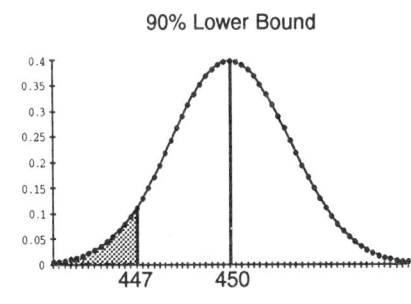

90% Lower Bound

90% LB = 446.7 = 447

§ 7.4

Confidence Intervals - Student t

1. Aw, shucks, out-of-room, problem 1 on the next page.

86

Nope, it doesn't make a lick of sense. As a rule, if you don't have the population. mean, you won't have the population std. dev. either.	1. The problems in the previous section (S 9.4) presented an unusual paradox. In these problems the population mean was not known, but the population standard deviation was known...does that make sense?
$\bar{X}$ estimates μ s estimates σ	2. A sample usually will produce two estimates: ( ) the sample mean, estimates ( ) the population mean. ( ) the standard deviation of the sample, estimates ( ) the population standard deviation.
degrees of freedom	3. In the case of the normal curve, we had the same distribution for every situation, regardless of sample size. In the case of the t distribution (when the population standard deviation is not known) we do not have a curve of the same shape. Instead the curve varies according to its _____ of _____.
n - 1	4. In the Student t distribution, the degrees of freedom are equal to _____.
True	5. In the case of the Student t, the degrees of freedom equal n-1 because the sample mean ($\bar{x}$) was used to calculate the sample standard deviation (s). True or False.
flatter	6. The Student t distribution is shaped much like the normal curve, the difference is that the Student t distribution is (flatter, taller, uniform, asymmetric) than the normal curve.
degrees of freedom	7. The Student t distribution is flatter than the normal curve, and the extent of its flatness varies with _____ of _____.
30	8. The Student t distribution starts out markedly flatter than the normal, but as the sample size increases it becomes progressively more normal. In fact, by the time that the degrees of freedom reaches about _____ the student t is almost identical with the normal distribution.

9. Because the Student t distribution becomes so close to the normal by the time the sample is as large as 30, the t distribution is usually thought of as used for and because of a small sample size. Technically, the use of the Student t has nothing to do with sample size. The use of the Student t is predicated around the substitution of _____ for _____.

s substituted for σ

10. The Student t distribution was given its name as a memorial to all of the students who flunked trying to learn it. True or False

False

11. The Student t distribution is named after a sharp student who thought it up one day in STAT 101 at State U. True or False

False. W.S. Gossett developed the t while working for the Guiness brewery. He published under the pseudonym "student".

12. A sample of 17 items was taken which produced a sample mean of 40 and a standard deviation of 10. Find the 95% confidence interval for the estimate of the true mean.

Student t 95% Confidence Int. df=16

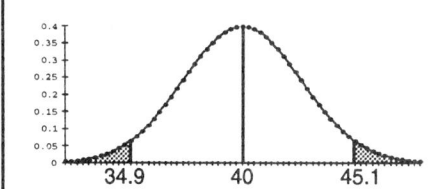

df = 16, t = 2.12
95% CI = 34.86 --- 45.14

13. A sample of 25 students produces a sample average of 104 with a standard deviation of 6. Find the 99% confidence interval for the estimate of the true mean.

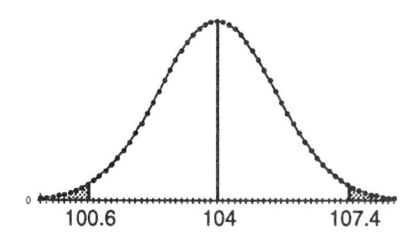

Student t 99% Confidence Int. df=24

df = 24, t = 2.797
99% CI = 100.6 --- 107.4

95% Confidence Int. Z distribution

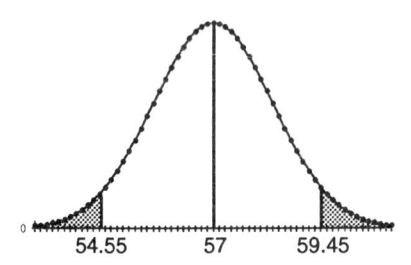

[graph showing normal curve with 54.55, 57, 59.45]

A trick?! Standard dev. came from pop., use Z
CI = 54.55 --- 59.45

14. Given a population with a mean believed to be around 60 and a standard deviation of 5, a sample of 16 items is taken which produces a sample average of 57. Find the 95% confidence interval for the estimate of the true mean.

Student t 95% Confidence Int. df=24

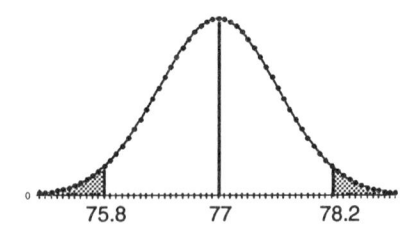

[graph showing normal curve with 75.8, 77, 78.2]

df = 24, t = 2.064
95% CI = 75.76 --- 78.24

15. A sample of 25 items is taken and a sample average of 77 with a standard deviation of 3 is recorded. Find the 95% confidence interval for the estimate of the true mean.

Student t 90% Confidence Int. df=7

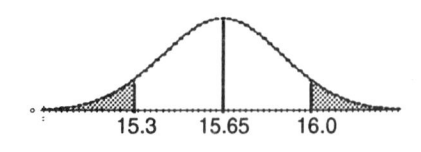

[graph showing normal curve with 15.3, 15.65, 16.0]

$\bar{x}$ = 15.65 s = .585
df = 7, t = 1.895
CI = 15.26 - 16.04

16. Washnot Paint Company is checking the amount of red dye being mixed into five gallon containers of Rose Blossom colored paint. The process specification calls for 15.5 ounces of red tint in each can. A sample of eight cans is selected and produces the following results: 15.2, 15.0. 15.7, 15.9, 15.8, 16.1, 15.6, and 15.9. Find the 90% confidence interval for the estimate of the true mean.

17. A shipment of copper ingots is received at the wire rolling mill. They are supposed to weigh 1000 pounds. A sample of 10 ingots was weighed and the mean is determined to be 982 pounds with a standard deviation of 18 pounds. Find the 95% confidence interval for the estimate of the true mean.

Student t 95% Confidence Int. df=9

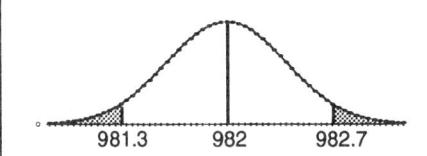

981.3   982   982.7

df = 9, t = 2.306
CI = 981.3 --- 982.7

18. A crushing plant was designed to process 35,000 tons of ore per day. A recent 7 day test period showed an average throughput of 33,000 tons per day with a standard deviation of 1500 tons. Find the 99% lower bound for the estimate of the true mean.

Student t 95% Lower Bound df=6

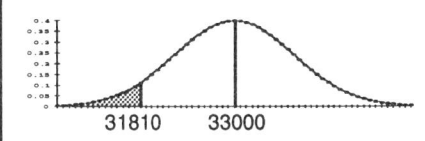

31810   33000

df = 6, t = 1.943
99% Lower Bound = 31810

Determining the Required Sample Size

§ 7.5

1. In sampling, the bigger the sample, the better the results. True or False

Not necessarily true. A small sample properly executed will be better than a larger sample done poorly.

2. Given the same degree of care, a larger sample will produce a more precise estimate of the population mean than a smaller sample. True or False

True.

3. The precision of the sample estimate can be controlled by variation of the sample size. True or False. Conversely, the required sample size can be determined for specified levels of precision. True or False

True.
True again, that is the point of this section.

90

95% sure within + or - 5
n = 61.46 = 62

95% sure within + or - 2
n = 384.16 = 384

99% sure within 100
  n = 23963 = 24,000

99% sure within 50
  n = 95852 = 96,000

Four times as many, because the estimate is twice as precise (50 vs. 100). Required sample size increases as the square of the increase in precision.

No.

No.

---

precision. True or False

4. A sample is taken to develop a more precise estimate of a population believed to have a mean of 100 with a standard deviation of 20. How large would the sample have to be in order to be 95% confident of being within 5 of the true mean.

5. For the above problem (mean = 100, standard deviation = 20), how large would the sample have to be in order to be 95% confident of being within 2 of the true mean.

6. Regarding the tire example discussed previously where the tires had an average life of 42,000 miles and a standard deviation of 6000 miles, how many tires would have to be tested to be 99% sure that the estimate was within 100 miles of the true average?

7. For the above problem (mean = 42,000 miles, standard deviation = 6000 miles), how many tires would need to be tested to be 99% sure that the estimate was within 50 miles of the true average?

8. Compare the results from problem 6 (estimate within 100 miles) and problem 7 (estimate within 50 miles). The required sample size in problem 7 was _____ times as large as problem 6...why?

9. Consider the situation in problem 6, 7, and 8 from above, does that seem like an economically intelligent thing to do...to test an additional 72,000 tires so that the confidence interval could be reduced from 100 miles to 50 miles? For that matter does it make business sense to test 24,000 tires so that the confidence interval can be as low as 100 miles?

10. For the tire (as in "I bet you are getting "tire-d" of this example problem") situation in the above problems, what would be the required sample size if they were willing to have a 99% confidence interval of 1000 miles?
  Let's work that problem the easy way by using the squared

that 24,000 tires would put us within 100 miles. So, 1000 miles is _____ times as many as 100. Therefore our sample could be reduced by 10 squared or _____. Therefore we need to take only one hundredth of the sample size needed for a confidence interval of 100 miles. Thus, 24000/100 = _____. That would mean a test of 60 cars, a much more reasonable figure.

10
100

240

11. The forest service has estimated there to be an average of 150 deciduous trees per acre in a given mixed pine forest. The standard deviation was 35. Should they desire a more precise estimate, how large a sample would be needed to obtain a 99% confidence level of being within 10 of the true mean?

99% sure within 10
n = 82

12. By the way, what is a deciduous tree?

A tree that loses its leaves in winter.

13. A sample needs to be taken to develop a more precise estimate of a population of test scores which are believed to have an average of 50 and a standard deviation of 3. How large a sample would need to be taken to be 95% confident of being within 1 of the true mean?

95% sure within 1
n = 35

14. Approximately 95% of the items in a normal curve will fall within plus or minus _____ standard deviations of the mean.

two

15. We can use the information from problem 14 (95% within plus or minus two standard deviations) with respect to the distribution of a set of sample averages because of the Central Limit Theorem. True or False

True. CLT says dist. of X-bar values will be normal.

16. Using the information from problems 14 and 15 we can develop a method for approximating the standard deviation. If you go two standard deviations to the left of the mean you will reach some of the lowest values generally encountered. If you go two standard deviations to the right of the mean you will reach some of the highest values generally encountered. Therefore our formula for approximating the standard deviation is an expected _____ value minus an expected _____ value, divided by _____.

High - Low
Four

No. Two std dev = 95%.
To get very highest and very lowest you need plus or minus three std dev. which is why you will often see this "trick" for est. the std. dev as SD ≈ range/6

4.25 inches

n = 30

7 points

estimate of standard deviation:
11/4 = 3.75 degrees

99% CI = 95.16 --- 98.64

§ 7.6

population

---

17. Would be expect those "highest" and "lowest" values to truly be the highest and lowest values which we would ever see in that distribution? (Hint, remember that plus or minus two standard deviations will delineate only 95% of the curve.)

18. You are trying to estimate the approximate standard deviation for the height of a certain group of men. The tallest men are usually around 6'7", and the shortest are around 5'2". What would be your estimate of the standard deviation?

19. For the above problem, how large a sample would you have to take to be 99% sure that your estimate of the mean height is within 2" of the true mean?

20. A certain football team (the "Fighting Opossums" to be exact) have hired a new statistician. He wants to determine how many points per game the 'Possums average. But he his also lazy, so he estimates the standard deviation from the highest and lowest values which are 28 and 0 respectively. What is his estimate?

21. An interested weather enthusiast has recorded the daily highs during the month of July for the current year. She found an average high of 96.9 degrees with the highest value 102 and the lowest value 91. Use this information to develop the 99% confidence interval for the estimate of the true mean daily high for July. (Assume that the current year is representative of July weather.) (Use Z...in one sense this should be a Student t problem since the standard deviation was based upon the sample and not upon the universe, however, since the standard deviation is only an approximation anyway, to use the Student t would seem a bit "pushy". In addition, the sample size is over 30.)

Other Sampling Procedures

1. The entire collection of items under investigation, all of the units which are available for sampling, this is called the _____.

2. Usually a single element taken from a population (although it can be a set of elements taken as a group) this is called a _____ unit.

sampling unit

3. The list of population elements from which the sample items will actually be selected is called the _____ frame.

sampling frame

4. A group of elements which forms a single sampling unit is often referred to as a _____.

cluster

5. Sometimes a group will be divided into distinct subpopulations or strata (from a synonym for the word "layers"). Samples are selected independently from each strata. This is called a _____ sample.

stratified

6. In order for a sample to be properly termed to be a "random sample", each available elementary unit in the population must have a _____ probability of selection.

known

7. In a "simple random sample", each available elementary unit in the population will have an _____ probability of selection.

equal

8. Taking a sample from a very large population (such as all the names in the phone book) can become quite a pain. Suppose a suggestion is made to take the first non-commercial name at the top of each odd-numbered page. This would be a variation of a _____ sample.

systematic

9. With respect to problem 8, with a true purist consider such a selection a "random sample"?

(As discussed in the answer section, a true purist might not consider such a systematic sample to be a random sample of even the names in the phone book. In turn, the phone book probably does not constitute an accurate population for either households or individuals.)

Perhaps not. Most business researchers would consider it a random sample, but technically speaking, a purist might not, since different pages might have different numbers of names, distorting the probabilities ever so slightly

10. Using a systematic sample can be dangerous if there are cycles (or periodicity) in the data. True or False

True.

True

heterogeneous

homogeneous

True

False

True

True

11. If there is no periodicity in the data, then a systematic sample will produce a suitably random sample which can be treated (statistically) as if it were a simple random sample. True or False

12. In a stratified sample, there are marked differences between the different strata...the strata are not like each other with respect to the specific characteristics being investigated. In this case, the strata are said to be (heterogeneous, homogeneous) with respect to each other.

13. But within an individual strata, the items are (hopefully) quite similar. So within strata, the items are said to be (heterogeneous, homogeneous).

14. In a stratified sample, each strata is sampled individually, with a separate mean and standard deviation developed for each individual strata. True or False

15. When taking a stratified sample, it is required that the same size sample be taken from each strata. So if the stratas were small, medium, and large clothing stores, then a sample of, for example, 100 stores of each type would have to be collected. True or False

16. In a stratified sample, if you have different sample sizes and different strata sizes, how do you combine them to form a single population estimate? Answer, by using a process similar to the weighted averages studied earlier in the book. True or False

17. In a stratified sample, each strata had been a distinctive subset of the population...a segment quite different from the rest of the population. The cluster sample is quite different, however. In a cluster sample, each cluster is (hopefully) a miniature duplicate of the population. For instance, if you wanted a sample of Rotarians, you might talk to members of several local clubs, operating on the assumption that these local clubs (clusters) are representative of all Rotary clubs. True or False.

18. Whereas the strata had been heterogeneous with respect to each other, the various clusters should be (heterogeneous, homogeneous) with respect to the other clusters (and with respect to the population as a whole. | homogeneous

19. Yet within the individual clusters there has been no attempt to segment the items, hence within clusters you should find the items to be (heterogeneous, homogeneous). | heterogeneous

20. The use of cluster sampling is often associated with what is referred to as "area cluster sampling".
For instance, rather than try to randomly sample from the entire United States, certain cities (clusters) will first be selected. It then might be desirable to have a stratified sample of the items within the clusters, and then a random sample of items within the stratas. This is known as multiple stage sampling. True or False. | True

CHAPTER 8

Hypothesis Testing for Mean and Variance of a Population

CHAPTER OBJECTIVES

Anytime a sample is taken to check the value of a population parameter, sampling scatter (sampling error) will be present. In other words, it is not reasonable to expect X-bar to exactly equal the true mean, although it should be close. But how close is "close enough"?

This chapter presents mathematical ways for determining how close is "close enough", along with the consequences of that determination. By the end of the chapter you should be able to:

1. Discuss what is meant by the terms "statistically significant difference" and "hypothesis test".

2. Test for significant difference for means and variances of a population.

3. Discuss the implications of a given decision from a hypothesis test.

HYPOTHESIS TESTING

§ 8.0 — A Look Back/Introduction

1. In the previous chapter we had attempted to estimate a population parameter such as (μ) by taking a small sample and using _____, the mean of the sample as an estimate of (μ).

X-bar

2. Because we have taken an actual sample, we now know the value of (μ). True or False.

False, all we have is an estimate of the mean.

3. We do not know the true value of (μ), but we can form a confidence interval. We now know that the true value of the mean must lie within that range. True or False.

False again, we are not sure (100% sure) that the mean is in the confidence interval, only 95% sure.

4. We assign probabilities to our confidence interval using the values from the normal curve. We can use the normal curve because the Central Limit Theorem states that the distribution of X-bar values will be normal. True or False.

True

§ 8.1 — Hypothesis Testing

1. The fact that we have to form confidence intervals illustrates the fact that there is no single value for the true mean. True or False.

It exists, but the only way to find it is to take a census.

2. We will usually start with a value which we believe to be the true mean, i.e. $\mu = 100$. This value becomes our "nil" hypothesis. True or False

False, not "nil"...null

3. After forming the null hypothesis, is it usually customary to state your option should you believe the null hypothesis to be false. This alternate hypothesis is called the "alternative hypothesis" (hmmmm, that sounds too easy). True or False

True

98

4. Let us suppose that someone has told us that the mean of a certain population is equal to 100. If the mean of that population really is 100, then a sample taken from it should produce a sample average of exactly 100. True or False.

False. X-bar should be close to mu, but it cannot be equal by definition.

5. When a claim is made concerning the value of the mean (i.e. mu = 16 oz.) that claim can either be true or false, and you as the one who hears that claim can either accept* it or reject it. If you accept* the claim and the claim is actually false, then you have committed what is known as a _____ error. On the other hand, if the claim were true, but you rejected it, that is known as a _____ error.
*Accept is not technically correct, it is only correct to say "fail to reject"...but more on that point later.

type II

type I

6. For the example above, a machine is making sticks of butter. Each stick should weigh one quarter of a pound, and the four sticks in the package should weigh exactly one pound (16 oz.). Suppose that you take a sample of 50 packages of butter and weigh them. The average of those 50 packages is 15.92 oz. You decide that a difference of .08 is surely close enough for your purposes so you fail to reject the claim. In actuality, the true mean is not 16 oz., but is 15.96 oz. Have you made an error? _____ And if so, what kind? _____

yes
type II

7. From a marketing perspective would you think that a difference of .04 would affect sales?

No, but that is not the purpose of the test.

8. You are the personnel director for a large firm. you have a job opening which would give the hired employee access to very sensitive material. Total honesty is a necessity. Thus there are two employee possibilities: either the employee is honest or he isn't...Likewise, you have two options, either to hire him, or not to hire him. If he is truly honest, but you reject him, that would be a type _____ error. If he is truly dishonest, but you hire him, that would be a type _____ error. In this case, which type of error would be more serious?

type I
type II
type II

9. An atheist is pondering the "big scheme of things". As he sees things, there are two possibilities, either God exists or he doesn't...and the atheist has two possibilities, either to accept God or reject God. If God exists and the atheist (as the name would imply) rejects him, he has made a type _____ error.

type I

100

type II
type I

alpha

tail (or tails)

5% or .05

.05
.01
critical

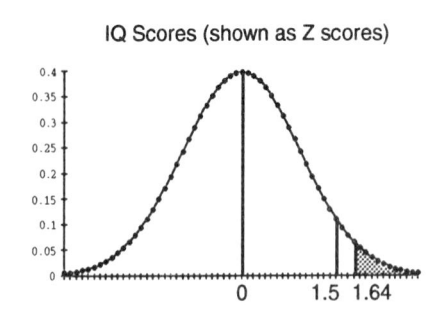

| If God does not exist and that atheist has a change of heart and accepts him, he has made a _____ error. In this case, which type of error do you think would be more serious?

10. The probability of a type I error is defined as _____.

11. In reality, alpha is quite related to the confidence intervals studied previously. Alpha is simply equal to the area that was in the _____(s) of the confidence interval.

12. If you had chosen a 95% confidence interval, this would imply that alpha equals _____.

13. One way to test for statistical significance would be to compute the confidence interval and then see if the actual value (i.e X-bar) fell within that range. More typically, the actual values are substituted into the Z equation and the observed value of Z is computed. This value is compared against the corresponding values from the table. Thus a Z value of at least 1.96 would be significant at the _____ level. A value of at least 2.58 would be significant at the _____ level. These values of 1.96 and 2.58 are called the _____ values.

14. A student claims that his high school is attended by students of above average intelligence. To test this claim, the standard IQ test is administered to 25 students selected at random. These students produce a sample average of 103. If previously published studies have been standardized at mean = 100, and standard deviation = 10, test this student's claim at alpha = .05.

Ho: μ ≤ 100
Ha: μ > 100

IQ Scores (shown as Z scores)

[Normal distribution curve with marks at 0, 1.5, and 1.64]

Z of 1.5 inside 1.64 critical value- no sig. difference- fail to reject Ho

15. In the above problem, a one tail test was used, why?

Student predicted <u>direction</u> of difference by claiming his school was <u>better</u>

16. Since we did not reject the null hypothesis, that means that we have shown that the mean is equal to 100. True or False

No, a X-bar of 103 has not shown the mean to be 100, we have simply been unable to show that the mean is sig. diff. from 100. That is why we use "fail to reject" rather than "accept".

17. Given a machine which is supposed to be filling beer bottles with exactly 12 ounces of beer. If the standard deviation is .5 oz., are we to conclude that the machine is still OK if a sample of 25 beers produces a sample average of 11.9 oz.? Let alpha equal .05.

Ho μ = 12.0 oz.
Ha $\mu \neq$ 12.0 oz.

Beer Bottles (shown as Z scores)
n = 25

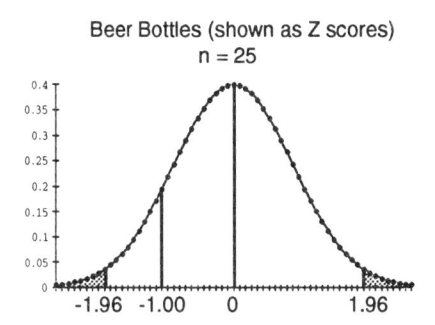

Actual Z = 1.0 inside
crit. value of Z = 1.96
no stat. sig. diff.
fail to reject

18. For the above problem involving the beer bottles, what would be your conclusion if a sample of 400 beers had produced an sample average of 11.9 oz.? Let alpha again be equal to .05.

(same hypotheses)

Beer Bottles (shown as Z scores)
n = 400

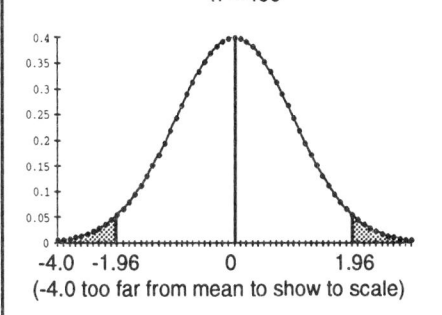

(-4.0 too far from mean to show to scale)

Actual Z = 4.0 outside crit. value of Z = 1.96
stat. sig. diff.
reject null hypothesis

True. Even trivial differences (of no managerial importance) will be stat. sig. if sample size is sufficiently large.

19. As illustrated in problem 18, the absolute magnitude of the difference (the difference between X-bar and the hypothesized mean) is not necessarily the "all-important" factor...sample size has much to do with whether a given difference will be statistically significant. In fact, any difference, no matter how small, can be shown to be statistically significant if the sample size is large enough. True or False

Two tail because an error can be made to either side:
too full = wasted beer
too empty = unhappy customers

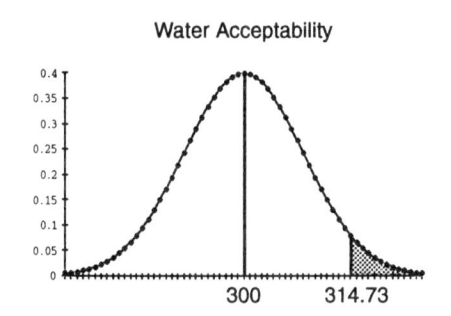

20. For the above beer bottle problems, a two-tailed test of statistical significance was used. Why?

Water Acceptability

one-tail, upper-bound
  equals 314.73

21. Water is judged to be acceptable if the microbe count is 300 units per cc. or less. If the standard deviation is 20, within what limits would samples of size 10 be considered acceptable if alpha = .01.

(This is basically a confidence interval problem.)

std. dev. from universe

22. In the above problem involving the water samples, samples of only 10 were being selected, why was the Student t distribution not used?

23. The desired value for a blood sample in a coulter hematology machine is 50 lambda. The standard deviation is 10 lambda. 15 samples are processed and they produce an average of 46 lambda. Is this value within the limits if alpha equals .01?

Ho μ = 50 lambda
Ha $\mu \neq$ 50 lambda

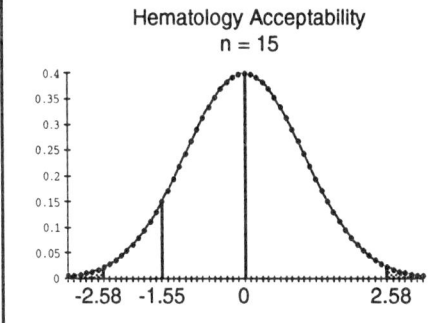

Hematology Acceptability
n = 15

Z = -1.55, inside critical value. of Z = -2.58
no stat. sig. diff.
fail to reject

24. For the problem above, what conclusion would you have reached if 250 samples had been selected? (let alpha remain at .01)

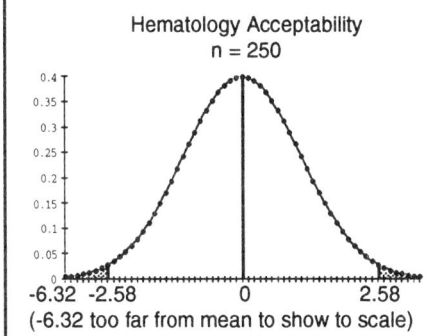

Hematology Acceptability
n = 250

(-6.32 too far from mean to show to scale)

Z = -6.32, outside critical value of Z = -2.58
stat. sig. diff.
reject null

25. A machine is taking bulk corn meal from a bin. It packages the meal in two pound (32 oz) packages with a standard deviation of .75 oz. A sample of 50 packages is weighed and the mean is determined to be 31.9 oz. Does the machine need adjustment? (let alpha equal .05)

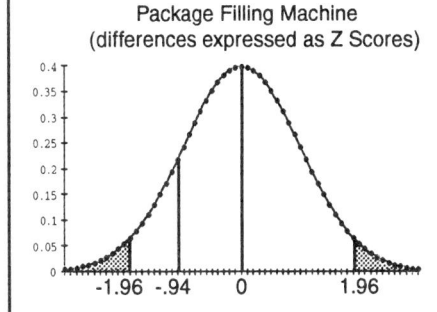

Package Filling Machine
(differences expressed as Z Scores)

Actual Z = .94, inside critical value Z = 1.96

Obviously yes, statistical testing measures only one dimension of product performance.	26. In the previous problem we determined that, statistically speaking, the machine did not need adjustment. As an aside, let us suppose that the machine also has a blown seal and is spraying oil all over the meal. Does the machine need adjustment?
Type II. To let a bad machine continue is worse than rechecking a good machine (maybe, depends what it costs to recheck).	27. For problems 25 and 26 above (the corn meal machine), which type of error would be the more serious, type I or type II? Explain.
False	28. For most problems, it is relatively easy to specify a precise value for alpha (the probability of a type I error). Beta (the prob. of a type II error) is also easy to specify. True or False

The Power of a Statistical Test

29. The power of the test is the probability of correctly rejecting the null hypothesis, if the null hypothesis is false. The power of the test is equal to _____.

1 - beta

30. The power of a hypothesis test must be refigured for each possible value which the true mean might assume (instead of the hypothesized value). For the corn meal problem (mean hypothesized to be 32, standard deviation equal to .75, and n = 50) what would be the power of the test if the true mean (rather than 32 oz.) were actually 31.95? (let alpha remain .05)

(Hint: 95% confidence interval is 31.79 - 34.21, round off to 31.8 and 34.2. You are trying to calculate the probability of getting a value lower than 31.8, when the true mean is 31.95)

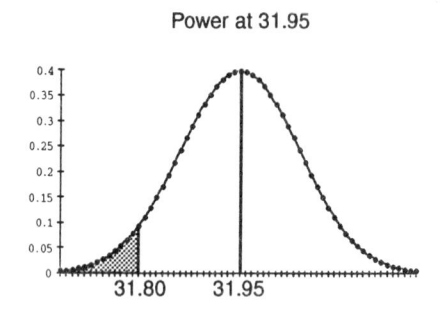

power at 31.95 = .08

31. As mentioned, the power of a hypothesis test must be refigured for each possible value which the true mean might assume (instead of the hypothesized value). For the corn meal problem (mean hypothesized to be 32, standard deviation equal to .75, and n = 50) what would be the power of the test if the true mean (rather than 32 oz.) were actually 31.9? (let alpha remain .05)

(Hint: Now you are trying to calculate the probability of getting a value lower than 31.8, when the true mean is 31.9.)

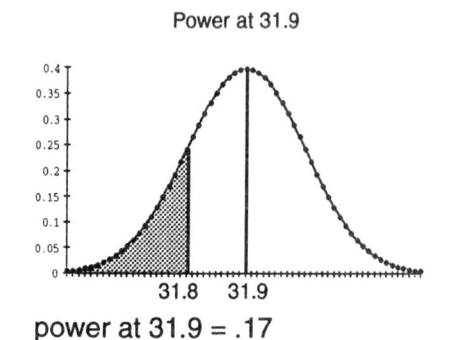

power at 31.9 = .17

32. Now that you are getting the hang of it, what would be the power of the test if the true mean had actually been 31.85.

(Hint: In this case, you will be trying to calculate the probability of getting a value lower than 31.8, when the true mean is 31.85.)

Power at 31.85

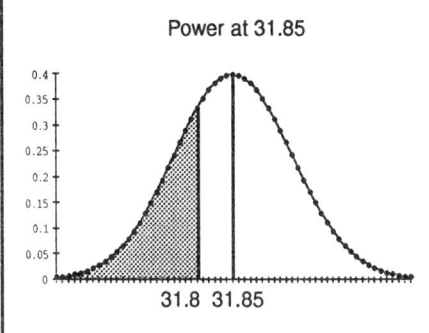

power at 31.85 = .32

33. What would be the power of the test if the true mean had actually been 31.8.

(Hint: Look at your picture before cranking too many numbers...this is an easy one.)

Power at 31.80

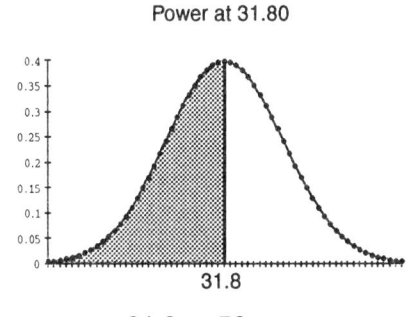

power at 31.8 = .50

34. No sense in quitting when you are having this much fun, right? What would be the power of the test if the true mean were actually 31.75?

(Hint: It is easy to lose track of what is happening. remember that we are still working from the original problem which had hypothesized a mean of 32.0 oz. For that situation, the 95% cut-off was approximately 31.8. This means that no matter where the true mean really happened to be, we would not reject the null hypothesis of μ = 32.0 unless we had a sample average below 31.8.

Therefore we are trying different possible means, 31.95, 31.90, 31.85, 31.80, 31.75, etc., and we are calculating what is the probability of a value below the 31.80 cut-off for each of these possible alternatives.)

(Special Hint: Before working the numbers, look at the similarity between this problem (mean = 31.75) and problem 32 (mean = 31.85).)

Power at 31.75

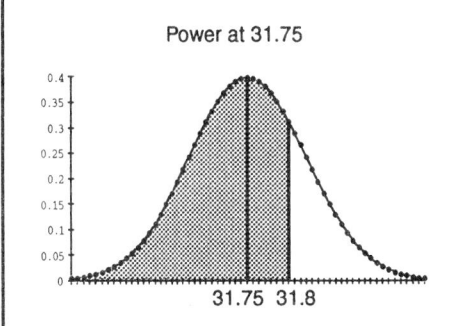

power at 31.75 = .68

106

Power at 31.7

power at 31.7 = .83

Power at 31.65

power at 31.65 = .92

Very True. We computed only six, non-trivial alternative means, whereas an infinite number of them exists.

35. I'll bet that you are really on a roll by now, so, what is the power of the test if the true mean were actually 31.7?

(Hint: As in the problem above, check the similarity between this problem (mean = 31.7) and problem 31 (mean = 31.9).)

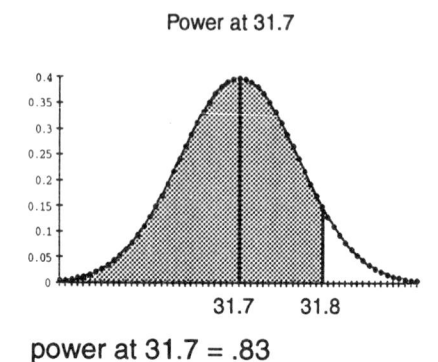

35. OK, one more and we will quit. What would be the power of the test if the true mean were really 31.65?

(Hint: Check similarity between this problem (mean = 31.65) and problem 30 (mean = 31.95).)

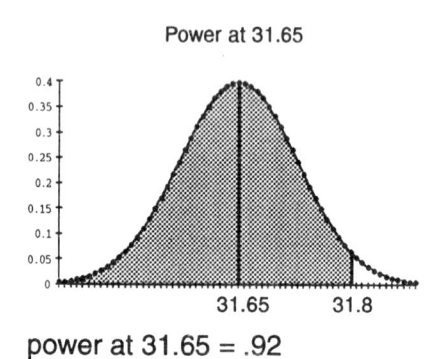

36. By now we have seen the following results for our determination of the power of the test for various assumed values of the mean. To wit

Mean	Power
31.95	.08
31.90	.17
31.85	.32
31.80	.50
31.75	.68
31.70	.83
31.65	.92

Computing the power of a test is a lot of work. True or False?

One-Tail vs. Two-Tail: One Tailed Test

§ 8.2

1. You should always look at your data before framing your hypotheses. In that manner you can make sure that you have phrased your alternative hypothesis properly. True or False

False. Frame your hypotheses <u>first</u>, then let the data dictate the conclusion.

2. For a given situation, using a one-tail test will cause a quicker rejection of the null hypothesis. The corresponding two-tail test will require a greater difference before a rejection of the null hypothesis is made. For this reason, the two-tailed test is considered to be a more statistically conservative procedure. True or False

True

3. Sometimes the null hypothesis will be rejected with a one-tail test, but fail to be rejected with the corresponding two-tail test. True or False

True

4. Likewise, sometimes the null hypothesis will be rejected at one level of significance (i.e. alpha = .05) but then fail to be rejected at a slightly different level of significance (i.e. alpha = .01). This proves that statistical testing is misleading and unreliable. True or False

False. Rejection is never absolute, always at a certain level. Such a situation would imply that you are 95% confident, but not 99% confident in rejection of the null hypothesis

5. If you are using a one-tail test you do not need to worry about using the Student t if the standard deviation came from a sample since you are only testing one-tail anyway. True or False

False

6. If you are using a one-tail test you do not need to worry about the finite population correction factor. True or False

False again, only the hypotheses and the critical values change.

Reporting Results Using a p-Value

§ 8.3

1. Previously, we have used "critical values" of Z such as 1.64 (.05, one-tail) and 1.96 (.05, two-tail) as cut-offs for the determination of statistical significance. Any Z value inside of those cut-offs was not significant at that level, any Z value outside those cut-offs was significant. Another approach is to compute the Z value, and then to look up the actual probability in the tail which is associated with that value. True or False

True

108

.0375
significant at .05, one-tail

2. A Z value of 1.78 has a p-value of _____. This would be significant at what level?

.0202
significant at .05, one & two tail

3. A Z value of 2.05 has a p-value of _____. This would be significant at what level?

.0075
significant at .01, one-tail

4. A Z value of 2.43 has a p-value of _____. This would be significant at what level?

.002
significant at .01, one & two tail

5. A Z value of 2.76 has a p-value of _____. This would be significant at what level?

number of standard deviations (away from the mean)

6. (Do you remember?) A score stands for the _____ of _____ _____.

it encompasses almost 100% (99.74)   p-value =.0013

7. A Z value of 3.00 is sometimes referred to as the "statisticians definition of certainty". Why? (Hint: what is the p-value for Z = 3.00 (two-tail)?)

True, the larger the sample, the tighter the confidence interval, hence, the stronger the rejection.

8. When p-values fall within the range .01 to .10 they are sometimes termed inconclusive since they are significant at some levels but not others. One solution to this dilemma is to take a larger sample. True or False

Very, very true. With a large enough sample, any difference, no matter how small, will be statistically significant.

9. It is possible to have a difference of very small absolute value which is statistically significant, but of no managerial importance. True or False

---

§ 8.4

Hypothesis Testing: Small Sample

True

1. When the sample size is large, it is possible to use the normal curve for testing of hypotheses, regardless of the shape of the underlying distribution. True or False

False

2. When the sample size is small, it is possible to use the normal curve for testing of hypotheses, regardless of the shape of the underlying distribution. True or False

3. Sometimes, hypotheses can still be tested under the assumption of normality, even when the distribution is not exactly normal. In this case, the test is said to be _____.

robust

4. A normal curve will exhibit a "pleasant", symmetric, bell-shape. Which is more critical, the lack of symmetry or the lack of bell-shape.

lack of symmetry

5. There are techniques which can handle distributions with strange (non-normal) shapes. These techniques are generally referred to as _____ techniques.

nonparametric

6. Usually the best (and often the easiest) way to check your data for normality is with a _____.

histogram, or some other type of graph

7. A population is believed to have a mean of 35. A sample of 17 items is selected which produces a sample mean of 40 and a standard deviation of 10. Test for significant difference at alpha = .05.

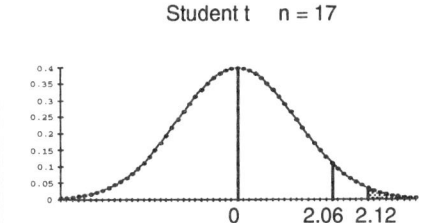

Student t   n = 17

actual t = 2.06
inside critical value of t = 2.12
fail to reject

8. A shipment of copper ingots is received at the wire rolling mill. They are supposed to weigh 1000 pounds. A sample of 10 ingots is weighed and the mean is determined to be 982 pounds with a standard deviation of 18 pounds. Test for significant difference at alpha = .05.

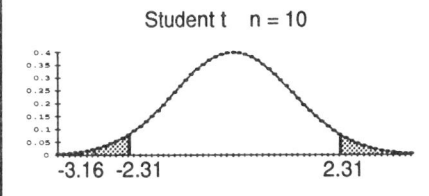

Student t   n = 10

actual t = -3.16
outside critical value t = -2.31
reject null

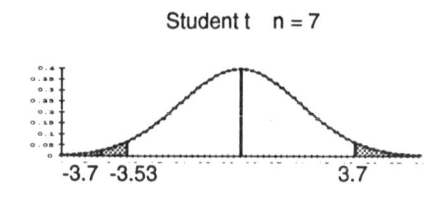

Student t n = 7

-3.7 -3.53   3.7

actual t = -3.53
inside critical value t = -3.707
fail to reject null

9. A crushing plant is designed to process 35,000 tons of ore per day. A recent 7 day test period shows an average throughput of 33,000 tons per day with a standard deviation of 1500 tons. Test for statistically significant difference at alpha = .01.

(Note: If problems 7, 8, and 9 seem vaguely familiar, that is good (compare the problems 12, 17, and 18 from chapter eight). Confidence intervals and hypothesis testing are opposite sides of the same coin.)

Note: If none of the problems seem even slightly familiar...you are in trouble.)

§ 8.5

Income Distribution HiLoTown

Income Distribution MiddleTown

Inference and Hypothesis Testing for the Variance

1. Suppose that two populations have exactly the same mean. There can still be important (managerial as well as statistical) differences if the variances (and distributions) of the populations are not the same. True or False

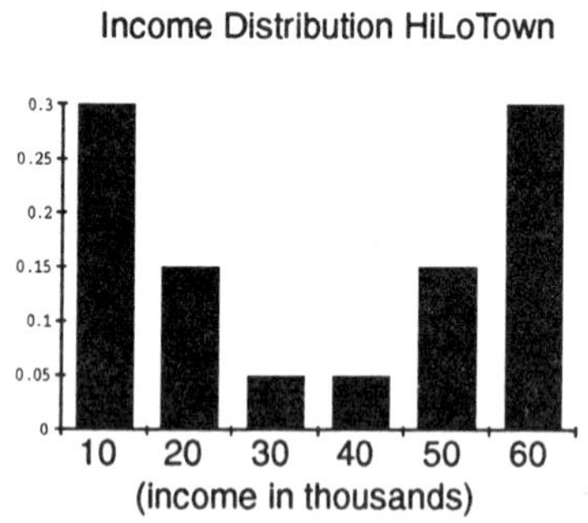

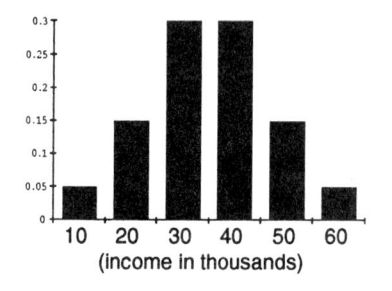

As shown in the two distributions at left, although the mean income of the two towns is the same, the distributions differ dramatically. One town might be a good market for Yugos and Lincolns, the other a good market for Chevy's and Fords.

2. The test of significance for the variance is more sensitive to the assumption of normality than was the test of significance for the mean. Thus it can be said that the test for variances is not as _____ as the test for means.

robust

3. When the standard deviation of the universe is not known, the student t distribution was used. Since it was derived on the basis of a sample standard deviation it is sometimes referred to as a _____ distribution.

derived

4. The testing of variances is performed using a distribution known as the "chi-square" distribution. The proper pronunciation of "chi-square" is:
   a. kye-square (hard "c", long "i", rhymes with lye)
   b. key-square (hard "c", short "i")
   c. chye-square (soft "c", like in cheek, long "i")
   d. chee-square (soft "c", short "i")

a. kye-square
   rhymes with lye

5. Like the normal curve, the chi-square is symmetric. True or False

False

6. Like the student t distribution, the shape of the chi-square changes with sample size (degrees of freedom). True or False

True

7. In the case of the chi-square test for population variance, the degrees of freedom are equal to _____.

n - 1

8. For a sample of 20, find the chi-square, one-tail, 95% critical value.

df = 19
chi-square = 30.1

9. For a sample of 20, find the chi-square, two-tail, 95% critical value.

df = 19
chi-square 8.91 - 32.9

10. For the chi-square critical values in problem 9 (8.91 and 32.9) find the confidence boundaries for the estimate of the variance. Assume that the sample of 20 had produced a sample mean of 85 and a sample standard deviation of 10.

95% CI for σ^2
5.77 - 21.3

95% CI for σ
2.40 - 4.62

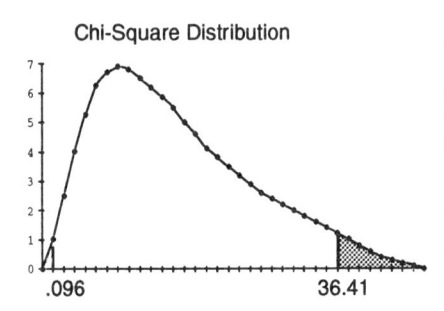

Chi-Square Distribution

.096 ———— 36.41

Actual chi-square = .096 within 36.41 (table) therefore fail to reject
(Did I trick you? Problem was testing variance, but I gave you the standard deviation.)

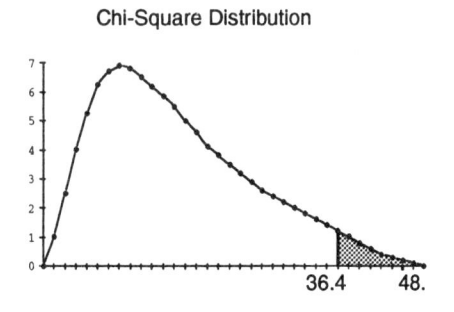

Chi-Square Distribution

36.4   48.

This is the problem you probably worked:
Actual chi-square = 48.0 is outside 36.41 cut-off

11. For the problem above, what would be the 95% confidence boundaries for the estimate of the standard deviation?

12. One-half inch bolts (obviously) have to be machined where that they will fit into one-half inch nuts. In this situation, the variance is virtually as critical as the mean. The specifications require that the variance be .001 inches or less. A sample of 25 bolts is selected and it produces a mean of .496 with a standard deviation of .002. Is the variance within the acceptable limit at alpha = .05.

13. For the problem above, work a student t test to see if the mean of .496 is acceptably close to the standard of .500 inches.

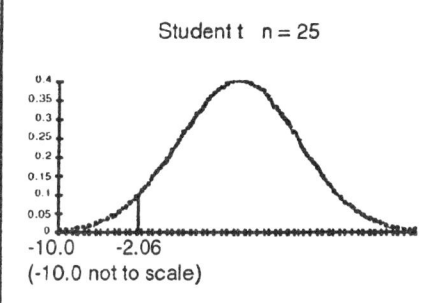

Student t n = 25

-10.0   -2.06
(-10.0 not to scale)

Actual t = -10.0
outside critical value t = -2.06
reject null, bolts are not close enough to the mean

CHAPTER 9

Inference Procedures for Two Populations

CHAPTER OBJECTIVES

Previous chapters have discussed the use of hypothesis testing for the testing of population means and variances. This chapter will extend that treatment to the testing of two means, such as the mean of sample one vs. the mean of sample two. This chapter will also discuss the situation presented by matched samples, such as a test-retest situation, where both means came from the same group of respondents. By the end of the chapter you should be able to answer the following questions:

1. Distinguish between dependent (matched) samples and independent samples.

2. How do you test for significant difference between means collected from independent samples?

3. How do you test for significant difference between means collected from dependent (matched) samples?

4. How do you test for significant difference between the variances of two samples from normal populations?

116

HYPOTHESIS TESTING FOR TWO MEANS

§ 9.0   A Look Back/Introduction

1. In statistical inference, the objective was to infer the probable location of a parameter such as µ on the basis of a sample statistic such as _____.

X̄ (X-bar)

2. In a hypothesis test the actual sample mean is tested against a range within which the mean is hypothesized to lie. If the actual sample mean falls outside that range we reject the null hypothesis. If the actual sample mean falls inside that range we accept the null hypothesis. True or False

False — say "fail to reject"

3. If a statistically significant difference is said to have occurred, that means that there is a really big difference between the means. True or False

False — the absolute diff may be quite small

4. When the null hypothesis is true, but you incorrectly reject it, you have made a _____ error.

Type I

5. When the null hypothesis is false, but you incorrectly accept it, you have made a _____ error.

Type II

6. The probability of a Type I error is defined as _____.

alpha

7. The probability of a Type II error is defined as _____.

beta

§ 9.1   Independent vs. Dependent Samples

1. When you compare two means from two different sample groups, this is an example of _____ samples.

independent

2. When you compare two means, but they came from the same sample group (such as a test-retest) this is referred to as _____ samples.

dependent

3. "Before and after" testing is one example of dependent sampling. Another situation which usually involves dependent sampling is when two samples have been constructed such that the items from each sample have matching characteristics. True or False

True

4. Sample items can be "matched" on a variety of characteristics. A couple of examples of matching characteristics are _____ and _____.

location and time

Comparing Two Means (Large Independent Samples)

§ 9.2

1. When comparing two populations we are not interested in the estimate of either µ1 or µ2, but rather in the difference between _____.

µ1 - µ2

2. The combined variance is formed by _____ the two variances.

adding

3. Because we are dealing with independent samples taken from large populations we can use the normal curve for determining the confidence intervals. We know this from the _____ _____ _____.

Central Limit Theorem

4. Given: A comparison between Chevrolets and Fords to test for gasoline mileage. A sample of 100 Fords and 100 Chevrolets is taken. The test results show the Chevrolets with an average mileage of 24.1 mpg and a standard deviation of 3 mpg. The Fords average 23.3 mpg with a standard deviation of 2 mpg. Find the 95% confidence interval for the estimate of the true difference.

95% Conf. Int. Ford vs. Chevy

95% CI around .80 diff
.09 to 1.51

Yes, the CI does not include zero diff.

5. Just looking at the confidence interval from the problem above, would you believe that there is a statistically significant difference between the Chevrolets and the Fords? Why?

95% Conf. Int. Reg. vs. LongLife Bulbs

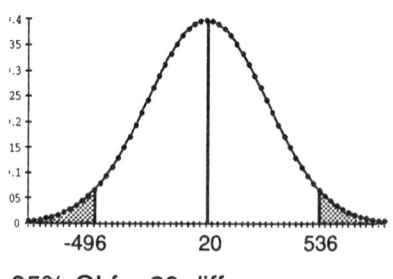

95% CI for 20 diff
 -496 to 536

6. Lightbulbs are rated with a standard lifetime of 1500 hours. Some bulbs claim to be "long-life" bulbs. To test this long-life claim, a sample of 50 "standard" bulbs is taken, as well as 50 "long-life" bulbs. The "standard" bulbs have a sample mean of 1680 hours with a standard deviation of 200 hours. The "long-life" bulbs have a sample mean of 1700 hours with a standard deviation of 400 hours. Compute the 95% confidence interval for the true difference between the two types of bulbs.

No, zero difference included in CI

7. Without doing a formal hypothesis test, but simply looking at the results from the problem above, does it look like there is a statistically significant difference between the two types of light bulbs? Why?

Actual Z = 1.26 within cut-off value of Z = 1.96
 no stat sig diff
 fail to reject

8. Two students are arguing over which school has the smarter students. A sample of 40 IQ scores is taken from each school. For school Ritesidetracks the average is 106 with a standard deviation of 8. For school Wrongsidetracks the average is 104 with a standard deviation of 6. Test for significant difference at alpha = .05.

Actual Z = 4.47 outside critical value Z = 1.28
 stat sig diff
 reject null

9. A fertilizer salesman claims his fertilizer will insure more bushels per acre. Field "C" is the control field. It consists of 40 acres and produces an average of 160 bushels per acre with a standard deviation of 10 bushels. Field "S" receives the fertilizer over its 40 acres and produces 170 bushels per acre with a standard deviation of 10 bushels. Test for significant difference at alpha = .10. (Note: Since we are dealing with a salesman's claim of increased yield, a one-tail test would be permissible. In that case one-tail Z value equals 1.28.)

10. What assumptions are implicit in the test of fertilizer efficacy?	Assume fields were same before the test and during test
11. Since problem 8 and problem 9 computed the actual Z values, it would be easy to determine the "p values" for each of these problems. a. What is the p-value for problem 8? b. What is the p-value for problem 9?	Z = 1.26, p = .1038 Z = 4.47, p = .0001
12. For problem 8 (the lightbulbs) what would be (in practical terms) the consequence of a Type I error? A Type II error?	Type I, reject null when null was true. Decide long-life are better, when they are the same. Type II, accept null when null is false. Decide long-life are same, but they are really better.
13. For problem 9 (the fertilizer) what would be the consequence of a Type I error? A Type II error? As before, try to state your results in as practical terms as possible.	Type I, buy fertilizer when it is really not helping. Type II, don't buy fertilizer, but it would have helped.

<u>Two Means, Small Samples, Normal Populations</u>	§ 9.3
1. When dealing with two small samples, if they are not normal then some type of _____ procedure needs to be used.	nonparametric
2. When dealing with two small samples, if they are normal, then you can use the _____ distribution to test for significant difference.	student t
3. The testing of small samples proceeds as for the normal curve, only the student t distribution is substituted. Actually, the use of the student t is not caused because the samples are small, the need for the t arises because _____ has been substituted for _____.	s σ

16.69
round down to 16

9+9 = 18

True

False

power

pooled

True

(n1 - 1) + (n2 - 1)

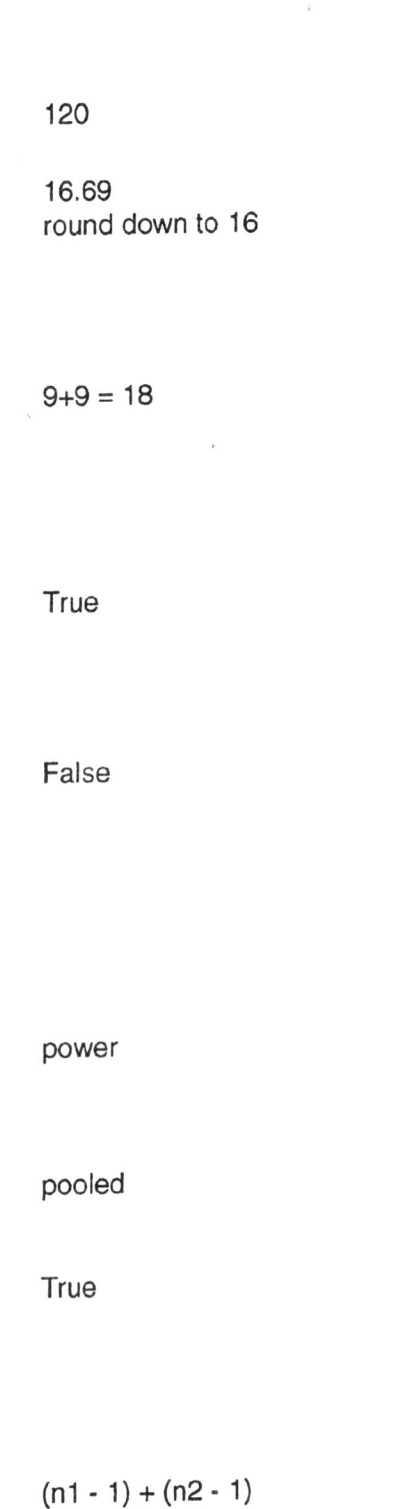

approximately

exactly

4. Suppose that two samples of size 10 (each) are selected. The standard deviation for the first sample is 3, and the standard deviation for the second sample is 4. What would be the degrees of freedom for this situation?

5. Some books recommend the following approximation for the degrees of freedom: df = (n1 - 1) + (n2 - 1). What would be the degrees of freedom with this formula?

6. When finding degrees of freedom, the values for s1 and s2 can be scaled to different magnitudes (i.e., .10 becomes 10) provided that they are both scaled in the same manner. True or False

7. In fact, in any problem, the standard deviation can be scaled in whatever manner suits your fancy. True or False

8. In some cases we can assume that the variances are equal. This is an advantageous situation in that it allows us to make a stronger hypothesis test. Technically speaking we can say that we are better equipped to correctly reject a false null hypothesis. This would mean that we have increased the _____ of the test.

9. When the variances are equal we simply combine the two variances. This is called a _____ variance.

10. Variances are additive. True or False

11. Earlier we had presented an approximation for finding degrees of freedom. This approximation represents the true degrees of freedom when the variances are equal. Degrees of freedom in this case is equal to _____.

12. When the variances are not equal, the test distribution follows a t distribution (approximately, exactly). When the variances are equal, the test distributions follows a t distribution (approximately, exactly).

13. The pooled variance simply represents the weighted average of the two variances and should lie between the two individual variances. True or False | True

14. The test of significance is sensitive to the assumption that the variances are indeed equal, hence the safest way to proceed is to simply proceed as if they might not be equal. True or False | True

15. Actually, the best way to proceed would be to first test whether the variances are equal, and then that would help you to determine which test you should use with respect to the means. True or False | True

16. One drawback to the idea presented in the previous problem (first test the variances, then test the means) is that if the two tests are performed upon the same sample (which was a small sample), then the tests are not statistically _____. This can result in biased results. | independent

17. Continuing with the discussion from above, to be truly technically correct, you actually need to take two samples, take one sample to test the variances, then a second sample to check the means. True or False | True

18. (Continuing) However, if you took two samples, how many items would you have selected? _____ If you were going to actually sample that many items, then it would make sense to just use a larger sample to begin with, dispensing with the use of the small sample t test procedures entirely, simply using the Z test. True or False | $n_1 + n_2$

True

19. (Continuing) After all, the degrees of freedom is equal (either approximately or exactly) to _____. Since the student t values begin to approximate the normal distribution at approximately df = _____ (it is around that value that the student t table begins to quit giving the value for each possible degree of freedom. This would mean that each one of the two samples would be around _____ or less. Although such small samples are seen in certain situations (rare diseases, or very expensive processes) most business situations are considerably more plentiful and considerably more mundane. | $(n_1 + n_2 - 2)$

df = 30

15

122

larger

20. (Continuing and concluding) In other words, the easy way to avoid all of this hassle, while producing better, more representative, and statistically more confident results, is simply to take _____ samples.

---

§ 9.4

Comparing Two Variances (Independent Samples)

ratio

1. When testing for significant difference between two sample means we looked at the difference between the two means. In the test for significant difference between two variances we look at the _____ of the two variances.

F distribution

2. The ratio of the two sample variances is distributed according to a distribution called the _____ distribution.

False, named after its developer, R. A. Fisher

3. The F distribution is a difficult and complex distribution. As a result many students Flunk this portion of statistics. For that reason, this distribution is called the "F" distribution. True or False.

False

4. The F distribution is symmetric. True or False

True

5. The F distribution varies in shape according to the degrees of freedom. True or False

Chi-Square

6. The F distribution has the greatest similarity to which distribution? _____

two

7. The biggest difference between the F distribution and the Chi-Square distribution, is that the Chi-Square distribution is based upon one set of degrees of freedom, while the F distribution is based upon _____ sets of degrees of freedom.

one

8. If the two variances are equal, then the F ratio would be equal to _____.

9. If the two variances were not equal, then the F ratio would be _____ than one (assuming we put the larger variance on top).

larger

10. (Obviously) the larger the value of the F ratio, the larger the difference between the two variances. True or False

True (obviously)

11. df_1 (also referred to as v1) is equal to _____. df_2 (also referred to as v2) is equal to _____.

$n_1 - 1$
$n_2 - 1$

12. Suppose that two samples of size 10 were taken. What would be the degrees of freedom? _____ and _____. The F value for a .05 level of significance would be? _____ The F value for a .01 level of significance would be? _____ 1

9
9
F = 3.18
F = 5.35

13. Continuing the preceding problem, suppose that the standard deviation of the first sample had been 20 and the standard deviation of the second sample had been 15 (sample size was 10 in each case). Would there be a statistically significant difference at alpha equal to .05?

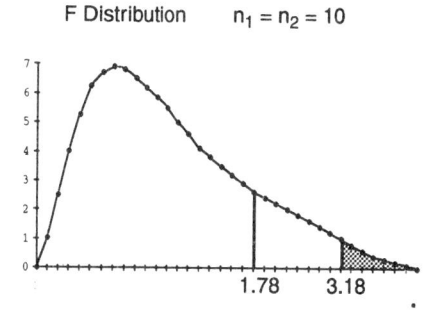

F Distribution $n_1 = n_2 = 10$

No. Actual value of F = 1.78 inside cut-off of F = 3.18.

124

F Distribution $n_1 = n_2 = 121$

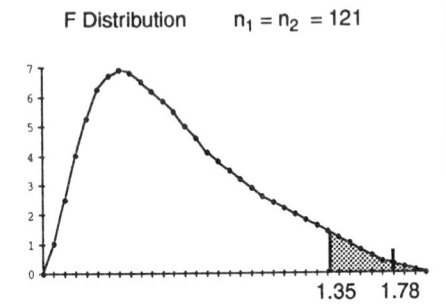

1.35   1.78

Actual F = 1.78 outside cut-off F = 1.35, sig diff, reject null, variances are different.

14. Given: two samples, both of size 121 (pretty tricky, huh? this way df = 120, the only value over 60 in the table). Once again, the standard deviation of sample one turned out to be 20, and surprise of surprises, the standard deviation of sample two just happened to be 15. Test for statistically significant difference at alpha equal to .05.

No.

Sample

larger

15. Comparing problem 13 with problem 14: Has the actual value of F changed? _____ The F test, like the Z test, the t test, and the chi-square test, is sensitive to changes in _____ size.

16. (Continuing) For the same difference between variances (i.e., standard deviation of 20 vs. standard deviation of 15), the _____ the sample size, the more significant that difference will be.

F Distribution $n_1 = 10$ $n_2 = 8$

2.78   3.29

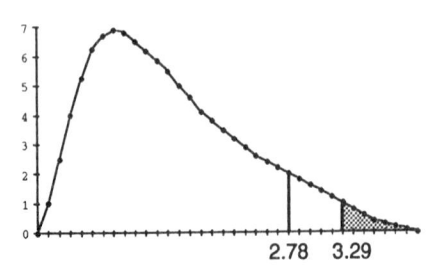

Actual 2.78 inside cut-off of F = 3.29. Therefore no stat. sig. diff.

17. Given: Two samples, one of size 10 with a standard deviation of 30, and a second of size 8 with a standard deviation of 50. Test for significant difference at alpha equal to .01.

18. These problems have been brilliantly designed so that the table will contain the degrees of freedom for which you are looking. But life is not always so kind. The only sample sizes which the table "truly" accommodates are: 1-13(really too small for most business situations) 16, 21, 26, 31, 41, 61, and 121. What should you do if your sample size does not happen to be one of these values? | Simply take the closest ones. The statistically conservative procedure would be to round your sample size down, that is, take the higher F value.

19. Generally speaking, the F table only gives the values for the right tail. However, with a little manipulation, the table can also be made to give the left tail values. Suppose that the degrees of freedom were equal to df1 = 8 and df2 = 6. What would be the right tail value for that situation? (let alpha = .05) _____ What would be the left tail F value for that situation? _____ | F = 4.15
F = .279

20. (Continuing) Suppose that for the situation described in problem 19, one standard deviation had been equal to 20 and the other standard deviation had been equal to 10. What would be the confidence interval for the F ratio of the two variances? | 1.22 - 14.28

21. (Continuing) Problem 20 found the confidence interval for the F ratio of the variances, what would be the confidence interval for the ratio of the standard deviations? (This would simply be a ratio, not an F ratio...an F ratio is a ratio of two variances.) | 1.10 - 3.78

22. By definition, an F ratio is a ratio of two _____. | variances

---

Comparison of Means (Paired Samples) | § 9.5

1. When the items selected in one sample are not related (paired) with the items in the second sample, then the samples are said to be _____. | independent

126

2. When the items selected in one sample are related (paired) with the items in the second sample, then the samples are said to be _____.

dependent or matched

3. As we have often done, we will assume that the population distributions follow a distribution what is essentially normal. If they are deviate substantially from normality, the alternative is usually some type of _____ test.

non-parametric

4. Since the event in question is a matched pair of numbers, we are no longer concerned with the actual values of the numbers, rather we are concerned not with the actual numbers, but rather the _____ between the values in each matched pair.

difference

5. The mean of the differences, is also equal to the difference of the means. True or False

True. You should write both formulas.

mean of diffs $\dfrac{\Sigma(X_1 - X_2)}{n}$

diff of means = $\mu_d = \mu_1 - \mu_2$

6. Given the following set of matched samples:

Sample One	Sample Two
5	4
6	3
3	7
7	5
5	8
9	6
6	9
2	4

Find the 95% Confidence Interval for the estimate of the true difference between the two samples.

avg diff $(\overline{X_1} - \overline{X_2})$ = -.375
CI = -2.33 to 1.58

7. For the previous problem, test for significant difference between the two samples at alpha = .05.

Actual t = .36, inside cut-off, t = 1.895 no stat. sig. diff.
 fail to reject

8. Given these two matched samples:

Sample One	Sample Two
16	45
23	47
24	76
42	64
53	55
24	64
13	45
17	66

Find the 95% Confidence Interval for the estimate of the true difference between the samples.

avg diff $(\bar{X}_1 - \bar{X}_2)$ = -31.25
CI = -33.2 to -29.3

9. For the problem above, test for significant difference between the samples at alpha = .05.

Actual t = 5.47, outside cut-off t = 1.895 stat. sig. diff reject null

10. It really does not matter whether a given pair of samples are treated as independent or dependent, the results are always very close. True or False.

False

11. By matching the samples, you created a stronger, statistically more powerful test. True or False.

True

CHAPTER 10

Estimation and Testing for Population Proportions

CHAPTER OBJECTIVES

The last several chapters have discussed the topic of hypothesis testing with respect to situations involving scalar numbers. This chapter applies those same techniques to situations involving percentages. By the end of the chapter you should be able to:

1. Construct confidence intervals for percentage estimates.

2. Perform tests of hypothesis on samples involving percentages.

3. Calculate the required sample size for situations involving percentages.

130 | ESTIMATION AND TESTING FOR PROPORTIONS

§ 10.0 — A Look Back/Introduction

1. In the process of estimation, a value from a sample, referred to as a sample _____, is used to estimate a value from the population, referred to as a population _____.

statistic
parameter

2. In the binomial, we dealt with Bernoulli trials, which was another way of saying that the event has just two outcomes, usually characterized as _____ or _____.

success
failure

3. The binomial distribution provided us a means of calculating the probability of obtaining "r" _____ in "n" _____, when the probability of each "r success" is _____.

successes
trials
p

4. Rather than trying to determine the specific number of successes, such as 4 out of 10, a binomial problem could be expressed as a percentage, in this case, 40%. True or False

true

---

§10.1 — Estimation and Confidence Intervals for Proportions

1. In the previous chapters we were concerned with estimates of population parameters involving scalar numbers. The value of the sample mean ($\bar{X}$ "X-bar") is used as the best single _____ _____ of (μ "mu") the population mean.

point estimate

2. When dealing with the estimation of a population mean, we used different symbols to differentiate between the sample mean and the population mean. We used ($\bar{X}$) to indicate a sample mean and we used (μ) to indicate a population mean. When estimating of a population percentage we also need different symbols to differentiate between the two situations. We use _____ to indicate a sample percentage and we use _____ to indicate a population percentage.

$\hat{p}$
p

3. For small samples, tables are available to compute the confidence intervals for the estimate of the percentage. What would be the 95% confidence interval if n = 8 and x = 6?

.349 - .968

4. If the sample showed a ratio of seven out of eight, what would be the point estimate for the estimate of the true percentage?

.875 = 87.5%

5. What would be the confidence interval for this estimate?

.473 -- .997

6. Is this estimate symmetric? Why or why not?

No. The tail values to one side are limited when p is close to zero or one.

7. The confidence interval for percentages is computed using essentially the same formula as before. The only real change is in the computational expression of the standard deviation. True or False

True

$$s_{\bar{p}} = \sqrt{(p)(q)/(n-1)}$$

8. A politician takes of sample of 101 voters (how convenient if you are using n-1...what an amazing statistical coincidence!) and finds that 60% of them favor him. Find the 99% confidence interval for the estimate of the true percentage.

95% Conf. Int. around p = 60%

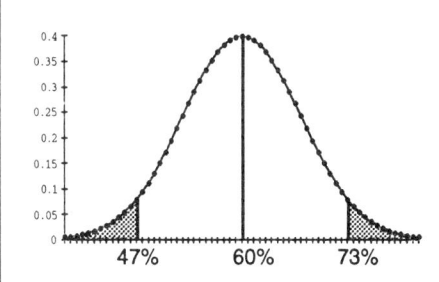

99% CI 47.36% -- 72.64%
or 47% -- 73%

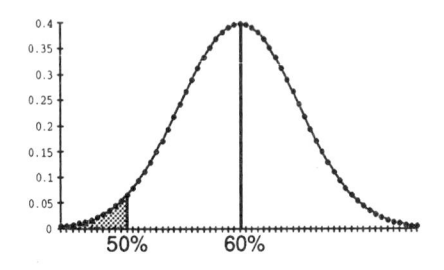

Probability less than 50%

Prob. less than 50%
= .0206 = .02 = 2%

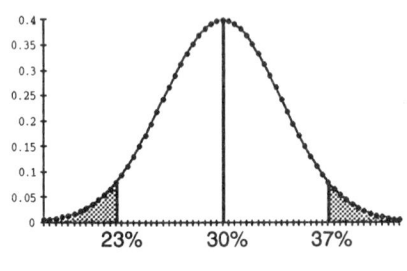

9. For the above situation, what is the probability that the true percentage is less than 50%

95% Conf. Int. around $\hat{p}$ = 30%

95% CI = 23.63% -- 36.37%
or   23% -- 37%

10. A manufacturer is estimating his brand share which he believes to be 30%. A sample of 200 consumers is taken. What is the 95% confidence interval for this estimate?

Obviously they would be happier with 33% than 28%, but both 33% and 28% are well within the CI.

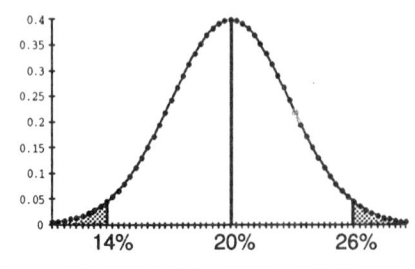

11. For the above problem (sample size = 200), what would be their conclusion if 56 people claimed to use the product. What would be their conclusion if 66 people use their product?

99% Conf. Int. around $\hat{p}$ = 20%

99% CI = 14.83% -- 25.17%
or   14% -- 26%

12. A quality inspector examines a sample of 400 products and finds that 20% of them are defective. What is the 99% confidence interval for the estimate of the true proportion of defective parts?

13. For the above problem, what is the 95% upper bound for the estimate of defective parts?

95% Upper Bound for $\hat{p}$ = 20%

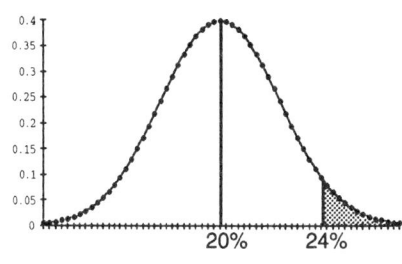

95% upper bound = 23.28 = 24%

14. In each of these problems, we rounded the confidence interval "outward". That is, rather than rounding to the nearest percentage we rounded the lower cut-offs downward (i.e. 14.83% went to 14% rather than 15%) and the upper cut-offs went upward (i.e. 25.17% went to 26% rather than 25%). Why?

The statistically conservative (proper) procedure is always to widen the Conf Int.

15. If the percentage of heads in a fair coin is 50% and a sample of 500 coin tosses is made, there is a 95% probability that the percentage of heads will be within what range?

95% Conf. Int. for p

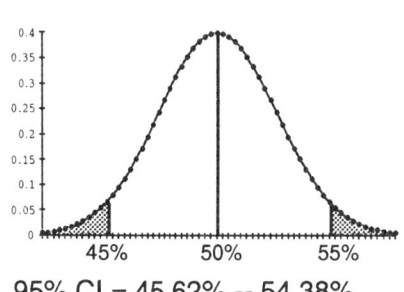

95% CI = 45.62% -- 54.38%
or   45% -- 55%

16. How close are the Nielsen Ratings? The Nielsen ratings try to estimate the percentage of viewers that are tuned into a given TV show. All of these ratings are close to 30%. The sample size is approximately 1200 homes. What would be the 95% confidence interval spread for an estimate centered at 30%?

95% Conf. Int. Nielsen Ratings

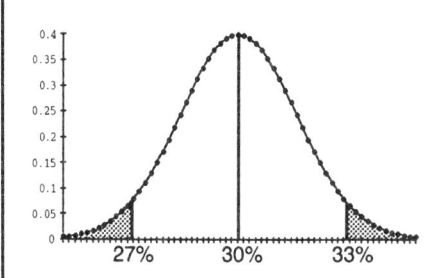

plus or minus 2.6%
CI = 27.4% - 32.6%

134

They probably will, but it is not a stat. sig. diff. Both 28 and 32 are within CI.

No. CI actually figured on basis of infinite population, FPC not applicable (n/N<5%), even at 100,000.

Qualitative problem? Is sample representative?

95% Conf. Int. Rainfall $\hat{p} = 20\%$

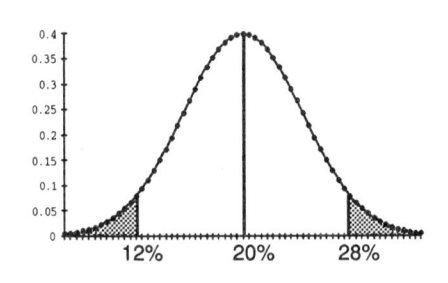

[Normal distribution curve centered at 20%, with shaded tails at 12% and 28%]

95% CI = 12.16% -- 27.84%
          12%   -- 28%

Depends. If you are in the month of May trying to decide whether to schedule the big church picnic for June or July, historical probabilities are probably as good a guide as anything else. On the other hand, if you are deciding that morning on a picnic that afternoon, check weather report for that day, ignore historical probabilities.

---

17. Suppose that during the recent TV season, ABC has registered a viewing percentage of 32% and NBC has registered a viewing percentage of 28%. Statistically speaking, can ABC claim to be truly better?

18. Some people get upset that the Nielsen ratings survey only 1200 homes out of a population of over 250,000,000. Statistically, is there any real difference between say 1200 out of 100,000 vs. 1200 out of 250,000,000? But what (hint: qualitative) problem might be caused by such as a small sample from such a large group?

19. A sample of weather records over the last 101 years shows rain on a certain day in June 20% of the time. What is the 95% confidence interval for the estimate of the true percentage?

20. (Continuing the problem above) Would this be a good way to plan a picnic on that given day?

21. A shopper buys a bag of 100 tomatoes at a discount only to discover that 30% of them are bad. If that bag can be considered to be representative of all of the tomatoes and the shopper, ever the glutton for punishment, is thinking about buying some more, what would be the 99% confidence interval for the estimate of rotten tomatoes?

95% Conf. Int.   Rotten Tomatoes

99% CI 18.12% -- 41.88%
         18%   --   42%

22. (Continuing...special bonus question) Is a tomato a fruit or a vegetable?

Although generally treated as a veggie, technically a tomato is a fruit.

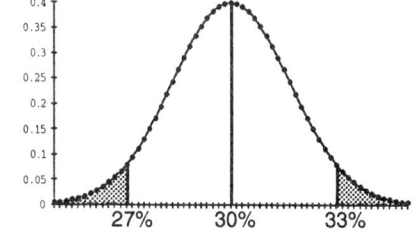

23. George Pinecone is the foreman for the Pixy-Stix toothpick company. George takes a sample of 1000 toothpicks and finds that 30% of the toothpicks are defective. What is the 96% confidence interval for the estimate of the true percentage of defective toothpicks?

96% Conf. Int.   Bad Toothpicks

96% CI = 27.02% -- 32.98%
   or   27%   --   33%

24. (Continuing) If there are 100 toothpicks in each box, what is the probability that a customer will get a perfect box? (Hint: set up as a binomial, work as a Poisson)

binomial (0, 100, p = .30)
Poisson (0, 30) = zero

No statistical way to know based on info in problem. But their quality control seems bad. P(given box) not good, P(each box) very small.

95% Conf. Int.   Mismarked Boots

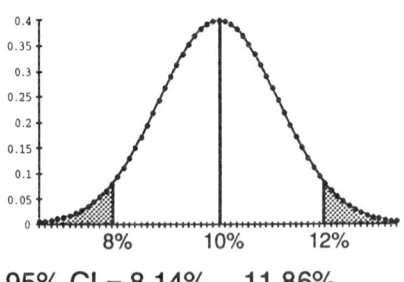

95% CI = 8.14% -- 11.86%
or   8% -- 12%

required n = 8067

Qualitative factors (TV on-no one watching, non-representative sample, etc) are easily worth a point, or two, or more. There is no sense in trying to measure an inherently imprecise situation so "apparently" precisely.

25. (Continuing) The above problem simply assumed that there would be 100 toothpicks in each box. What is the probability of there actually being 100 toothpicks in a given box? What is the probability of 100 toothpicks in each box?

26. A sample of 1000 boots was taken and 10% of them are found to be marked the wrong size. What is the 95% confidence interval for the estimate of the true percentage of boots marked the wrong size?

27. (Continuing the saga of the TV ratings) A new executive has arrived at the Nielsen company (or the networks...at any rate, some big important place). This executive has decided that an estimate of plus or minus 3 percentage points is simply too great a spread, especially when all of the networks are so close, and when each ratings point is worth tens of millions of dollars of advertising revenue. The executive decides that the estimate should be within 1 percentage point. How large a sample must be taken to attain that level of precision?

28. Although this sample (roughly 3 times as accurate) has required almost 9 times as large a sample (remember the effect of the square root sign (3 squared = 9), it is still a manageable size sample, especially given the importance of the situation. Yet Nielsen continues to sample only 1200...why?

29. How large a sample would you have to take to be 95% confident that your estimate is within 2 percentage points of the true proportion if the percentage you are trying to estimate is believed to be around 50%?	2401
30. How large a sample would you have to take to be 95% confident that your estimate is within 2 percentage points of the true proportion if the percentage you are trying to estimate is believed to be around 40%?	1537
31. How large a sample would you have to take to be 95% confident that your estimate is within 2 percentage points of the true proportion if the percentage you are trying to estimate is believed to be around 30%?	864
32. How large a sample would you have to take to be 95% confident that your estimate is within 2 percentage points of the true proportion if the percentage you are trying to estimate is believed to be around 20%?	384
33. How large a sample would you have to take to be 95% confident that your estimate is within 2 percentage points of the true proportion if the percentage you are trying to estimate is believed to be around 10%?	96
34. How large a sample would you have to take to be 95% confident that your estimate is within 2 percentage points of the true proportion if the percentage you are trying to estimate is believed to be around 5%?	24
35. One more, how large a sample would you have to take to be 95% confident that your estimate is within 2 percentage points of the true proportion if the percentage you are trying to estimate is believed to be around 2%?	2...2?!
36. (Continuing) Problem 35 specified that a sample of only 2 was required, does this make sense?	No. That is why the text said that for the CLT formulas to be applicable we needed (np) GT 5 and (nq) GT 5.

138

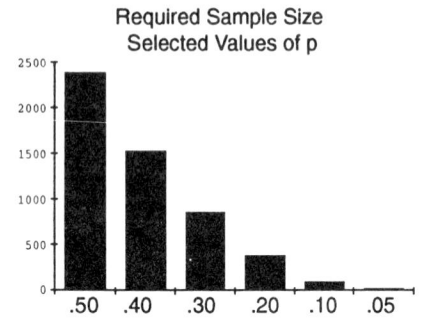

[Bar chart: Required Sample Size, Selected Values of p — values at .50, .40, .30, .20, .10, .05 showing decreasing required sample sizes from ~2400 down to near 0]

The closer p/q = 50/50, the larger sample is required.

37. Graph the results from problems 29 through 35. (Realize that 40% would be the same as 60%, 30% would be the same as 70%, etc.) What conclusion can be drawn from this?

---

§ 10.2

True. Conceptually the problem is the same.

True.

True.

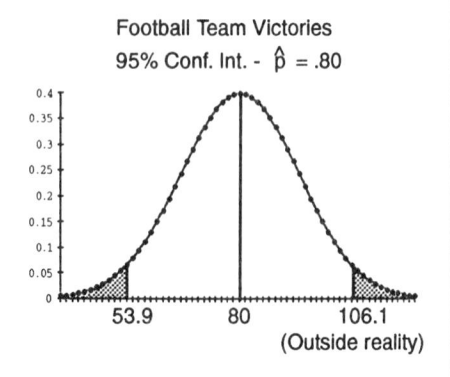

[Bell curve: Football Team Victories, 95% Conf. Int. - $\hat{p}$ = .80, with marks at 53.9, 80, 106.1 (Outside reality)]

CI ≈ 54% -- 100%

Hypothesis Testing for a Population Proportion

1. Hypothesis testing for a proportion is conceptually identical to the hypothesis testing procedures we used for testing means and variances. The only difference is that previously we had tested a scalar number such as a mean, now we are testing a percentage. True or False

2. As before, we cannot "prove" that the percentage is equal to a certain value...or for that matter that it isn't equal to a certain value. We simply try to set the limits of "normal sampling scatter", and pick the conclusion that seems "most probable".

3. (Continuing) The desire to express results in terms of what seems to be "most probable" explains why we use confidence intervals and alpha values which are essentially probabilities.

4. A certain football team has recently been winning 80% of its games. Assuming a ten 1-1 game season, what would be the 95% confidence interval for the season?

5. (Continuing) The team suffers a rather mediocre season, winning only 6 of their 10 games. The coach claims (the baying of the hounds of his critics notwithstanding) that the team has shown no statistically significant difference, and that you cannot statistically claim that this team with a 6-4 record is significantly different from their normal 8-2 team. Is the coach correct?

Statistically, yes. But you would have a hard time telling that to a rapid alumni group.

6. (Continuing) Then the coach went on to say, "And furthermore, boys (speaking to the newsreporters) the fact that no statistical difference has been found, proves that this team is equal to our teams of the past." True or False

Uh-oh, now the coach has gone too far. We have not shown teams to be equal, simply unable to show statistically unequal.

7. A baseball player claims that he can bat 300 (.300). So far this season in 300 bats (strange coincidence?) he is batting 290 (.290). If alpha equals .10 are we to reject his claim? (Hint: this problem can be confusing, remember that batting 300 = .300 = 30%)

Baseball Batting Test
90% One-tail Test

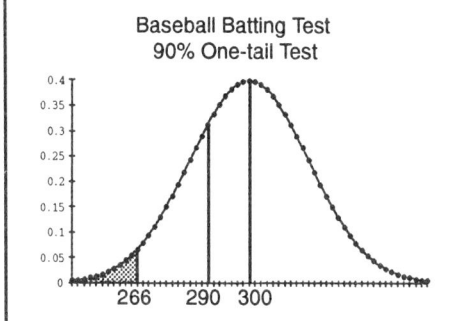

average of .290 inside
cut-off of .266
no stat. sig. diff.
cannot reject his claim

8. A baseball helmet manufacturer claims that its helmet design is 99% effective against head injuries when a player is struck in the head by a baseball. To test this claim they line up 100 washed-up minor league baseball players in front of a pitching machine and fire the baseballs directly at the helmets of the players. Only 2 players suffer concussions. If alpha = .01 is that within acceptable limits?

Baseball Helmet Test
99% One-tail Test

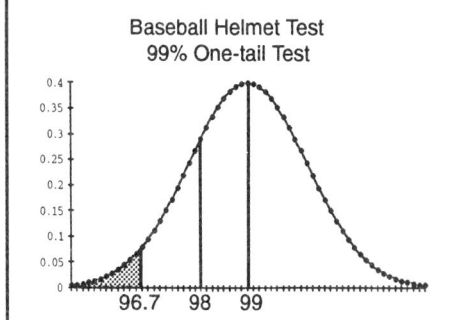

Yes. 98% inside cut-off of 96.67%.

Drug Efficacy Test   n = 100
(Differences expressed as Z scores)

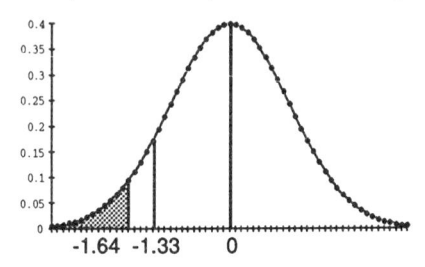

[Graph showing normal curve with -1.64 and -1.33 marked]

for n = 101
actual Z = 1.33 inside cut-off Z = 1.64 no stat. sig. diff. fail to rej. 90% claim

Drug Efficacy Test   n = 200
(differences expressed as Z scores)

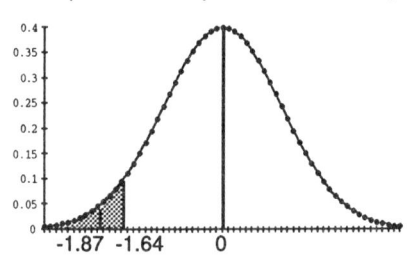

[Graph showing normal curve with -1.87 and -1.64 marked]

for n = 201 actual Z = -1.87 outside cut-off Z = -1.64
stat. sig. diff.
reject 90% claim

Razor Refunds
99% Conf. Int. for p

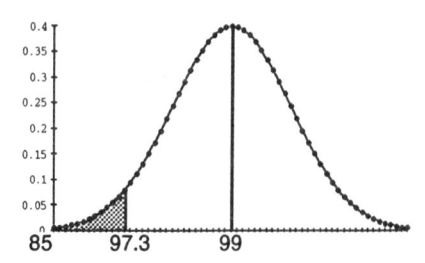

[Graph showing normal curve with 85, 97.3, and 99 marked]

Not necessarily. Stat. sig. (85% outside 97.3% cut-off). However, you can't equate satisfaction with return. Many unhappy customers will not hassle with a refund.

9. A drug company claims its drug is 90% effective. A test of 101 volunteers shows only 86% effectiveness. If alpha equals .05 is that within the acceptable limits for 90% effectiveness?

10. (Continuing) Suppose for the above problem, the sample size had been 201. What would your conclusion be if the rate of effectiveness has still been 86%?

11. The president of a well known electric company boasts a satisfaction rate of 99% based upon razors returned for the money-back guarantee. A survey of 100 recent purchasers indicated that 15 of them were unhappy with their razor. At the 99% level are we to conclude that the quality of the product has dropped?

12. Hypothesis testing can be accomplished in one of two basic ways: you can either check the actual Z value against one of the cut-off values (i.e. Z = 1.64, or Z = 1.96), or you can check the actual Z value to determine its precise level of significance. This precise determination is referred to as checking the _____ .

p value

Hypothesis Tests for Two Proportions

§ 10.3

1. Brand A claims to be superior to brand B in relieving sinus congestion. Brand A is administered to 80 people of which 60 claim relief. Brand B is given to 60 people of which 40 claim relief. Test at alpha = .01.

Sinus Medicines   Brand A vs. Brand B
(differences expressed as Z scores)

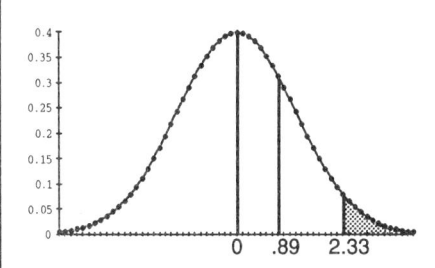

Actual Z = .89 inside cut-off Z = 2.33 ergo, no stat. sig. diff fail to reject null, claim of superiority is not supported

2. An extremely scientific research test, conducted under the strictest laboratory conditions at the Barrel House (a local tavern) investigates the ability of persons to correctly identify unmarked beers. In a two beer test, 54 out of 100 participants correctly identify Budweiser. In a second sample, 52 of 100 participants correctly identify Miller. Test for significant difference between Budweiser and Miller at alpha = .10.

Beer Taste Test   Budweiser vs. Miller
(differences expressed as Z scores)

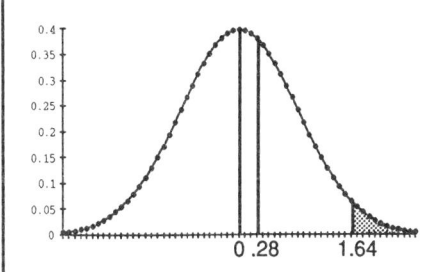

Actual Z = .282, far inside cut-off Z = 1.64 no stat. sig. diff.

**Test of Dandruff Medication Efficacy
99% One-tail Test**

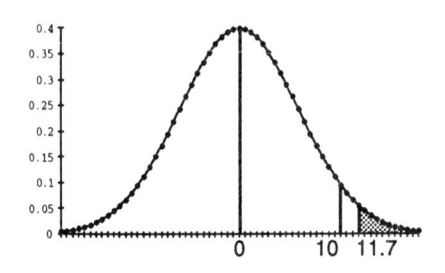

[Normal distribution curve with cutoff at 11.7, actual value at 10]

No stat. sig. diff. Actual diff of 10% inside 11.71% cut-off

Not necessarily. Remember, tests of sig. are very sensitive to sample size. Had this same diff. been seen over a sample of size 400 it would have been quite significant. Also remember, fail to reject, not equivalent to equal.

**Computer Preference IBM vs. Apple
(differences expressed as Z scores)**

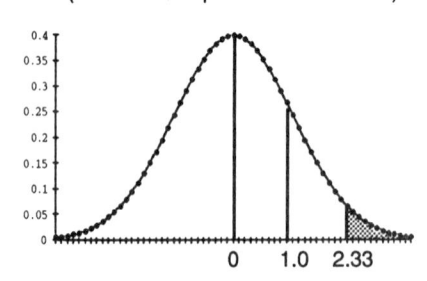

[Normal distribution curve with cutoff at Z = 2.33, actual Z = 1.0]

Actual Z = 1.0 inside cut-off Z = 2.33 no stat. sig. diff.

3. The famous German dandruff chemist, Dr. Ludwig von Flakenitchenscratchen, has developed a new medication for the relief of dandruff. He claims that it is better than the leading product. To prove this he gave his new dandruff tonic to 100 severe sufferers where it was effective in 90% of the cases. The leading competitive product was also given to a control sample where it was shown effective in 80% of the cases. Test for significant difference at $\alpha = .01$.

4. (Continuing) Because of the result above (no statistically significant difference, fail to reject null hypothesis) are we to conclude that his medication is really not any better? (Weigh your answer carefully, the survival of planet earth hangs in the balance. Should he fail to receive the credit he believes he deserves, Dr. Flakenitchenscratchen threatens to release a rabid, fast-multiplying dandruff virus on the world, thereby burying the world in an avalanche of white flakes, destroying all life as we know it on this planet.)

5. A comparison is made to determine if IBM computers appeal to more "professional" types than Apple computers. A sample of 50 professionals is questioned concerning IBM machines, 30 persons express interest in the IBM machine. A second sample of 50 professionals is queried concerning the Apple machine, with 25 persons expressing an interest. Are we to conclude that IBM has more "professional appeal" at alpha = .01?

6. Would the results be the same if it had been the same group of 50 professionals?	No, would not be independent samples.
7. Determine the required sample sizes if we wish to be 95% confident of being within 5 percentage points when p1 is believed to be around 20% and p2 is believed to be around 30%.	n1 = 528 n2 = 605
8. If we are totally at a loss for the possible (probable values of p1 and p2) what value should be use for p1 and p2?	50% for p1 and p2
9. What happens to the values of A, B, and C if p1 and p2 are the same?	if p1 = p2 then A = B = C
10. (Referring back to problem 7) What would be the required sample sizes if p1 and p2 were unknown and 50% was used in place of each? (Let the confidence interval remain at 95% and the error remain at 5%.)	n1 = 769 n2 = 769

CHAPTER 11

Analysis of Variance

CHAPTER OBJECTIVES

Previous chapters have presented various techniques for testing for significant difference between two means. This chapter will introduce a technique for mathematically testing for significant difference between two or more means.

The completely randomized design (one-factor ANOVA), the randomized block design, and the two-way factorial design are discussed. Procedures for constructing confidence intervals for mean differences using these designs are described along with a test for equal variances using the completely randomized design. Multiple comparison procedures are also introduced.

By the end of the chapter you should be able to:

1. Explain what is meant by 'analysis of variance', form confidence intervals and test for significant differences between means.

2. Use Hartley's test for testing variances.

3. Discuss the assumptions behind the use of an experimental design. Explain the experimental design technique of randomized block design.

4. Perform multiple comparison procedures.

146

ANALYSIS OF VARIANCE

§ 11.0

A Look Back/Introduction

1. In previous chapters we investigated techniques which could be used to test for significant differences between either one mean vs. some standard, or between _____ means.

two

2. Suppose that there were 3 means to be compared. Rather than Ford vs. Chevy, it is Ford vs. Chevy vs. Chrysler. To say Ford vs. Chevy vs. Chrysler is not to say that we are comparing Ford vs. Chevy, and Ford vs. Chrysler. Our null hypothesis simply states: the means are all equal, the alternative hypothesis simply states, the means are not all equal. True or False

True

3. As discussed in problem two, if you have four different means and you want to test for significant difference between means, the proper approach is to use analysis of variance to test all four of the means, simultaneously against each other. It is not appropriate to make 'individual' two-way tests between each of the four means (1 vs. 2, 1 vs. 3, 2 vs. 3, etc.) (Actually the word "appropriate' is probably not a good choice of words. There is nothing 'wrong' with performing a series of two-way tests, such tests can be quite informative...perhaps it would be most correct to simply say that a series of two-way tests gives the answer to a different question than the 'all-at-once' analysis of variance test.) Review question: suppose that you did have 4 means and you decided to perform all of the two-way tests possible between those four means...how many two-way tests would there be?

From previous chapters:
combination of 4 draw 2
= six combinations

4. In analysis of variance, we will be making inferences about the means by examining the _____.

variance

---

§ 11.1

Comparing Two Means: Another Look

1. In previous chapters a clear distinction was made between situations in which the variances between samples could be

147

pooled (the variances were believed to be approximately equal) and situations in which the variances could not be pooled (the variances were not believed to be equal). However, one of the assumptions behind the technique of analysis of variance is that the variances of the populations are _____.

equal

2. Actually, there is a technical term for the situation where the variances are equal, the term is homoscedasticity. True or false.

True...but I wouldn't want to say it very loudly.

3. The assumption of homoscedasticity (equality of variances) is a very critical assumption since the analysis of variance test is very sensitive to deviations from strict homoscedasticity. True or False

False, the test is not very sensitive, esp. if sample sizes are equal.

4. In the traditional Z or t test between means, we would test between Ford vs. Chevy. In analysis of variance the items are broken into two groups (or levels) based upon what is referred to as a _____. In this case, the factor might be called "car type". If formally we had said that there was a significant difference between the two groups, now we would conclude that "car type" is a significant _____.

factor

factor

5. Phrased in terms of analysis of variance, the traditional Z or t test could only examine _____ (how many) factor at _____ (how many) levels.

one
two

6. One of the advantages of analysis of variances is that it can be easily(?) (the computation is rough, but theoretically it is a simple extension) extended to multiple factors at multiple levels. True or False

True, the ability to test multiple factors and multiple levels is main advantage of ANOVA.

7. Since the phrase "Analysis of Variance" is a bit cumbersome, it often goes by the acronym _____.

ANOVA

8. When we are looking at the difference between means, we are really looking at a type of variation or scatter...in this case the variation between means. It is the purpose of analysis of variance to analyze the variation in the data set and to pinpoint its source. In traditional analysis of variance, the variation in

148

between within	the data set is broken into two sources, variation _____ and variation _____.
sum of squares	9. A variance is simply a set of squared differences, since the pinpointing (computation) of variances is of such importance, the computation of these squared differences is of corresponding importance. These sets of squared deviations are referred to as _____ of _____, or SS.
factor	10. The between groups sum of squares measures the variation between the means of the various groups (or levels). Perhaps a more descriptive name, would be to say that it measures the variation attributable to the _____.
error	11. The within groups sum of squares measures the variation within each group (or level). Perhaps a more descriptive name, would be to say that it measures the variation attributable to _____ (that is, the 'natural' scattering of the items within each group).
between within	12. The total sum of squares will be equal to the _____ plus the _____.
True	13. There will be a different degree of freedom for each sum of squares. True or False
number of levels (groups) minus one, often written (n_g - 1)	14. The degrees of freedom for the "between" or "factor" sum of squares is _____.
sample size minus # of levels often written (n_s - n_g)	15. The degrees of freedom for the "within" or "error" sum of squares is _____
sample size minus one often written (n_s - 1)	16. Not only does the total sum of squares represent the sum of the between sum of squares plus the within sum of squares, but in addition, the degrees of freedom for the total will equal to the sum of the degrees of freedom within, plus degrees of freedom between. This will be equal to _____.

17. For a given sum of squares, the mean square error is the _____ divided by its respective _____.

sum of squares / df

18. The ultimate result of all of this pushing and shoving is the production of the F ratio. The F ratio is the result of the mean square error _____ divided by the mean square error _____.

between (factor)
within (error)

19. To determine the appropriate values of significance for the F test, you must investigate both degrees of freedom. True or False

True

20. Even though it has gotten more complicated, an F ratio is simply a ratio of two variances. True or False

True

21. Given two groups (levels), each with 5 members, one group with an average of 4.0 and the other with an average of 6.0. Use ANOVA to test for significant difference between these two groups (levels). (Or if you prefer, to test if group membership is a significant factor in distinguishing performance.)

Group 1 (level 1)   Group 2 (level 2)
       3   7
       4   6
       6   8
       4   5
       3   4

avg = 4.0   avg = 6.0

SS(factor) = 10.0
df(factor) = 2-1 = 1

SS(error) = 16.0
df(error) = 10-2 = 8

$F = \frac{10/1}{16/8} = 5.0$

F values from table
df = 1 and 8
.05 = 5.32   01 = 11.3

To guide you in your efforts, set up your work in the ANOVA table below:

Source	df	SS	MS	F
factor				
error				
total				

F Distribution   Two Groups ANOVA

5.0 5.32

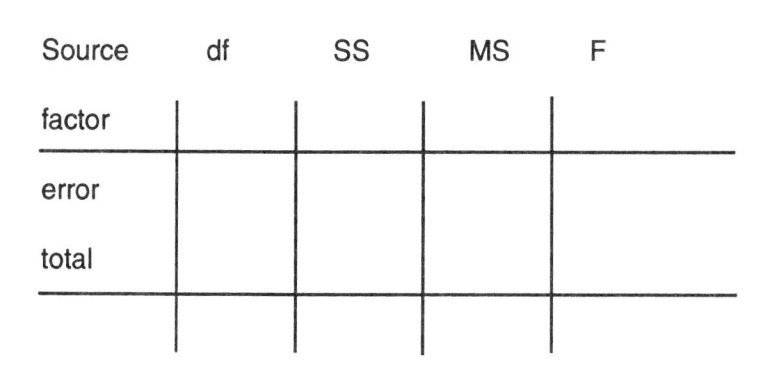

Actual value inside of cut-offs, therefore no stat. sig. diff. between means (factor is not significant)   fail to reject

22. Given the following scores for two groups, test for significant difference at alpha = .05 using ANOVA.

Group 1 (level 1)	Group 2 (level 2)
6	15
6	16
4	15
6	17

avg = 5.5   avg = 15.75

SS(factor) = 210.13
df(factor) = 2-1 = 1

SS(error) = 5.75
df(error) = 8-2 = 6

$F = \dfrac{210.13/1}{5.75/6} = 219.26$

F values from table
  df = 1 and 6
  .05 = 5.99
  .01 = 13.74

F Distribution   Two Groups   ANOVA

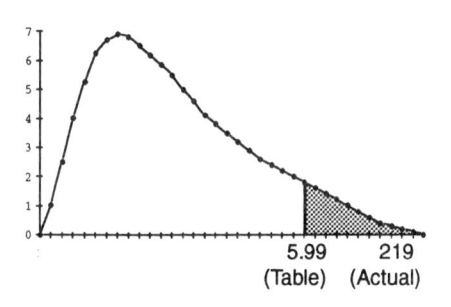

5.99   219
(Table)   (Actual)

Actual F, outside of cut-offs, therefore stat. sig. diff. (factor is sig) reject null

Here again is the ANOVA table to help organize your results.

Source	df	SS	MS	F
factor				
error				
total				

23. Given the following scores for two groups, test for significant difference using ANOVA. (Although the assumption of homoscedasticity holds up better with equal sample sizes, the variances are close, and besides, it would be instructive to see that equal sample sizes are not necessary for the technique to work.)

Group 1 (level 1)	Group 2 (level 2)
2	1
1	1
8	1
5	9
	9
	9
avg = 4.0	avg = 5.0

Here again is the ANOVA table to help organize your results.

Source	df	SS	MS	F
factor				
error				
total				

SS(factor) = 2.40
df(factor) = 2-1 = 1

SS(error) = 126.0
df(error) = 10-2 = 8

$$F = \frac{2.40/1}{126/8} = .15$$

F values from table
df = 1 and 8
.05 = 5.32
.01 = 11.3

F Distribution   Two Groups   ANOVA

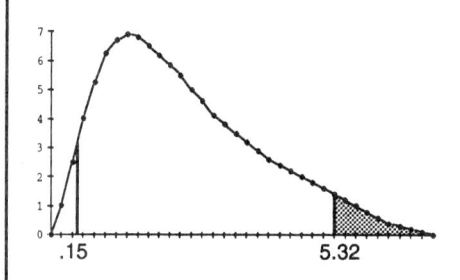

Actual value inside of cut-offs, therefore no stat. sig. diff. between means (factor is not significant) fail to reject

152

SS(factor) = 1081.6
df(factor) = 2-1 = 1

SS(error) = 48.0
df(error) = 10-2 = 8

$F = \frac{1081.6/1}{48.0/8} = 180.3$

F values from table
 df = 1 and 8
 .05 = 5.32
 .01 = 11.3

F Distribution   Two Groups   ANOVA

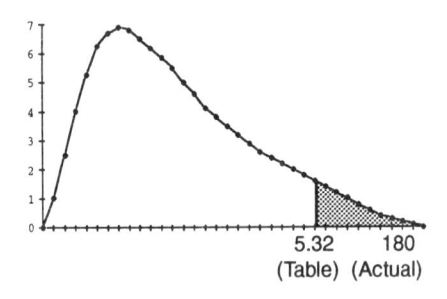

Actual F, outside of cut-offs, therefore stat. sig. diff. (factor is sig) reject null

large
is

small
is not

24. Given the following two groups, test for significant difference using ANOVA.

Group 1 (level 1)	Group 2 (level 2)
16	42
18	37
22	36
19	40
17	41
avg = 18.4	avg = 39.2

Here again is the ANOVA table to help organize your results.

Source	df	SS	MS	F
factor				
error				
total				

25. When the variance between- (attributable to the factor) is large, and the variance within (attributable to the error) is small, then the resulting F ratio will generally be _____, indicating that there (is/is not) a statistically significant difference.

26. On the other hand, when the variance between- (attributable to the factor) is small, and the variance within (attributable to the error) is large, then the resulting F ratio will generally be _____, indicating that there (is/is not) a statistically significant difference.

153

27. Suppose that you were told the following "facts":

   BGSS = 4
   WGSS = 30
   Two Groups, n1 = 5, n2 = 5

   What would be the resulting F ratio, and would it be statistically significant?

$df_1 = 1$, $df_2 = 8$

$F = \dfrac{4/1}{30/8} = 1.07$

not significant

28. Continuing, now suppose we change the sample sizes:

   BGSS = 4
   WGSS = 30
   Two Groups, n1 = 200, n2 = 200

   What would be the resulting F ratio, and would it be statistically significant?

$df_1 = 1$, $df_2 = 398$ (use df_2 = infinity for table)

$F = \dfrac{4/1}{30/398} = 53.1$

quite significant

29. In general, for a given difference, the larger the sample - the more significant the results using the F test. True or False
In this respect the F test is much like the Z and the t test. True or False

True

True

30. Using the Z table, what is the two-tail, .05 value for Z?

1.96

31. Using the t table, what is the two-tail, .05 value for t at df = infinity?

1.96

34. Using the F table, what is the two-tail, .05 value for F at df1 = 1, and df2 = infinity? What would be the square root of this value?

3.84
1.96

35. When df1 = 1, the value which you will compute for F will be equal to the _____ of the t value.

square

36. Since the value of F is simply equal to the value of t squared, and since the F was considerably more work, why not just use the t distribution and forget about the F entirely?

$F = t^2$ only when df1 = 1
t only works for 2 groups

154

§ 11.2

ANOVA: More than Two Means

1. In this section we have several levels, but still only one factor. An example would be to investigate whether cigarette smoking was a factor in life expectancy and to test this we had three groups: Light, Medium, and Heavy smokers. True or False

True

2. Now consider this situation: Same basic problem, and investigation of life expectancy. Only this time we are looking at smoking, eating and exercise. Would this be a one-factor problem?

No - 3 factors, each with their own levels

3. ANOVA makes three assumptions:
   1. The values are obtained _____ of each other.
   2. The observations in each distribution follow a _____ distribution.
   3. All of the populations exhibit homoscedasticity that is, _____ of _____.

independently

normal

equality of variances

4. If we let the symbol "k" stand for the number of levels, then we have the following computations for the various degrees of freedom:
   df_1 = _____
   df_2 = _____
   df-total = _____

k - 1
n - k
n - 1

Where df_1 relates to the variance attributed to _____, and df_2 relates to the variances attributed to _____.

factor (between groups)
error (within groups)

5. As before, the "mean square errors" are simply the _____ divided by their respective _____.

sum of squares / df

6. As before, the F ratio is simply the _____ divided by the _____.

MSE(factor) / MSE(error)
of
MSE(between) / MSE(within)

7. Given the three groups shown below, test for significant difference between means using ANOVA.

Group 1 (level 1)	Group 2 (level 2)	Group 3 (lev 3)
10	6	3
9	7	4
11	7	5
10	8	2
	7	1
		3
avg = 10.0	avg = 7.0	avg = 3.0

The ANOVA table:

Source	df	SS	MS	F
factor				
error				
total				

SS(factor) = 122.4
df(factor) = 3-1 = 2

SS(error) = 14.0
df(error) = 15-3 = 12

$$F = \frac{122.4/2}{14.0/12} = 52.46$$

F values from table
df = 2 and 12
.05 = 3.88
.01 = 6.93

F Distribution   Three Groups   ANOVA

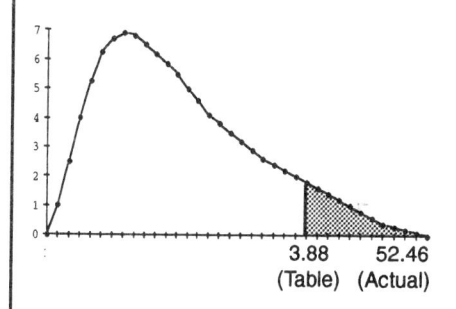

3.88   52.46
(Table) (Actual)

Actual value outside of cut-offs, therefore
stat. sig. diff. between means (factor is significant) reject null

SS(factor) = 9.80
df(factor) = 3-1 = 2

SS(error) = 26.87
df(error) = 12-3 = 9

$$F = \frac{9.80/2}{26.87/9} = 1.64$$

F values from table
df = 2 and 9
.05 = 4.26
.01 = 8.02

F Distribution   Three Groups   ANOVA

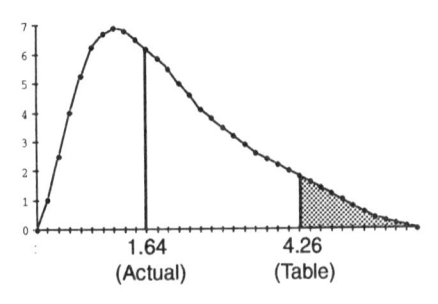

[F distribution curve with 1.64 (Actual) and 4.26 (Table) marked]

Actual F, inside of cut-offs, therefore no stat. sig. diff. (factor is not sig) fail to reject null

8. Since you had so much fun, how about this set of overall performance scores for Toyota, Honda and Nissan (each vehicle ranked on a score of 1 to 7, with four persons testing the Toyota, 5 persons testing the Honda, and 3 people testing the Datsun.)

Toyota	Honda	Nissan
6	3	5
6	1	5
4	7	6
6	2	
	5	avg = 5.33
avg = 5.5	avg = 3.6	

The ANOVA table:

Source	df	SS	MS	F
factor				
error				
total				

9. Now try this one with four groups:

Group 1	Group 2	Group 3	Group 4
15	4	1	17
16	2	1	18
15	9	9	18
17	avg = 5.0	9	avg = 17.7
16		avg = 5.0	
avg=15.8			

The ANOVA table:

Source	df	SS	MS	F
factor				
error				
total				

SS(factor) = 500.27
df(factor) = 4-1 = 3

SS(error) = 93.47
df(error) = 15-4 = 11

$$F = \frac{500.27/3}{93.47/11} = 19.63$$

F values from table
df = 3 and 11
.05 = 3.59
.01 = 6.22

F Distribution Four Groups ANOVA

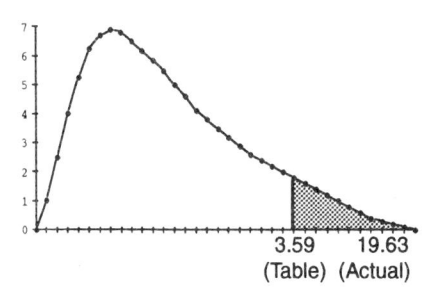

3.59   19.63
(Table) (Actual)

Actual value of 19.63 is outside F value cut-offs, therefore stat sig diff, reject null hypothesis that all of the means are the same.

Note that in this situation not all four means are different from each other, in fact, two of them are exactly the same, but when viewed "as a whole", not all four means appear to have been taken from the same population.

158

variances | 10. In its most simple expression, an F ratio can simply be said to be the ratio of two _____.

Hartley | 11. When there are multiple variances, a simple F ratio can be formed by simply dividing the largest variance among the groups(levels) by the smallest variance among the groups. This test is called the _____ test.

7.11 | 12. Suppose that you have 5 samples with 10 in each sample. What would be the cut-off value for the Hartley statistic?

F = 6.25
  inside 7.11 cutoff
  no stat sig diff
| 13. (Continuing) And suppose that the largest variance among those 5 groups was 39.4, and the smallest variance among those 5 groups was 6.3. What would be the value of the F ratio, and what what you conclude about these samples?

True | 14. In problem 9 (previous page) we determined that somewhere in the four means there was a significant amount of difference, although we were not sure if there was a significant difference between any particular pair of means. True or False?

multiple comparison | 15. Tests which compare all possible pairs of means in such a way that the probability of making one or more Type I errors is alpha are known as _____ _____ tests

Uh...False. | 16. One of the more popular tests is Tukey's test. Tukey's test is usually conducted around Thanksgiving when everyone gets together to see who cooked the best bird. True or False?

The four groups have unequal sample sizes. | 17. As much as we would really like too, we can't perform Tukey's test on the data in problem 9 ... why?

---

§ 11.3 | Experimental Design

dependent | 1. In most situations a variable on interest is to be affected by some phenomena. This variable is the _____ variable.

2. Consider four groups. If samples are drawn from the four groups in a way in which none of the sample observations are related to each other in any way, this is considered to be a _____ _____ design. | completely randomized

3. In a completely randomized design, all of the sample values are _____ of each other. In a randomized block design the values are _____ _____ of each other. | independent
not independent

4. In the randomized block design, the data have been grouped or paired in some manner. The criterion on which the data pairs have been paired is the _____ factor. | blocking

5. In a two-way factorial design, there are two dependent variables which are believed to affect the situation. True or False? | True

6. Suppose you were concerned with the effect of two factors, education and height on income (it's true, taller people tend to make more. . . alas, as you might have guessed. . . I am rather short.) In the two-way factorial design it is possible to test for the effect of education on income, the effect of height on income, and the _____ between the two. | interaction

---

The Randomized Block Design | § 11.4

1. In the previous sections we have assumed independence, that is the selection of sample items from one group (and the values from that one group) were not related to the values in the other groups. However, in some situations this is not the case, there is a relationship between the items in the various groups. These samples are said to be _____. | dependent

2. A good example of dependent groups would be if the same person were to rate three kinds of cola...this process being repeated for however many persons were in the sample. In this case, each person would be called a _____, and the experiment would be termed a _____ _____ design. | block
randomized block

160

factor
error

blocks

SS-factor = 1.14
df-factor = 2
MS-factor = .57

SS-blocks = 23.14
df-blocks = 6
MS-blocks = 3.857

SS-error = 4.86
df-error = 12
MS-error = .41

F-factor = 1.41
F(2/12) = 3.89
not sig

F-blocks = 9.53
F(6/12) = 3.00
sig diff

Therefore we conclude that there is no sig diff between the brands of beer, but that there is a sig diff between the persons rating the beers.

---

3. In analysis of variance, it is the purpose of analysis of variance to look at all of the variance which is present between the various scores, and to then determine the source of the variance. In the example above (the cola) some of the variation might be due to differences between colas, this would be the _____ variance. Some of the variation might be purely random, this would be termed the _____ variance. And some of the variation might be due to differences between the persons performing the test. This would be the _____ variance.

4. Consider the following situation: Seven persons have been asked to rate three beers on a 1 to 5 scale with 5 being best and 1 being worst. Perform analysis of variance to determine whether there is either a significant difference between beers, as well as whether there is a significant difference between blocks (persons). (let alpha = .05 for both tests)

Person	Budweiser	Miller	Shiner
1	4	4	5
2	3	4	5
3	2	1	2
4	3	2	2
5	4	3	4
6	5	5	4
7	4	4	5
average	3.57	3.29	3.86

The ANOVA table:

Source	df	SS	MS	F
factor				
blocks				
error				
total				

(Note that this table has an extra row for the "blocks" effect.)

5. This analysis of variance was done on rating scores which had values of 1 to 5. What problem might this present?

Might be considered to be ordinal data. In that case it is technically not appropriate for ANOVA.

6. (Special Bonus Question!) What brewery produces Shiner beer? In what town is this brewery located? Where in tarnation is that town?

Spoeltz Brewery Shiner, Texas 'Bout halfway between San Antonio and Houston

7. Now consider this situation: Eleven golfers have been invited to the golf course to test four brands of golf balls. They take one drive off the tee with each of the four balls. The distances were recorded and are provided below. Use ANOVA to test for significant difference (alpha = .05) between groups and between golfers.

Golfer	Wilson	Spaulding	MacGregor	Soyus1
1	290	280	270	190
2	260	250	260	160
3	270	270	280	180
4	230	220	230	130
5	250	250	240	140
6	210	200	200	110
7	220	210	220	110
8	280	270	280	170
9	310	300	300	200
10	300	310	310	210
11	260	260	250	150
avg	247.1	240.0	242.9	145.7

SS-factor = 82170.4
df-factor = 3
MS-factor = 27390.2

SS-blocks = 45468.2
df-blocks = 10
MS-blocks = 4546.8

SS-error = 1004.5
df-error = 30
MS-error = 33.48

F-factor = 817.9
F(3/30) = 2.92
quite sig

F-blocks = 135.8
F(10/30) = 2.16
also sig diff

Conclude that there is a significant difference between golfers and between brands of golf balls

The ANOVA table:

Source	df	SS	MS	F
factor				
blocks				
error				
total				

SS-factor = 169.7
df-factor = 2
MS-factor = 84.8

SS-blocks = 33884.8
df-blocks = 10
MS-blocks = 3388.5

SS-error = 696.9
df-error = 20
MS-error = 34.8

F-factor = 2.43
F(2/20) = 3.49
not sig

F-blocks = 97.24
F(10/20) = 2.35
sig diff

The blocks effect is still significant, indicating a significant difference between golfers However, the factor effect is no longer significant indicating no sig diff between brands of golf balls.

8. (Continuing) In problem number 7 (the golf balls) we concluded that there was a large difference between golfers, and a very large difference between the brands of golf balls. However, if we remember our null hypothesis, we remember that the ANOVA test is looking for any difference between means, anywhere. Furthermore, if we 'eyeball' the averages we can see that three of the means are quite close, only one of them seems to be noticeably different.

Retest the golf scores but this time omit the Soyus1 scores (use just three groups).

Golfer	Wilson	Spaulding	MacGregor
1	290	280	270
2	260	250	260
3	270	270	280
4	230	220	230
5	250	250	240
6	210	200	200
7	220	210	220
8	280	270	280
9	310	300	300
10	300	310	310
11	260	260	250
avg	247.1	240.0	242.9

The ANOVA table:

Source	df	SS	MS	F
factor				
blocks				
error				
total				

Two-Way Factorial Design

1. Previous work in this chapter has focused upon problems with only one factor...that is, only one independent variable which is felt to be causing the changes in the dependent variable. In two-way factorial designs, we are concerned with the effects of two, independent variables. True or False

§ 11.5

True. And furthermore, not only are we concerned with these two independent variables, we are also concerned with any possible **interaction** effects between the two independent variables.

2. Consider this example: At a certain university, records are made of the time spent (in hours per week) doing homework. (Actually, there was some confusion...the researchers are not sure whether these numbers represent the numbers of hours doing homework, or the number of hours spent watching TV. Not wishing to appear sexist, you may decide which phenomena has been monitored.)

Anyway, the data was collected (broken-down) by two different classification factors: **gender** and **class standing**. In performing the two-way factorial test, we can test for statistically significant difference with respect to three hypotheses. These three hypotheses are: (state in the traditional "null" hypothesis format)

1. Gender
   Males vs. Females
   H_o $\mu_m = \mu_f$

2. Class Standing
   Between Classifications
   H_o $\mu_f = \mu_{so} = \mu_j = \mu_{sr}$

3. Interaction between Gender and Classification

3. Because of the way in which the degrees of freedom are calculated, the two-way factorial design demands that there be multiple observations for each classification subgroup. These multiple observations are called _____.

replicates

4. In this current design the factor for gender has (hopefully) two levels. The factor for school classification has four levels. Thus our design has _____ subgroups.

8

5. If the experiment featured four replicates in each subgroup, that is, four-male-freshmen, four-female-freshmen, four-male-sophomores, four-female-sophomores, etc., the total sample size would need to be _____.

4 x 8 = 32

6. Enough suspense. Here are the numbers:

	Fr	So	Jr	Sr
M	14,13,15,14	12,11,12,13	10,9,11,10	8,7,9,8
F	6,5,7,6	8,7,9,8	10,9,11,10	12,11,13,12

As in previous problems we need to arrange our work in an ANOVA Table.

The ANOVA table:

Source	df	SS	MS	F
factor				
Rows(sex)	1	32	32	48
Cols(class)	3	0	0	0
Interaction	3	160	53.3	80
error	24	16	.67	
total	31	208		

What are our conclusions with respect to the three hypothesis tests?

7. Actually, one of the easiest ways to check for the interaction effects is by graphing the data points. Graph the subcell averages for each subcell and see what you get.

Interaction effects are indicated by the presence of lines with different slopes (lines that cross).

If the lines are basically parallel, then there is probably no interaction effect.

If the lines are parallel and (also) close together there is probably no difference on that factor either (in this case gender). If the lines are parallel and far apart, there probably is a significant difference for that factor.

1. Male vs. Female
   df1 = 1, df2 = 24
   .05 cut-off, F = 4.26 (table)
   Actual F = 48.0
   Statistically significant diff.

2. Classifications
   df1 = 3, df2 = 24
   .05 cut-off, F = 3.01 (table)
   Actual F = 0.00
   No stat sig diff (no difference at all. unlikely to occur in "real life", but this is obviously a "teacher-designed" problem)

3. Interactions
   df1 = 3, df2 = 24
   .05 cut-off, F = 3.01 (table)
   Actual F = 80.0
   Statistically significant difference (quite significant)

ANOVA Graph
Looking for Interaction Effects

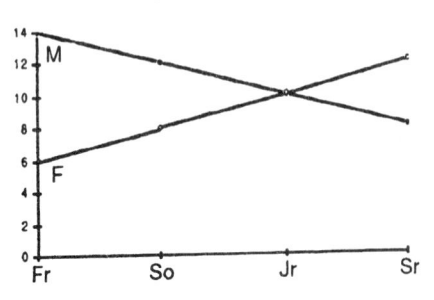

CHAPTER 12

Quality Improvement

CHAPTER OBJECTIVES

This chapter introduces the philosophy and many of the techniques related to quality improvement and quality assurance. The basic principles of total quality management (TQM) are discussed. The philosophy and criteria of the Malcolm Baldrige National Quality Award (MBNQA) are outlined. Various quality improvement tools such as control charts, variables sampling and attributes sampling, process capability and process cabability ratios are discussed. By the end of this chapter you should be able to:

1. Tell what is meant by "quality". How is it defined? How is it measured?

2. Explain the history, intent and criteria associated with the Malcolm Baldrige National Quality Award.

3. Develop and use Control Charts. Develop and interpret "Xbar-charts", "R-charts", "p-charts" and "c-charts".

4. Develop and use Process Capability Charts and process cabability ratios.

166

§ 12.0	A Look Back/ Introduction
variability	1. Quality Control is the study of _____.
Baldrige	2. Evidence of the emphasis upon Quality (in the United States) can be seen in the Malcolm _____ Award, given by the US Department of Commerce.

§ 12.1	Quality Improvement: Concepts and Strategies
False, in statistics, quality does not relate to "costliness".	1. In statistics, "quality" means general excellence, and how expensive. For instance, most would agree that Nieman-Marcus is a higher quality store than K-Mart. True or False
True	2. In statistics, "quality" is defined in terms of standards. Does the product conform to the standards that have been set for it? True or False
True, although scorned in the US, Dr. Deming's techniques were heartily embraced in Japan.	3. The "father" of quality control procedures is an American Statistician, W. Edwards Deming. True or False
1. iden. cust. and their needs 2. innovate to meet these needs 3. entire corp orientation to meeting these customer needs	4. Another major spokesman for the quality movement is Joseph Juran. The core of Juran's philosophy is contained in the Juran Trilogy: Quality planning, quality control and quality improvement. Quality planning concentrates on:
quality is free	5. Philip Crosby is the most 'marketing oriented' (as opposed to statistical process control oriented) of the three. He is best known for the slogan: _____ is _____.
stable, chance	4. Some variation is inherent in every production process. This is referred to as a _____ system of _____ causes.
process	5. Any combination of people, machinery, material and methods that produces a product or service is a _____.

6. Features of a product that describe its fitness for use, such a length, weight, taste, appearance, reliability, etc., are referred to as _____ _____.	quality characteristics
7. The application of statistical quality control to measuring and analyzing the variation found in processes is called _____ _____ _____.	statistical process control or SPC
8. The procedure of accepting or rejecting a large lot (batch) based on the results of a sample from the lot...is called _____ _____.	acceptance sampling
9. A statistical chart used to monitor various aspects of a process (such as the process average) and to determine if the process is in-control (stable) or out-of-control (unstable) is called a _____ _____.	control chart

The Malcolm Baldrige National Quality Award	§ 12.2
1. Whereas the Deming award is given in Japan to the company that best demonstrates quality improvement, the Malcolm Baldrige Award is given to _____ companies that demonstrate noteworthy quality.	American
2. The Malcolm Baldrige award is named after Malcolm Forbes who thought of the idea of a quality award while driving over a large, treeless mountain called 'bald ridge'. True or False	False. It is named after the former Secretary of Commerce.
3. The biggest drawback for a company trying to win the Baldrige award is that you may not win. Applying for the award takes a great deal of effort (money) and if you don't win, then all of that effort has been wasted.	The biggest drawback is that a company may try to win the award without really making a total corporate commitment to improving quality. If a firm does make that commitment, value has still been gained regardless of who wins the Baldrige.

Quality Improvement Tools	§ 12.3
1. One of the keys to improvement is to chart or graph what is happening so that you can observe whether various activities are remaining within the set standards. True or False	True, you must monitor, the use of graphs is an important tool for seeing where things are amiss.

168

True, "what you can't measure, you can't manage."	2. One of the biggest advantages to the initiation of a quality program is that if forces management to actually measure and monitor what is happening in a firm in an objective manner. True or False
Pareto	3. A popular quality improvement tool is the _____ Chart. These charts are enhanced bar charts that are useful for identifying the quality problems with the largest impact, and for displaying the relative importance of different categories.
True. In a 'narrative' description, steps may be omitted. If they are omitted in a flowchart, you have a branch with nowhere to go.	4. Flowcharts are very useful in describing the operations and sequence of an operation. They are very powerful because they prevent any activity from being overlooked. True or False
False. The name comes from the shape of the chart, where the primary and secondary causes form a fishbone pattern.	5. Cause and Effect Diagrams are often called <u>fishbone diagrams</u> because a problem in an organization is like a fishbone that gets caught in your throat. True or False

---

§ 12.4

Process Variation and Control Charts

in-control

1. If the observed variation is due to inherent or natural variability...that is the cumulative effect of many small, essentially uncontrollable events, the process is said to be _____ _____.

out-of-control

2. If the observed variation is due to some relatively large variation that can be traced to an assignable cause the process is said to be _____ _____ _____.

center line

control limits

upper control limit

lower control limit

3. A Quality Control Chart usually features three lines. In the middle is the _____ _____ which represents the average value of the quality characteristic corresponding to the in-control state. The other two lines are the _____ _____, which are the same distance from the center line. The top line is the _____ _____ _____, if the process is in-control, the items should not be above this line. The bottom line is the _____ _____ _____, if the process is in-control, the items should not be below this line.

4. When measuring a quality characteristic which is continuous data (such as average weight), the resulting values are referred to as _____ _____. When measuring a quality characteristic which is discrete (such as number of defects per lot) the resulting values are referred to as _____ _____.	variables data attribute data

Control Charts for Variables Data: the X̄ Chart and the R Chart   § 12.5

1. A plot of the average values for a sample is referred to a _____ _____, where X̄ represents the averages of the samples.	X̄ chart
2. A control chart for the variation is referred to as a _____ _____, where R represents the _____ _____.	R chart sample range
3. If the sample size is small (10 and under) a good estimator of the variation within the sample would be the _____ _____ or more simply, the _____. If the sample size is large (over 10) the more preferred estimator of variation within would be _____ _____ or _____.	sample range, range standard deviation, s
4. In a three sigma control limit, a Z value equal to _____ is used. This would correspond to a _____ confidence interval.	3.0 99.74% (That seems like virtually 100%, but consider the millions of cans that Coke makes. Six sigma would mean 2600 defective cans in each million units.)

5. Consider the following production of 8 oz frozen pizzas. They were wondering if certain times of the day were more prone to out-of-control performance. (Note: this is a non-union factory where the workers must work every day of the week.) Develop the control chart for the this data (the first thing that will be needed is the averages and the ranges).

Control Chart for 8 oz Pizzas

Time	Mon	Tues	Wed	Thrs	Fri	Sat	Sun
8:00	8.4	8.3	8.2	8.7	8.4	8.6	8.8
8:30	7.9	8.1	8.0	7.9	7.9	8.1	8.0
9:00	7.8	7.9	8.0	8.1	8.0	8.1	7.9
9:30	8.0	7.8	7.9	8.1	8.1	7.9	8.0
10:00	7.8	7.6	7.5	7.4	7.6	7.3	7.2

Pizza Production Values

Time	Avg	Range
8:00	8.4857	.6
8:30	7.9857	.2
9:00	7.9714	.3
9:30	7.9714	.2
10:00	7.4857	.6
Overall	7.98	.38

170

$$\sigma = \frac{R}{d_2} = \frac{.38}{2.704} = .1405$$

Center Line = 7.98

UCL = avg - 3(sigma)
UCL = 7.98 + 3(.1405) = 8.40

LCL = avg - 3(sigma)
LCL = 7.98 - 3(.1405) = 7.56

Xbar Control Chart: UCL, LCL & Cnt Line

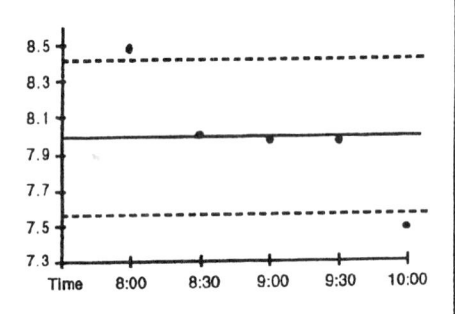

Average R = .38

using the values from the table
UCL = (1.924)(.38) = .7311
LCL = (.076)(.38) = .0028

Range Control Chart: UCL, LCL & Cnt Line

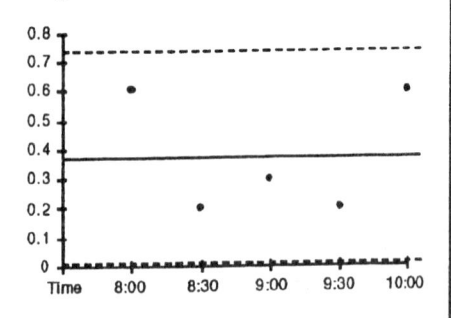

pattern analysis

Yes
8:00AM (just getting started?)

What is the estimate of sigma (σ)?

Develop the three sigma control chart around the process average.

Develop the three sigma control chart for the range.

9. The procedure of looking at the points to spot possible causes of out-of control production is called _____ _____.

10. Do any of the periods seem out-of-control? Why? (suggest possible causes)

10. Reasons for deviation, continued	10:00 (hurrying to get through for coffee break?)
11. Does this bring the UCL and CLC we have determined under suspicion?	yes

---

Control Charts for Attribute Data - p chart §12.6-1

1. A "p chart" is a control chart kept by the urologists at the hospital. True or False

False

2. A "p chart" is a control chart for "p", the proportion of items that are _____.

non conforming

3. The Barnyum's Company is very concerned that its animal cookies do not end up looking like a paraplegic zoo. Eight batches of twelve dozen cookies are inspected* and the following results are found: (find the percentage of defective)

"p" chart for Barnyum's animal crackers

Sample	# def
1	4
2	7
3	5
4	18
5	4
6	7
7	9
8	5

"p" chart for Barnyum's

samp	# def	# insp	% def
1	4	144	0.028
2	7	144	0.049
3	5	144	0.035
4	18	144	0.125
5	4	144	0.028
6	7	144	0.049
7	9	144	0.063
8	5	144	0.035
TOT	59	1152	
AVG	7.38		0.051

*Each animal must be inspected separately. Round animals with short limbs such as bears and lambs are seldom broken. Animals with long limbs such as zebras and giraffes are frequently broken. This particular group of eight batches is composed of camels.

4. Compute the Upper Control Limit

$UCL = .051 + 3(\sqrt{(.051 \times .949)/144})$
$= .051 + 3(.01833)$
$= .106$

172

LCL=.051-3($\sqrt{(.051 \times .949)/144}$)
 = .051 - 3(.01833)
 = -.0039999
 = -.04

zero

5. Compute the Lower Control Limit

since the LCL is negative, it is set to _____

Control Chart ("p") for Barnyum's

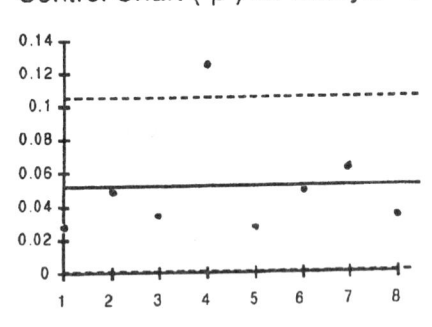

6. Construct the "p chart" for Barnyum's.

Yes, #4 is above the limit.

Are any of the samples outside the limit?

No, 15 defects = .1042
inside cut-off of .1059
do not adjust

7. Continuing the problem with Barnyum's Animal Crackers, suppose that the next batch produces 15 defective camels. Should the process be declared out-of-control and process adjustment be attempted?

Yes, 16 defects = .1111
outside cut-off of .1059
check process

8. Continuing...suppose the subsequent batch produces 16 defective camels. Should the process be declared out-of-control and process adjustment be attempted?

---

§ 12.6-2

Control Charts for Attribute Data - c chart

binomial

Poisson

1. In the "p chart", the nonconforming units were assumed to be distributed according to a _____ probability distribution. In the "c chart", the nonconforming units are assumed to be distributed according to a _____ distribution.

μ = np
σ = $\sqrt{npq}$

2. For the binomial, the mean = _____
 and the standard deviation = _____

For the Poisson, the mean = _____
and the standard deviation = _____

μ
$\sigma = \sqrt{\mu}$

3. Whereas the "p chart" looked at the proportion of defective units within some sample of units, the "c chart" looks at the _____ of defects per _____.

number, unit

4. The Lottasparks Computer Company is inspecting its computers as they come off the assembly line. Each computer is treated as a single unit. Although it is hoped that each computer would be absolutely perfect, rigorous inspection of 10 units has uncovered the following number of defects:

"c" chart for Lottasparks Computers

Sample	# def
1	47
2	65
3	59
4	84
5	93
6	43
7	34
8	27
9	56
10	78
AVG	58.6

Compute the UCL and LCL, and draw the "c chart"

average = 58.6
variance = 58.6
standard deviation = 7.65

UCL = 58.6 + 3(7.65) = 81.55

LCL = 58.6 - 3(7.65) = 35.56

c chart for Lottasparks

5. Are any of the units out-of-control?

(Note that the smallest # of defects is 27. A process may be consistent (in-control) yet producing items that are unacceptable.)

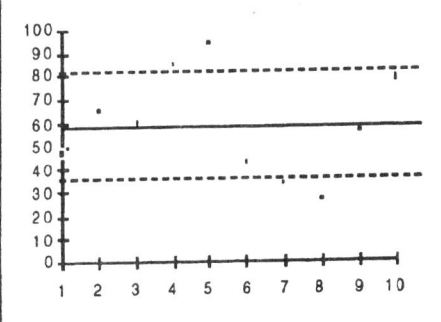

Yes, units #4 and #5 are too high

units #7, #8 are too low
(too low? probably not a matter of serious concern)

6. Suppose that problem 14 (Barnyum's Crackers) was reworked as a "c chart" by treating the 144 cookies as one unit.

"c" chart for Barnyum's animal crackers*

Sample	# def
1	4
2	7
3	5
4	18
5	4
6	7
7	9
8	5

mean = 7.38
std dev = 2.72

7. Compute the UCL.

UCL = 7.38 + 3(2.72)
UCL = 15.53

8. Has there been any change in the units deemed out-of-control?

No. Unit #4 is, once again, the only unit out-of-control.

9. Unit #4 seems to be considerably different from the other units. Suppose that it was discovered that someone had sat on that box of cookies thereby causing the large number of crushed camels. Since this is an assignable cause, it can be removed from consideration as part of the normal process. Refigure the UCL with Unit #4 removed.

mean = 5.857
std dev = 2.42

UCL = 5.857 + 3(2.42)
UCL = 13.12

all units are in-control

---

§ 12.7

Process Capability

1. A process may be in control and yet still be producing parts which are unacceptable if they do not meet the process requirements, referred to as the _____ _____.

specification limits

2. The process control limits (measuring variability) had been referred to as the UCL (upper control limit) and the LCL (lower control limit). The specification limits are the USL (_____ _____ _____) and the LSL (_____ _____ _____).

upper specification limits
lower specification limits

175

3. The difference between the UCL and the LCL is referred to as the _____ _____. Mathematically it is usually set to _____ standard deviations, or _____ _____.

process spread
six
six sigma

4. The Process Capability Ratio looks at the variability of the process (the standard deviation) in comparison to how much variability is allowed. True or False

True

5. Let's go back to the pizzas (Problem #8, §12.4) At that time we estimated sigma (σ) to be .1405 ounce. Suppose that the process specifications had been 7.5 for the LSL and 8.5 for the USL. Before determining the Process Capability Ratio, what three assumptions must be made?

a. process centered within specs (in this case, mean of 7.98 is very close to spec of 8 oz.)
b. normally distributed
c. stable, in control

6. Compute the Process Capability Ratio.

$$C_p = \frac{USL - LSL}{6\sigma} = \frac{8.5 - 7.5}{6(.1405)} = 1.18$$

7. What is the rule for interpreting the Process Capability Ratio? How do the pizzas fare according to the rule?

$C_p \geq 1.33$ good
$1 \leq C_p < 1.33$ adequate
$C_p < 1$ inadequate

The Pizza C_p is adequate

8. A new foreman, Easy Ed, has taken over. He sets the limits of the USL at 9oz, and the LSL at 7oz. Compute the C_p and comment (assume that production remains the same as the original sample).

$C_p = 2/(.843) = 2.372$
Ratio classified as "good"
(pizzas may show a great deal of variability but process will almost always be declared up to specs)

9. After a few months, Easy Ed is replaced by his cousin, Nitpicky Ned, who promptly sets the limits at USL = 8.1 and LSL at 7.9oz. Compute the C_p and comment (assume that production remains the same as the original sample).

$C_p = .2/(.843) = .237$
Ratio now classified as "inadequate".
(Unless improvement is made in the variability of the production, the process will almost always be judged as inadequate, not up to specs.)

True, the process specifically may not be centered on the specification mean.

False, we compare to the nearest spec limit, since that is the one that is the one that is the most danger of being exceeded.

$R_L = \dfrac{7.98-7.5}{3(.1405)} = \dfrac{.48}{.422} = 1.138$

$R_H = \dfrac{7.98-8.5}{3(.1405)} = \dfrac{.52}{.422} = 1.233$

The critical side is the LCL, although it is still above 1.0 and would be considered "capable".

$R_L = \dfrac{7.8-7.5}{3(.1405)} = \dfrac{.30}{.422} = .71$

$R_H = \dfrac{7.8-8.5}{3(.1405)} = \dfrac{.70}{.422} = 1.66$

The low side has not become in real jeopardy of violating the LCL, and such a ratio would be declared "incapable".

$Z_{(LSL)} = \dfrac{7.98-7.5}{.1405} = \dfrac{.48}{.1405} = 3.42$

$Z_{(USL)} = \dfrac{8.5-7.98}{.1405} = \dfrac{.52}{.1405} = 3.70$

10. In computing the Process Capability Ratio, it was explicitly assumed that the process was centered on the specification mean. In computing the Process Capability Ratio, C_{pk}, it is <u>not</u> assumed that the process is centered properly. True or False

11. In computing the C_{pk} we compare the point where the process is centered with the farthest specification limit, since we are most concerned about large differences. True or False

12. Refer to problem #8, S12.2. In that case the sample mean had been 7.98. Recompute the Process Capability Ratio using that mean if the USL = 8.5 and the LSL = 7.5. Which is the critical side?

13. Continuing the problem above, suppose that the mean had been 7.8oz rather than 7.98. Recompute the Process Capability Ratio once again using USL = 8.5 and SLS = 7.5. Comment on the ratios.

Determining the Percent Non-Conforming

14. Using the mean and standard deviation, Z scores (or standard scores, or standardized scores) can be created. Rework problem 12 to compute standardized scores. To refresh: mean = 7.98, std dev = .1405, LSL = 7.5, USL = 8.5

15. Continuing problem 14, what is the probability that is associated with those Z values?

Z = 3.42, p = .49916
Z = 3.70, p = .49989

16. What would be the the probability of a randomly occurring value exceeding those limits?

Probability of exceeding
  Z = 3.42, is .00084

Probability of exceeding
  Z = 3.70, is .00011

17. Those probabilities sound pretty low, but suppose that a drug company was making a fairly common, yet very serious item such as insulin. If the company made three million units, how many of them would be too weak (below the LSL)? How many units would be too strong (above the USL)?

2520 units too weak
 330 units too strong

a total of 2850 incorrect units

CHAPTER 13

Applications of the Chi-Square Statistic

CHAPTER OBJECTIVES

Previous chapters have performed tests of significance with respect to continuous data. This chapter investigates the use of the Chi-Square statistic for performing tests of significance upon frequency distributions that is, data arranged in classification tables.

The Goodness of Fit test for the multinomial situation as well as the test for determining whether a set of sample data is from a particular distribution are described. The test of independence is extended to cover the test of homogeneity for several populations By the end of the chapter you should be able to:

1. Use the Chi-Square to test whether a series of data fits a given probability distribution such as the binomial, multinomial, Poisson, or normal.

2. Use the Chi-Square to test whether an observed distribution fits an expected distribution (goodness of fit test).

3. Use the Chi-Square to test whether the values in a classification table seem to be related to each other (independence of classification test).

180

§ 13.0

A Look Back/Introduction

1. The last few chapters have dealt with data which is been continuous and generally ratio in strength. This chapter works with the Chi-Square distribution. The chi-square distribution can work with data which is in the form of classification tables. This would include _____ data (the lowest strength) of data.

nominal

2. We had previously used the chi-square distribution to test the _____ of a normal population.

variance

3. As with the t distribution and the F distribution, the shape of the chi-square distribution is determined by the _____ __ _____ inherent in the situation.

degrees of freedom

---

§ 13.1

Chi-Square Goodness of Fit Test

1. The Chi-square distribution can be used to test if some observed distribution fits the distribution that we would logically (mathematically) expect to see given that situation. True or False

True

2. The binomial distribution had been used for situations where we were trying to determine the probability of _____ successes in _____ trials, when the probability of a success on each trial was equal to _____.

r
n
p

3. The binomial features "Bernoulli trials", this indicates an event which is characterized by having only _____ outcomes, usually referred to as _____ and _____.

two
success & failure

4. The chi-square test works with frequency distributions, that is, the number of items that fall into each category, or class, or cell. True or False

True

5. In the case of the chi-square the shape of the distribution (the degrees of freedom) is determined by the number of _____.

categories
 (or cells, or classes)

6. At the heart of the chi-square test lies the chi-square statistic. The chi-square statistic is computed by taking the square of the difference of the frequencies in each cell of the _____ distribution minus the frequencies in the corresponding cell of the _____ distribution, divided by the frequency of the items in the expected cell. This procedure is repeated for all of the cells in the distribution. The chi-square statistic is the sum of these squared differences.

observed
expected

7. In problem 9, section 12.3, it was mentioned that a variance is basically a set of squared deviations. Notice that in the case of the chi-square, we also have a set of squared deviations. The difference is that in the case of the chi-square, rather than having the differences between individual items, we have the differences between the frequencies of various _____.

cells

8. Consider this situation: a coin is supposed to have a 50/50 ratio of heads to tails. But you suspect that your "friend" may have some type of trick coin. You quickly flip the coin twenty times, observing 12 heads and 8 tails. Use the chi-square test to test for statistically significant difference at alpha = .05.

df = 1
 table value = 3.84

(Your problem would look like this:)

Observed

12
8

Expected

10
10

Chi-Square Distribution   Coin Toss

.80   3.84
(Actual)   (Table)

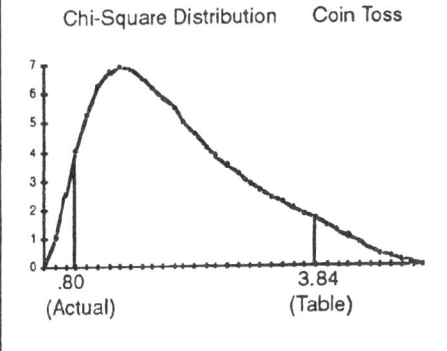

actual chi-square = .80
inside cut-off
no stat sig diff
don't accuse friend of cheating

181

182

3.84
1.96

3.84
1.96

1.96
3.84

1.96
3.84

Uh...not really.

df = 5
table cut-off = 11.07

Chi-Square Distribution 50 Coin Tosses

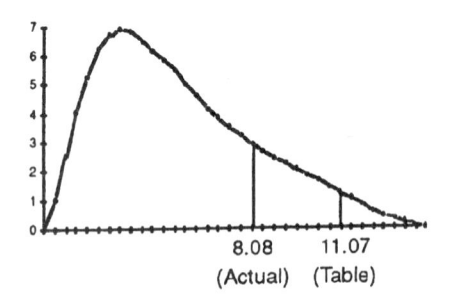

8.08   11.07
(Actual) (Table)

Actual chi-square = 8.08
 actual inside of cutoff
 therefore no stat sig
 diff, fail to reject

---

9. What is the .05 cut-off value for the chi-square statistic when df = 1? _____ What is the square root of this value? _____

10. What is the .05 cut-off value for the value of the F ratio when df1 = 1 and df2 = infinity? _____ What is the square root of this value? _____

11. What is the .05 cut-off for the value of Z? _____ What is the square of this value? _____

12. What is the .05 cut-off for the value of t when df = infinity? _____ What is the square of this value? _____

13. Obviously there is a strong degree of relationship between these various tests. Chi-square can actually be defined as Z squared. And the F-test can be defined as a ratio of two chi-squares. Don't you find this to be absolutely fantastic?

14. OK, so you would rather be watching Gilligan's Island reruns...alas, such are the fates of student and professor alike! At any rate, your "friend", the one with the suspicious coin, now wants to roll some dice. You suspect one of the dice has been, shall we say, modified. You make a test of the suspected die by rolling it 50 times (don't ask me how you got your friend out of the room long enough to roll it 50 times, but that is what you did). The observed distribution is provided below, along with the structure of the expected distribution. Test at alpha = .05.

Value	Observed	Expected
1	12	
2	12	
3	10	
4	8	
5	4	
6	4	

15. (Continuing) Suppose that the friend was gone a bit longer, let's say long enough for you to roll the die 500 times. The results of that experiment are shown below. Test at alpha = .05.

Value	Observed	Expected
1	120	
2	120	
3	100	
4	80	
5	40	
6	40	

df remains at 5
cut-off remains at 11.07

But now, actual chi-sq
 equals 80.8
 Outside cut-off,
 Stat sig diff

Chi-Square Distribution 500 Coin Tosses

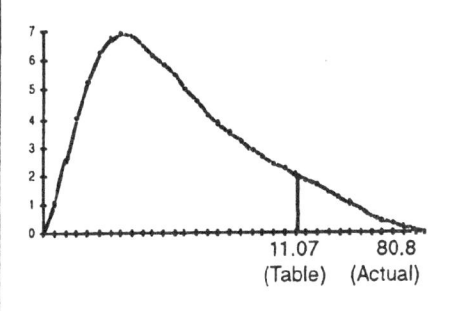

11.07   80.8
(Table) (Actual)

16. As we have seen previously, as the same difference is maintained over larger sample sizes, that difference becomes increasingly significant. True or False

True with chi-square as with the other distributions

17. When categories are "pooled", that means that if there are cells with very small numbers of values, that those small cells should be combined with other cells to form a smaller number of larger cells. True or False

True

18. The rule of thumb is to combine (pool) cells if the expected value in a given cell is less than _____.

5

19. In some cases you wish to determine whether a distribution follows some specified distribution such as a Poisson or a Normal, but you don't know the parameters (ie, the mean). You could use the sample information to 'bootstrap' yourself into the problem (just as we did in the Student t, when the standard deviation of the sample was used as the estimate of the standard deviation of the mean). However, when this is done

184

degree of freedom
 parameter

We have to estimate the mean (5) from the data.

Form Poisson with mean = 5. Must collapse first 3 cells and last 3 cells.

df = 7-1-1 = 5
chi-sq, table = 15.09

Chi-Square Distribution   Football Coach

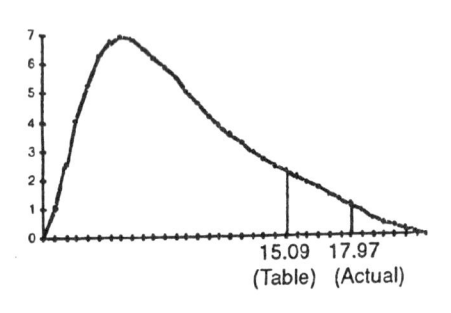

15.09 17.97
(Table) (Actual)

Actual chi-sq = 17.97
 actual outside cut-off
 stat sig diff
 does not follow Poisson

Encouraged that victories are not Poisson dist. Coach leads team to 11 and 0 record and wins national championship. Credits it all to chi-square test, thoroughly baffling news media.

No, however, it is very true that what you do **believe** can make a difference in what you can achieve.

---

you lose a _____ __ _____. In general, you will lose one degree of freedom for each _____ you estimate on the basis of sample information.

20. A most perplexed football coach is wondering if the victories (in a given season) at his college follow a Poisson distribution. He checks the records for the last 50 years and finds the following distribution.

Number of Victories	Number of Seasons
0	2
1	5
2	8
3	10
4	8
5	7
6	4
7	3
8	2
9	1
10	0

Use the chi-square to determine if the distribution follows a Poisson distribution. Let alpha = .01.

21. In recent years (under this most perplexed coach) the team has not done well (3-47-0 over the last five years). The coach feels that if he can demonstrate that the team victories follow a Binomial distribution that this will really help him turn the team around. Do you agree?

22. Consider the quarterly sales figures shown below. Use the chi-square to test those sales against the model of equal sales throughout the four quarters of the year. Let alpha = .05.

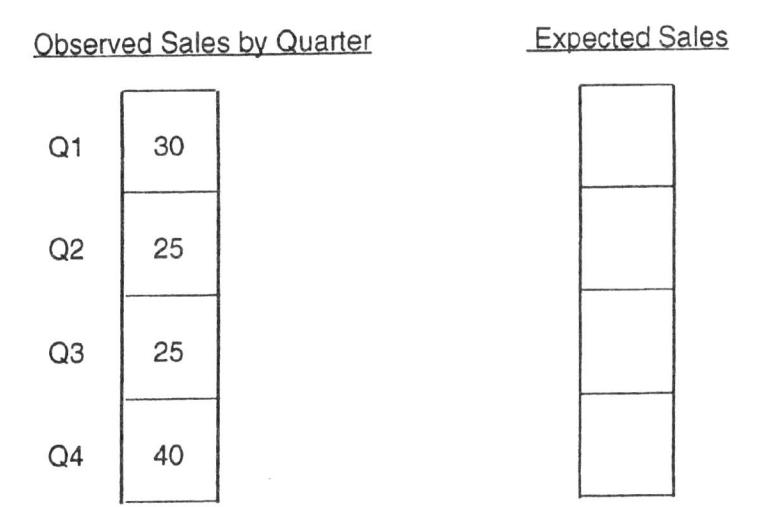

Observed Sales by Quarter

Q1	30
Q2	25
Q3	25
Q4	40

Expected Sales

df = 3
table cut-off = 7.81

Actual chi-sq = 5.00

Chi-Square   Test of Quarterly Sales

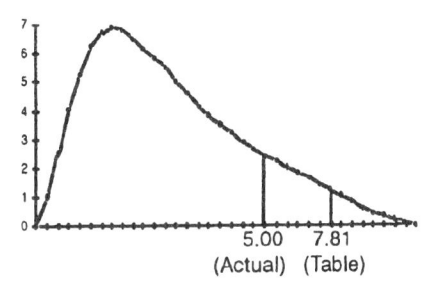

actual inside cut-off
no statistically significant diff
fail to reject the
hypothesis. that quarters
are equal.

23. Suppose that the director of the student union dance committee claims that twice as many lower classmen attend dances as upper classmen. A random sample of 120 persons is selected from those attending a recent dance and their classification is recorded. Test for significant difference at alpha equal to 10%. (Hint: Remember to allocate the total 120 students in such a manner that Fr and So are <u>twice</u> the expected cell values of Jr and Sr.)

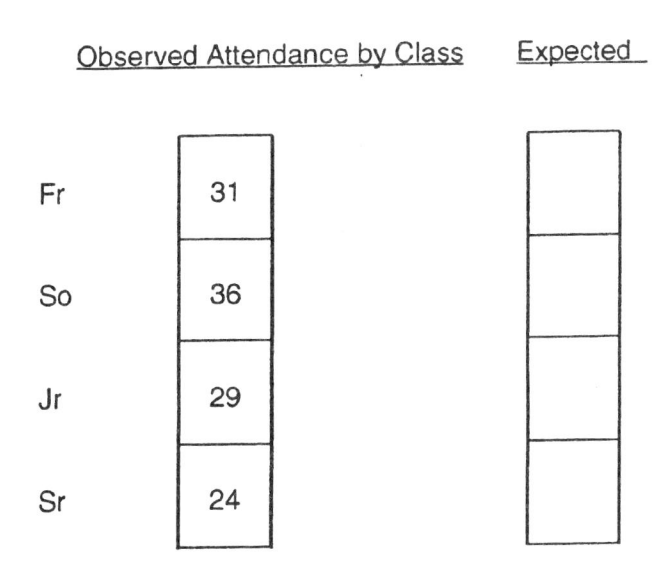

Observed Attendance by Class

Fr	31
So	36
Jr	29
Sr	24

Expected

df = 3
table cut-off = 6.25

Actual chi-sq = 7.28

Chi-Square   Student Union Dance

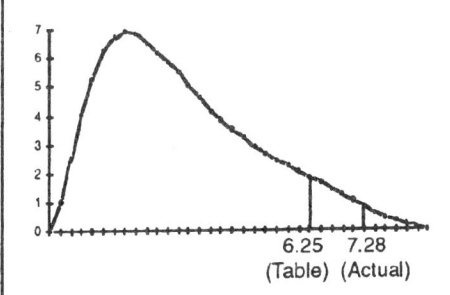

sig diff at .10

(note .05 table = 7.81 therefore 90% sure that observed do not fit expected, but not 95%)

186

df = 4
05 table = 9.488
01 table = 13.277

Actual chi-sq = 10.59

Therefore sig diff at .05 not sig diff at .01

We are 95% sure that they are not contributing equally, but not 99% sure.

The chi-square test works with frequencies. Frequencies of occurrence as recorded in classification tables.

Chi-square is not designed to work with percents, rates, and so forth.

---

24. On a certain basketball team the average per game point totals of the starting five members of the team are as shown below. Test that performance against the hypothesis that all members of the team are contributing equally to the scoring. Test at the 95% and 99% levels.

Observed Scoring by Player   Expected

Center	20
Forward	20
Forward	10
Guard	25
Guard	10

25. Consider this problem:
For a grocery store, we can establish certain "ideal" profit contribution percentages. Compare the observed percentages against the expected percentages (shown below).

Observed Percentages   Expected Percentages

grocery	70%	65%
meat	10%	15%
produce	7%	5%
other	13%	15%
TOTAL	100%	100%

What is wrong with this problem?

26. Consider this problem:
A certain golfer wants to test whether he is playing "par golf". To test this he shoots 5 rounds as shown below (also shown the expected or "par" value).

	Observed Scores	Expected (par)
round 1	81	72
round 2	74	72
round 3	71	72
round 4	79	72
round 5	74	72

What is wrong with this problem?

Note that total of exp. = 360, total of observed =379 (avg round = 75.8).

The chi-square test is not designed to test whether the total number of observations. is equal to the total number of exp (in fact, they must be equal), rather, the chi-sq tests whether the distribution of the set of observed scores is unusual. For the above problem, the observed rounds (total= 379) could be tested against the avg of 75.8 per round to test the consistency with which the golfer had played.

27. With the Chi-Square test, virtually any set of observed frequencies can be tested against any set of expected frequencies. If the expected distribution features equal numbers of items in each of the cells this is termed a _____ distribution.

uniform

Chi-Square Test of Independence

§ 13.2

1. In the previous section all of the tests were one-dimensional, that is, the items were broken down according to only one criterion (ie. in problem #22 sales were broken down by quarter, in problem #23 the students were broken down by classification, in problem #24 the basketball players were

188

broken down by position) (Talking about the phrase "broken down" reminds me of the story of the employer who was filling out a questionnaire. The question said, "Show number of employees broken down by sex", he replied, "To my knowledge none have been broken down by sex, alcohol is a much bigger problem in our shop."...hmmm, I seem to have gotten off the subject, oh well) In this section we will look at classification tables where the respondents have been classified on two variables. We will be testing to see if there is a relationship between the classifications. This type of test is referred to as an _____ of _____ test.

independence of classification

2. A "cross-classification" table is sometimes referred to as a _____ table.

contingency

3. In a contingency table, the values in the expected table are computed from the totals which were present in the observed table. The formula for computing the value of a given cell in the expected distribution is _____ x _____ / _____.

cell = $\frac{\text{RowTot} \times \text{ColTot}}{\text{Grand Total}}$

4. Because the expected cell values are computed using the products of the totals around the margin of the observed table, this method is sometimes referred to as the method of marginal products. True or False

True

5. In a contingency table, the degrees of freedom are equal to _____.

(r-1) x (c-1)

6. With contingency tables you should still pool values for expected cells with less than 5. True or False

True

7. Consider the classification table shown below which gives the breakdown between sex and test score. In this test we will be trying to determine whether or not the males have the higher scores. Although it appears that way from the table, we wish to test the proposition mathematically. (Note: and do not jump to conclusions and call me a male chauvinist pig for using an example with males having higher scores. The table does not say with what those scores were concerned, it might be that the males scored higher on an alcoholic tendency test. I mention

this to make the point that one must always look behind the scenes when analyzing numerical data and avoid making assumptions which may prove to be false.)

Observed

Scores
Hi   Lo

Sex
	Hi	Lo
M	14	7
F	12	23

Expected

Scores
Hi   Lo

df = 1

Chi-square table cut-offs
.05 = 3.84
.01 = 6.64

Actual chi-sq statistic
= 5.53

sig at .05
not sig at .01

95% sure M not equal to F
not 99% sure

8. (Continuing) Suppose that the researcher was bothered by the somewhat ambiguous results from the problem above (95% significant, not 99% significant). to provide greater information, a much larger sample is taken. The results of that sample are shown below:

Observed

Scores
Hi   Lo

Sex
	Hi	Lo
M	140	70
F	120	230

Expected

Scores
Hi   Lo

Now what is your value for the chi-square statistic? What effect does sample size have on this test?

Same df = 1
same .05 = 3.84
and .01 = 6.64

But now actual
chi-square = 55.3

very sig at .05 and .01

As before, if the same absolute diff is maintained over larger samples, the chi-square statistic increases proportionately and the level of significance increases.

Of course, if there was really no intrinsic difference between Males and Females, as the sample got larger, the difference would be expected to narrow dramatically.

df = 4
chi-sq table cut-offs
.05 = 9.48
.01 = 13.27

Actual chi-square statistic = 22.5

Therefore, actual chi-sq outside allowable therefore stat sig diff

Conclude that there is a relationship between the size of the eggs and the amount of bacon

9. A manager of a grocery store wants to see if there is a relationship between the size of the eggs that a customer buys and the amount of bacon which he buys. To determine if there is indeed a relationship, he monitors 100 customers and makes a chart of his findings. Test for significant difference at the 95% confidence level.

Observed

Bacon
	none	1lb	2lb
S	12	3	0
M	12	22	6
L	6	25	14

EGGS

Expected

Bacon
	none	1lb	2lb
S			
M			
L			

(Note: One of the expected cells is below 5, however, I would ignore it since there is only one and it is so close.)

10. Consider this classification table showing the relationship between age and adult TV watching. Test for significant difference using the chi-square independence of classification test.

Observed

TV Viewing
	Lo	Hi
20-30	5	10
30-50	10	10
50-80	6	9

Expected

TV Viewing
	Lo	Hi
20-30		
30-50		
50-80		

df = 2
chi-sq table cut-offs
.05 = 5.99
.01 = 9.21

Actual chi-square statistic = 1.01

Actual inside of cut-offs therefore no stat sig diff, no relationship between age and TV.

11. Given this classification table showing the relationship between classification in school vs. grade, test for independence of classification.

Observed (only)

	A	B	C	D	F
Lower classmen	6	3	2	3	6
Upper classmen	2	8	6	3	1

df = 4
chi-sq table cut-offs
.05 = 9.48
.01 = 13.27

Actual chi-square statistic = 9.84

Therefore significant diff at .05 (95% sure there is a relationship)

No sig diff at .01 (not 99% sure there is a relationship)

12. Given the data below comparing age to income levels for a group of 75 salesmen. Use the chi-square test to test for significant difference.

Observed

Income
	Lo	Med	Hi
20-30	5	10	15
30-50	5	5	10
50-80	10	10	5

Expected

Income
	Lo	Med	Hi
20-30			
30-50			
50-80			

Once again, df = 4 chi-sq table cut-offs
.05 = 9.48
.01 = 13.27
(notice that contingency tables with markedly different shapes can have the same degrees of freedom)

Actual chi-square
statistic = 7.305

Conclude no stat sig diff
Fail to reject,
cannot show that there is a relationship.

192

True

True

powerful

normality and
equality of variance
(homoscedasticity)

nonparametric or
distribution free

· test of homogeneity

13. The Chi-square test can work with nominal data, which is the lowest type of data. True or False

14. Because the chi-square test works with nominal, and because data can always be broken down from a higher form down to a lower form, the chi-square test can (if you arrange things correctly) be applied to every data collection situation. True or False

15. Of course, when you break data from one form to a lower form your statistical test is not as _____.

16. But aside from applicability and convenience, another reason why it is sometimes desirable to break data down into a lower form is that the chi-square test makes no assumptions about the nature of the data, assumptions such as _____ or _____.

17. Tests such as the chi-square which make few if any assumptions about the shape of the underlying distributions are referred to as _____ tests or _____ tests.

18. When the number of observations is determined in advance (for each row or column...not just the total sample size) this is referred to as a _____.

CHAPTER 14

Correlation and Simple Linear Regression

CHAPTER OBJECTIVES

The concepts of linear regression and correlation are introduced in this chapter. Formulas are discussed for computing and testing the sample correlation and least squares line. Confidence intervals for the mean value of the dependent variable and prediction intervals for individual values of the dependent variable are discussed. Procedures for detecting influential sample observations and unusual independent values are discussed. By the end of the chapter you should be able to:

1. Describe what is meant by "bivariate analysis".

2. Describe what is meant by a "scatter diagram".

3. Compute the correlation coefficient, the measure of covariance, and explain the meanings of these measures.

4. Explain what is meant by "least squares analysis".

5. Compute the regression equation, test the significance of the regression equation, make predictions using the regression equation, and make confidence intervals for those predictions.

6. Identify influential observations and detect outlying observations that have an unusually large or small value of the dependent or independent variable.

§ 14.0

two
two

True

True

A Look Back/Introduction

1. We have already investigated the topic of "bivariate" data from a couple of directions in the text. Reduced to its most simple terms, the word "bivariate" means that _____ variables and the relationships between those _____ variables is under investigation.

2. Chapter Two was concerned with graphical presentation. This meant that the relationship between two variables was presented pictorially. True or False

3. Chapter Thirteen presented the chi-square test. The independence of classification test had also looked at the relationship between items that had been measured on two dimensions. True or False

---

§ 14.1

two

pairs

same

positive

Bivariate Data and Correlation

1. You encounter bivariate data when each observation (each subject) has provided data on _____ variables.

2. Because each subject has responded with data on two variables, these sets of responses are sometimes referred to as data _____.

3. These data pairs, however, represent a different situation from the paired data (dependent data) we have studied before. Those situations represented (for instance) a test-retest of the _____ variable. Here we are talking about pairs of variables where the variables are entirely different, such as age (measured) in years, and income (measured in dollars).

4. If both variables increase together, then there is said to be a _____ relationship.

194

5. In one variable is increasing while the other variable is decreasing, then the variables are said to show an inverse or _____ relationship.

negative

6. A simple measure for determining the strength of relationship between two variables is the _____ coefficient.

correlation

7. The correlation coefficient is also defined as a measure of linearity because it provides a measure of how well a _____ would fit through the data.

line (in this chapter a straight line)

8. The values of the correlation coefficient range from _____ to _____.

-1.00 to +1.00

9. A value of -1.00 for the correlation coefficient says that there is _____ correlation between the two variables. In this case as one variable goes up, the other variable goes _____.

perfect (negative)

down (with every point falling on a straight line)

10. A value of 0.00 for the correlation coefficient says that there is _____ correlation between the two variables. In this case as one variable goes up, the other variables goes _____. (Note: just because the correlation coefficient is zero does not mean that there is no relationship between the movement of one variable and the movement of the other variable...it might be that we are trying to describe the relationship with the wrong model. It is analogous to radio and TV waves. Radio and TV waves bombard us constantly. But we are not aware of them unless we activate a radio receiver or a TV receiver. In this chapter we will be attempting to model the relationship with a straight line. A value of zero for the correlation coefficient is saying (in this chapter) that the variables do not fit a linear model. That is not to say, however, that some other type of model might not show some significant relationships.)

zero or no

who knows?

11. The correlation coefficient can be computed in several ways. One way, which can be conceptually viewed as an extension of some of the calculations which we had been doing in the section on analysis of variance, is to form the correlation

196

XY

X
Y

coefficient as the ratio of the cross-products of _____ divided by the square root of the sum of squares of _____ times the square root of the sum of squares of _____.

12. Consider this set of X and Y data pairs

X	Y
3	12
4	13
6	11
4	15
7	16
8	13
9	15

correlation coefficient
r = .3475

Use the sum of squares formula for finding the correlation coefficient just discussed to find r.

13. We will have more to say about this statistic later, but a quick way to gauge the strength of the correlation coefficient is to take the square of the value. This value r^2 is known as the coefficient of determination and tells the percent of explanation in Y provided by X. In this case the correlation coefficient was _____. Thus the square of that value would be _____, and the percentage of explained variance would be approximately _____ percent.

.3475
.1207
≈12%

14. Another commonly used measure of the association between two variables, X and Y, is the covariance, which is written _____.

cov(X,Y)

15. The covariance will have the same sign as the correlation coefficient. True or False

True

16. The covariance is based upon the same values (the same sums of squares) which the correlation coefficient was based. The covariance is simply the sum of squares for _____ divided by _____.

XY
n-1

17. One reason that the correlation coefficient is more often calculated and reported than the covariance is that the magnitude of the covariance is a function of the values of X and

Y, and hence can be extremely large (if dealing with miles between planets for X and gallons of gasoline for Y), or extremely small (atomic weights for X and volts of electricity per atom for Y), or anywhere in between. The value of the correlation coefficient, on the other hand, must be between _____ and _____. Because all correlation coefficients have this same magnitude, this facilitates comparisons.

-1.00 to +1.00

18. The correlation coefficient can also be considered to be the covariance between the standardized values of X and Y. A standardized value is the value minus the _____, divided by the _____.

mean,
std deviation

Least Squares

19. One of the best ways for determining what type of model should be used (whether a straight line might be appropriate) is to make a sketch of the data points. Such a sketch is called a _____ _____.

scatter diagram

20. An infinite number of lines can be drawn through the data set. The closeness of the fit can be summarized by measuring the distance between the predicted point on the line (often designated $\hat{Y}$) and the actual data point (often designated Y_i). When the line is fitted according to the least squares criterion it will produce a line such that the sum of the _____ of these distances ($Y_i - \hat{Y}$) is a _____.

square
minimum

21. An additional characteristic of this line is that the sum of these distances ($Y_i - \hat{Y}$) (unsquared) will be equal to _____.

zero

22. Another name for this distance ($Y_i - \hat{Y}$) would be the _____ or _____.

error or residual

23. Therefore, another name for this squared total (first mentioned in question 20) would be the _____ _____ of _____.

error
sum of squares

197

198

$SCP_{XY} / SS(X)$

slope

X

Ybar - (b_1)Xbar
(avg of Ys) - (b_1)(avg of Xs)

Y intercept
(some authors refer to it as "a")

line
Y axis

zero

$b_0 = 11.94$
$b_1 = .2777$

SSE = 17.33

24. The least squares regression equation can be determined from the sum of squares (X, Y, and XY) which were used in the computation of the correlation coefficient. The value of b_1 is equal to _____ (give formula).

25. The term b_1 is also called the _____. It represents the rate of the rise or fall in the line.

26. Another way to define the slope is to say that it is the change in Y per each unit change in _____.

27. In continuing the computation of the least squares regression line, the value of b_0 is equal to _____ (give formula)

28. Another name for the term b_0 is the _____.

29. The Y intercept is the point at which the _____ crosses the _____.

30. To say that it crosses the Y axis is the same thing as to say that X has a value of _____.

31. Using the data we had used previously, compute the values for the regression coefficients (b_0 and b_1).

X	Y
3	12
4	13
6	11
4	15
7	16
8	13
9	15

32. The residual error for the regression line, the error sum of squares, can also be computed from the sum of squares totals. Compute the SSE for the above set of data.

33. In a regression situation, a causality relationship is assumed...that is to say that the value of one variable depends upon the value of the other variable. In specific, regression analysis assumes that the value of _____ will be determined by the value of _____.

Y
X

34. (Continuing) For this reason, Y is often referred to as the _____ variable, because its value depends upon the value that X has taken.

dependent

35. (Continuing) Likewise, X is often referred to as the _____ variable, because its value does not depend (is independent of) the values taken by Y.

independent

The Simple Linear Regression Model

§ 14.2

1. If your model is wrong, your answers are _____.

wrong

2. The simple linear regression model provides for a certain mode of handling the data points. The term simple means that just one _____ variable is going to be used to predict the Y variable. For example if we were trying to predict life expectancy, we might have just one factor, say amount of cigarette smoking. (This contrasts with multiple regression where we might have two independent variables, i.e., smoking and weight control which are used to predict life expectancy.)

X, or independent var.

3. There are many kinds of lines, a curve is a line, a circle is a line. In simple linear regression we are concerned with the fitting of a _____ line through the data points.

straight

4. Even if the data can be modeled reasonably well with a straight line, most real world situations will show some scattering (or error) between the actual Y_i values and the predicted $\hat{Y}$ points along the regression line. True or False

True, some scattering is always present, especially in business research situations.

5. The statistical model which we employ is _____.

$Y = \beta_0 + \beta_1 X + e$

200

deterministic

random

sample

minimum

zero

normal

equal

homoscedasticity

6. In this model, "$\beta_0 + \beta_1 X$" is called the _____ part of the model.

7. In this model, "e" is called the _____ part of the model.

8. In most business situations, the true values for the regression coefficients (β_0 and β_1) (that is the true population values) will remain unknown. An estimate of these values will be made from a _____. We have two sources of error in our prediction: One, the scatter naturally present in the situation itself (the random part of the model). Two, the scatter caused by taking a sample estimate rather than census.

9. The simple linear regression model makes a number of assumptions: One assumption is that the mean of all the errors is zero (we have already discussed that the sum of $(Y_i - \hat{Y})$ is zero (and that the squares of these deviations is a _____).

10. (Continuing) The previous question had been concerned with the scattering of all of the Y_i values at all possible values of X_i, along the entire length of the line. But the regression model also makes critical assumptions about the scattering of points at each individual X_i. The regression model assumes that for each individual X_i value the mean of the errors (the actual Y_i points vs. the predicted $\hat{Y}$ point on the line) will be _____.

11. (Continuing) Furthermore, not only will the average of the error around these points be zero but, in addition, the distribution of these errors will be _____.

12. (Continuing) And still furthermore, not only will the average of the errors around these points be zero, and not only will the distribution be normal, but in addition, the variances of the various points will be _____.

13. When variances are equal, they are said to exhibit _____.

14. When variances are not equal, they are said to exhibit _____.

> heteroscedasticity

15. Many moons ago, we studied a measure called the coefficient of variation, which measured the standard deviation as a percentage of the mean...in a sense, providing a relative or proportional measure of dispersion. Could such a measure be used to satisfy the assumption of homoscedasticity? That is, even if the variances were not equal, they were proportionately equal...the persons with incomes of $50 had an error of $10, the persons with incomes of $500 had an error of $100...same variance, 20%...right?

> wrong, data must show homoscedasticity with the data in absolute units, not relative.

16. (Continuing) We have seen that the regression model assumes that the mean of the errors around each point is zero, that these errors are normally distributed, and that the variance of these errors is the same for each X_i value. Yet a fourth assumption is that the errors are _____ of each other.

> independent

17. (Continuing) The assumption of independence says that if an estimate of Y_i is made from X_i and the estimate is too big...and if a prediction of Y_i+1 is now made from X_i+1, we have no reason to think that this estimate will also be too high, or p(high) = _____.

> 50%

18. Based upon these assumptions we can say that the predicted values of each $\hat{Y}$ represent a random normal variable with a mean equal to _____ and a variance equal to _____.

> mean of $Y_i = \beta_0 + \beta_1 X$
> σ^2_e

19. It would be advantageous for the value of e, the error or residual term, to be as _____ as possible. This would indicate that our line is providing very good prediction.

> small

20. In estimating the error variance based upon the error sum of squares we use the equation _____.

> SSE / (n-2)

202

β_0 and β_1

21. (Continuing) In this situation we lost two degrees of freedom because (and we are assuming that our values of X and Y represent a sample and not the universe) we estimated two population parameters on the basis of sample information. These two parameters are _____ and _____.

Y intercept

22. (Lest we forget) The common name for b_0 is the _____.

slope

23. (Lest we forget) The common name for b_1 is the _____.

$\dfrac{17.33}{(7-2)} = 3.466$

24. Earlier, in problem #32, S 14.1 we computed the value of SEE for the data set originally presented in problem #12, S 14.1. What would be the value of the estimate of the error variance?

1.86

25. What would be our estimate of the standard deviation of the error?

95%

26. The "Empirical Rule" (Z table approximation) says that _____ percent of all values will fall within (approximately) plus or minus two standard deviations.

3.72

27. Applying the Empirical Rule to the above situation (especially the answer from problem #25) we could say that 95% of the data items (values of Y) should fall within _____ of our predicted value of Y.

normally

28. We can apply the Empirical Rule because one of our assumptions was that the values were _____ distributed about any point on the line.

3.46

29. Extending the Empirical Rule, we can say that 99.73% (virtually 100%) of all items in a normally distributed population should be within plus or minus three standard deviations of the mean. Applying that rule to the answer obtained in problem #25 we could say that we would expect virtually all of our values of Y_i to fall within plus or minus _____ of the predicted value of Y.

Inference Concerning the Slope

§ 14.3

1. It is important that there be some slope, that is to say, that the value of b_1 not be equal to _____.

zero

2. If the slope is equal to zero, that means that we get the same prediction for _____ regardless of the value of _____. Thus knowing that the value of X is high, versus knowing that the value of X is low has given us no information.

Y
X

3. We can perform a statistical test upon the value of b_1 to test if it is significantly different from zero. In this case we know from the assumptions of the simple linear model that b_1 is a _____ random variable. Hence it can be tested with the t test.

normal

4. Because we have estimated two parameters, once again the t test has _____ degrees of freedom.

n-2

5. Referring back to problem #31, § 14.1, what was our estimate for the value of b_1?

.277

6. We wish to use the data from problem #31 and #32, § 14.1, to test if our estimate for b_1 is significantly different from _____.

zero

7. In this case we have a student t with _____ degrees of freedom. The 95% two-tail cut-off value for t would be _____.

(7-2) = 5

2.571

8. The 'actual' value of t based upon the numbers in the sample is _____

$\frac{.277}{1.86/5.55} = \frac{.277}{.335} = .827$

9. (Continuing) The value of t was .827 and the cut-off was 2.571. What is our conclusion regarding the value of b_1?

not statistically significantly different from zero

204

60
(Pretty clever to choose 62, eh? A sample of 60 would have produced df=58, not in the table.)

10. As we have seen so many times, the significance of a given result is very sensitive to changes (increases) in sample size. Go back through this problem and change the sample size from 7 to 62. This would change the degrees of freedom from 5 to _____.

17.33 / 60 = .289

11. The error variance was equal to SSE divided by degrees of freedom. This number had originally been equal to 17.33/5 = 3.466. The error variance is now equal to _____ which equals _____.

.537

12. (Continuing) Therefore our estimate of the standard deviation of the error would be _____.

$\dfrac{.277}{.537/5.55} = \dfrac{.277}{.096} = 2.86$

13. The value of t (assuming that the value of b_1 stayed the same would now be _____.

2.00
significant difference

14. The .05 cut-off t value for 60 degrees of freedom is _____. Therefore our conclusion would now be a claim of _____.

linear

15. When we failed to declare that there was a significant regression relationship in problem #9 (directly above), that can not be taken as conclusive proof that no relationship of any kind exists between the two variables,.merely that the data did not exhibit a relationship when tested with a _____ model.

scatter diagram
residuals

16. To detect the presence of a possible non-linear relationship two methods are suggested: One, a plot of the data, also referred to as a _____ _____. Two, a plot of the differences (Y-Ŷ) also referred to as _____.

True

17. When the residuals are examined, there should be a totally random pattern to their distribution. (That is to say, the pattern will be random if the data has been modeled with the appropriate model.) True or False

18. Examination of the residuals can not only tell if an incorrect model has been used, but it can also spot deviations from the assumption of independence of errors (assumption number 4). True or False | True

19. Another way to generate a more narrow confidence interval is to increase the variance of SSX, the variation in the _____ variable. This can be accomplished by taking a large number of small X values, a large number of large X values, and few X values in the middle. | X

Measuring the Strength of the Relationship | § 14.4

1. The correlation coefficient can be thought of from several directions. Earlier in this chapter we used it as a measure of the amount of linear association (did the data fit a straight line?). Another way to think of the correlation coefficient is as a measure of the _____ of the relationship between the two variables. | strength

2. The values of "r" and "b₁" will always have the same _____. | sign

3. In addition to having the same sign, the values of "b" and "r" are quite related mathematically. In fact, the value of the test statistic t, for the test of b_1 will be exactly the same as the value of t for the test of r. This formula for t is written _____. | $t = \dfrac{r}{\sqrt{\dfrac{1-r^2}{n-2}}}$

4. In problem #13, S 14.1 we computed a value for "r" for the set of X and Y pairs we have been using throughout this chapter. That value of r was _____. Plug that value of r into the formula from problem #3 (directly above) and compute the value of the t test. The value is _____. Compare this value with the t value computed in problem #8, § 14.3 | r = .3475

t = .827
they are the same

5. Thus both tests are mathematically equivalent, and obviously they both answer the same question: "Is the model statistically significant?" Given that they both answer the same question with exactly the same answer, which is the easier way to test? a) To compute b_1 and test b_1?
   b) To compute r and test r? | b) compute and test "r"

205

False. Correlation merely shows association, it does not show (or prove) causality.

6. High statistical correlation is proof of a cause and effect situation. True or False

Y bar (the average of the Ys)

7. The total variation in the dependent variable is measured by the sum of the variation between the individual Y_i values and _____, the (sample) mean of the Y values. This term is denoted SSY.

unexplained variance

8. The ratio between the unexplained variation (SSE) and the total variation (SSY) tells the percentage of _____ _____.

explained variance

9. One minus the percentage of unexplained variance gives us the percentage of _____ _____.

r^2

10. The percentage of explained variance also happens to be equal to _____, the correlation coefficient squared.

coefficient of determination

11. Another name for r^2 is the _____ of _____.

$(.3475)^2 = .1207$
or about 12%

12. (We introduced this topic briefly before) The correlation coefficient computed in problem #13, S14.1 was equal to .3475. Based upon this value, what percentage of the variation in Y is explained by the variation in X?

factor
error

13. In analysis of variance the total sum of squares was partitioned into the sum of squares _____ and the sum of squares _____.

regression
error

14. In regression sum of squares, the total sum of squares is partitioned into the sum of squares _____ and the sum of squares _____.

error
SSE

15. The variation of the points about the regression line can be measured by the _____ sum of squares, written _____.

16. If all of the Y_i data points fell exactly on the line, the value of SEE would be _____.	zero
17. Furthermore, if all of the Y_i data points fell exactly on the line, the value of r would be _____.	1.00
18. In 'real life" there is always at least some scattering of the data points. True or False	True
19. In problem 12 (above) we found that the variation in X had explained only 12% of the variation in Y. Would this be unusually low for a market research project involving a consumer survey (for instance, to correlate income with who watches the Jay Leno show)?	Probably not...very seldom, in real life, do you have a single variable explaining a very large percentage of the variance. Life is like a giant 500-piece jigsaw puzzle. It takes lots of pieces to see the picture. You will not have any one piece explaining (showing) 60%, 70%, 80%, etc. of the picture.

Estimation and Prediction	§ 14.5-1
1. The regression equation can be used to make (identical) predictions under two different situations. One situation involves the estimate for the _____ value of Y for a specified value of X. The other type of situation involves the estimate of an _____ value of Y for a specified value of X.	average individual
2. Although the value which will be generated will be the same in either case, the difference comes with respect to the confidence interval which is created for that estimate. When we are concerned with the prediction of the average of all Y values for a specified value of X, the interval is called a _____ interval. When we are concerned with the prediction of a specific, individual value of Y for a specified value of X, the interval is called a _____ interval.	confidence prediction
The confidence interval in this situation is not a set of parallel lines, but rather, the width of the confidence interval is determined (in part) by the distance which the specified X_i (the Kvanli text uses X_0) value is from the mean of the X values.	

The farther the specified X is from the mean, the wider the confidence interval becomes. For a line with a positive slope, the confidence interval would look roughly like the sketch below:

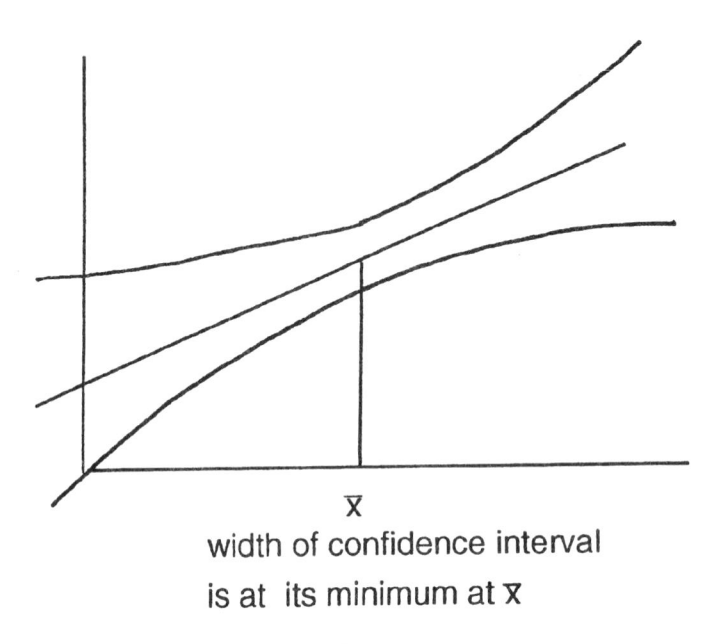

$\overline{X}$
width of confidence interval
is at its minimum at $\overline{X}$

---

§ 14.5-2

Confidence Intervals for the Average Value of Y

1. The width of the confidence interval (a confidence interval for the estimate of the average value of Y at the specified X_i (or X_o) value) is dependent upon three things:

observations
variance
X_i (or X_o)

a. the number of _____ in the sample
b. the amount of _____ in the sample
c. the specific value of _____ (the distance between X_i and X-bar (the average of the Xs).

2. Two of these three elements we have seen before. In our classic formulas for Z and t, we had the standard deviation which corresponds to _____ in problem #3 (above). We had the sample size which corresponds to _____ in problem #3. The only new term is the distance between X_i and X-bar (the average of the Xs). It is this new term which gives this confidence interval its distinctive curved shape.

b(variance)
a(sample size)

3. Consider the data, originally presented problem #13, § 14.1. The regression equation had been computed to be _____.

$\hat{Y} = 11.94 + .2777(X)$

4. What would be our prediction for the average value of Y when X was equal to 9?

at X=9, Y(avg)=14.44

5. In this case the degrees of freedom would be equal to _____. Thus a .05 two-tailed confidence interval t value would be _____.

df = 5
t = 2.571

6. Find the confidence interval for the estimate of the average value of Y when X equals 9.

14.44 (+ or -) 3.25
11.19 to 17.69

7. What would be our prediction for the average value of Y when X was equal to 6?

at X=6, Y(avg)=13.61

8. Find the confidence interval for the estimate of the average value of Y when X equals 6.

13.61 (+ or -) 1.81
11.80 to 15.42

9. Where was the confidence interval wider...at $X_i=9$ or $X_i=6$? Why?

wider at X=9
since farther from Xbar ($\bar{X}$)

10. Where would the confidence interval be its very smallest?

CI smallest at X_i = Xbar ($\bar{X}$)

11. Suppose that all of the numbers from the previous problem remained the same, the only difference is that the sample size was 1000. What would be the confidence interval for the estimate of the average value of Y if X_i were equal to X-bar (the average of the xs)? (Don't worry with the t, use Z equal to 1.96.) Notice how small the confidence interval has become.

if n = 1000
13.57 (+ or -) .115
13.45 - 13.68

Prediction Interval for Estimate of Individual Y

§ 14.5-3

1. We are using the term "prediction interval" rather than the term "confidence interval" because we are estimating a random variable rather than a _____.

parameter

210

1.00

at X=9 $\hat{Y}$=14.44
(same value)

14.44 (+ or -) 5.783
8.65 to 20.22

at X=6 $\hat{Y}$=13.61
(again, same value)

13.61 (+ or -) 5.112
8.50 to 18.72

zero

zero

one

extrapolation

interpolation

extrapolation

2. Actually the formulas for computing a "prediction interval" versus computing a "confidence interval" are very similar. The only difference is that the prediction interval includes a _____ under the square root radical.

3. Previously we had computed the estimation for the average value of Y when X = 9. What would be our specific prediction for Y when X = 9?

4. Find the prediction interval for the value of Y when X = 9.

5. Previously we had computed the estimation for the average value of Y when X = 6. What would be our specific prediction for Y when X = 6?

6. Find the prediction interval for the value of Y when X = 6.

7. Suppose that Xi=X-bar (the average of the xs) (which makes the value of the (Xi-X-bar (the average of the xs)) term equal to _____). And suppose that we begin to increase sample size towards infinity. The limiting value of the "square root term" for the confidence interval will move towards _____. The limiting value of the "square root term" for the prediction interval will move towards _____.

8. For any given data set, the values of X will lie within a certain range. If an attempt is made to make a prediction for a value of X which is outside of that range it is referred to as _____.

9. (Continuing) When a prediction is made for a value of X which is within the range of X values in the original data set, this is referred to as _____.

10. Of these two procedures (extrapolation and interpolation) the more dangerous procedure is _____.

11. Extrapolation is dangerous because you are outside the range of the observed data...you can only hope that the values outside of the observed range will continue to behave in the manner of those inside the observed range. True or False	True

Examining the Residuals

§ 14.6-1

1. In the format of simple linear regression, a residual is the difference between _____ vs. _____, or in mathematical notation form, _____ minus _____

actual data point vs. point predicted by regression line
$(Y_i - \hat{Y})$

2. By examining the residuals you can see how well the regression equation has modeled the data. In the case of simple linear regression, we are trying to model the data using a _____ _____.

straight line (with only one predictor variable)

3. The values of the residuals will all be positive in a 'good' (models the data nicely) regression equation, but may be negative in a 'bad' regression equation. True or False

False. The points should be scattered around the line, some points above, some points below.

4. Like the correlation coefficient, the sum of the residuals $\Sigma(Y_i - \hat{Y})$ will be between zero and one, with one being a 'good' residual score, and zero being a 'bad' residual score. True or False

False. The total distance above will equal the total distance below. $\Sigma(Y_i - \hat{Y})$ = zero. This is similar to $\Sigma(X_i - \bar{x})$ = zero. The regression line goes through the 'average' of the data points.

5. When examining residuals, you would like to see a 'random' pattern of negative and positive residuals...a point above the line, a point below the line, a couple above, one below, one above, a couple above, etc. True or False You could even use the 'runs test' §19.1 to see if the data alternated back and forth between positive and negative residuals with the proper frequency. True or False

True...kinda. You would not want to see the points flop back and forth every observation, +,-,+,-,+,-,+, etc. But you would like some alternation.

True, again.

6. What you do not want to see in the residuals is long strings of consistently increasing or decreasing values. This indicates that the simple linear regression model is not doing a good job of modeling the data. True or False The examination of the residuals can also check to see if the original assumptions of the regression model are valid. True or False

True

True, again.

211

where $\hat{Y} = 11.94 + .2777(X)$
(You must substitute each X into the reg. equ. to compute Yc.)

Y_i	$\hat{Y}_i$	$(Y_i - \hat{Y}_i)$
12	12.7731	-0.7731
13	13.0508	-0.0508
11	13.6062	-2.6062
15	13.0508	1.9492
16	13.8839	2.1161
13	14.1616	-1.1616
15	14.4393	0.5607

No, and no. The data set appears to be without any noticeable pattern.

No, but close, $\Sigma(Y_i - \hat{Y}_i) = .0343 \approx 0$
Difference due to rounding with the values of b_0 and b_1

---

§ 14.6-2

Yes, by definition. Since $\Sigma(Y_i - \hat{Y}_i) = 0$, avg $= \Sigma(Y_i - Y_c)/N = 0$

Seven data points is not enough to chart a histogram, but points do not appear to be skewed seriously in either direction with four negative values and three positive values.

---

§ 14.6-3

3	-0.7731
4	-0.0508
4	1.9492
6	-2.6062
7	2.1161
8	-1.1616
9	0.5607

Residuals seem to be OK

---

7. For the data set that we began using in problem 12, compute the residuals. (For convenience, here is the data set again.)

X	Y
3	12
4	13
6	11
4	15
7	16
8	13
9	15

Computing residuals (by hand) is a very tedious job. For each X value, you must substitute that value into the regression equation ($\hat{Y} = b_0 + b_1(X)$) and compute the point on the regression line, Yc. Then the actual value of Y_i is subtracted from Yc to form the residual.

8. From a simple visual inspection, how do these residuals look? Does there seem to be any noticeable pattern to the data set?

9. The sum of the residuals is supposed to equal to zero, that is $\Sigma(Y_i - \hat{Y}_i) = 0.00$. Does it?

Examining the residuals for tests of the original assumptions
Assumption #1 Normally distributed, mean of zero.

1. Is the mean of the residuals zero?

2. Are the residuals normally distributed?

Examining the residuals for tests of the original assumptions
Assumption #2 Homoscedasticity, variance of errors is constant

1. Do the residuals change predictably with changes in the value of X? In particular, do the residuals get larger as the values of X get larger?

2. When the residuals are increasing as the values of X are increasing this is sometimes referred to as a _____ _____, because of the pattern the residuals will show if graphed. | shotgun blast

---

Examining the residuals for tests of the original assumptions
Assumption #3 The errors are independent | § 14.6-4

1. Visually inspecting the data set, does it look like the residual observed for one X value is related to the residual from the previous X value? | No, the residuals look quite random with no apparent pattern.

2. When adjacent residuals are related to each other this is called _____. | autocorrelation

3. The degree of autocorrelation in a data set can be measured using the _____ _____ statistic. | Durbin-Watson

---

Checking for Outliers and Influential Observations | § 14.6-5

1. The fellow in town that is the least trustworthy is called the 'out-liar' because he can 'out-lie' everybody else. True or False | False

2. An outlier is a value that does not seem to fit with the rest of the data points. It seems unusual or peculiar. True or False | True, it **lies out**side the usual scattering of points.

3. Outliers can be caused by rare, but still regularly occurring events such as: (a. try to think of one).

Outliers can be caused by exceedingly unusual events such as: (b. try to think of one).

Outliers can also simply be mistakes in coding, data entry, or tabulation. | a. Gamblers hitting the jackpot at the slot machines. The machines are programed to pay-off with certain frequencies, so a major jackpot is to be expected, although it will mess-up the receipts for that week.

b. The comets that crashed into Jupitor 7/94. The normal spectometer readings for that week were greatly affected.

214

leverage

4. A value that is at a distance from the other variables is said have high _____.

True

5. Leverage for the independent variable can be determined by comparing each value of X against the overall mean of the X values (X-bar). True or False

True

6. Leverage for the dependent variable can be determined by examining the standardized residuals. True or False

False

7. An influential observation is a remark made by an opinion leader since their comments tend to cause people to change their behavior. True or False

True

8. An influential observation is one that (singlehandedly and) markedly affects the regression equation. The regression equation will be quite different due to the inclusion of this observation. True or False

Cook's Distance Measure

9. The presence of an influential observation can be statistically determined using _____ _____ _____.

CHAPTER 15

Multiple Linear Regression

CHAPTER OBJECTIVES

The last chapter investigated the situation in which the value of a given phenomena was being predicted by a single predictor variable. In the chapter attention will turn to the situation in which the value of the dependent variable will be predicted by two or more predictor variables. Hypothesis testing is introduced for a set of predictor variables (F test) or teh predictive ability of individual predictors (t tests). Additional topics are discussed, including multicolinearity, dummy variables stepwise procedures and examination of residuals. By the end of the chapter you should be able to:

1. Explain what is meant by multiple regression, distinguish between simple and multiple regression and understand the various assumptions behind the sue of a multiple regression model.

2. Explain the meaning of R^2, the coefficient of determination.

3. Explain what is meant by multicollinearity, why it occurs, and what can be done about it.

4. Explain what is meant by stepwise regression. Construct and evaluate various regression models.

5. Explain "dummy variables", and tell how they are used.

216

§ 15.0	A Look Backward/Introduction
one	1. The previous chapter dealt with the topic of simple linear regression. It was defined as simple regression because there was only _____ X (independent, predictor) variable being used to predict the Y (dependent, criterion) variable.
deterministic random	2. The statistical model which was introduced consisted of two parts, the _____ component, and the _____ component.
$Y = \beta_0 + \beta_1 X + e$	3. The full model can be written as _____.
$Y = \beta_0 + \beta_1 X$	4. The deterministic part of the model is _____.
e	5. The error part of the model is _____.
residual	6. The error is also referred to as the _____.
§ 15.1	The Multiple Linear Regression Model
several, at least two, more than one	1. In the multiple regression model, there are _____ independent (or predictor) variables.
False, there will always be some error (scatter)	2. With multiple predictors, there should be no need for the error or residual term. True or False
straight line	3. In the case of simple linear regression, the deterministic component of the regression model could be sketched as a _____.
plane	4. In multiple linear regression, if the model contains only two predictor variables, the deterministic component of the regression model could be sketched as a _____.

5. If you had a multiple linear regression model with 8 predictor variables it could be sketched as a _____.

who knows?

6. For all practical purposes the widespread use of multiple regression as a statistical technique had to wait for the development of the computer. True or False.

True, there is just too much number crunching to do it by hand.

Multiple Regression Example Problem

Let's consider the following situation: We are trying to develop a model for life expectancy. Three predictor variables have been suggested:
1. Cigarette smoking (measured in cigarettes per day)
2. Weight control (measured in pounds overweight)
3. Exercise (measured in minutes per day)

We have data from 10 persons (who amazingly enough did everything in fives...smoked in units of 5, put on weight in units of 5, exercised in units of 5, even died in units of 5...hey, we have been telling you that statistics is amazing! Now you have proof!) Here is the data set:

Age	Smoking	Weight Control	Exercise
60	20	20	15
70	10	10	30
55	40	30	15
70	5	20	60
80	0	20	90
75	0	10	60
65	0	10	60
60	20	20	30
70	30	0	90
75	5	0	60

For the moment, however, let's assume that we are still back in chapter 14 (simple linear regression) and let us form the simple regression equation for each of these predictor variables.

Life Expectancy predicted by Smoking

$$\hat{Y} = 73.3 - .406(X)$$

$R^2 = 51.9\%$

$s = 5.804$

$F = 8.62$

(Life Expectancy predicted by Smoking, continued)

thus, if you smoked two packs a day
$\hat{Y} = 73.3 - .406(40)$
$\hat{Y} = 57.06$ years, estimated life expectancy

What would be your estimate of life expectancy if a person smoked one pack a day?

$\hat{Y} = 73.3 - .406(20)$
$\hat{Y} = 65.18$ years

Age predicted by Weight Control

$\hat{Y} = 74.2 - .44(X)$

$R^2 = 29.1\%$

$s = 7.045$

$F = 3.28$

thus if you were 30 pounds overweight
$\hat{Y} = 74.2 - .44(30)$
$\hat{Y} = 61.0$ years, predicted life expectancy

$\hat{Y} = 74.2 - .44(5)$
$\hat{Y} = 72.0$ years

What would be the estimate of life expectancy if a person was only 5 pounds overweight?

$\hat{Y} = 74.2 - .44(-10)$
$\hat{Y} = 78.6$
But be careful, extrapolating outside of original data range

What would be the estimate of life expectancy if a person was 10 pounds underweight?

Age predicted by Exercise

$$\hat{Y} = 56.5 + .226(X)$$

$R^2 = 62.3\%$

$s = 5.136$

$F = 13.2$

thus if you exercised an average of 15 minutes/day
$$\hat{Y} = 56.5 + .226(15)$$
$$\hat{Y} = 59.89$$

What would be the estimate of life expectancy for a person who exercised 30 minutes a day?

$\hat{Y} = 56.2 + .226(30)$
$\hat{Y} = 63.28$ years

We can tell a good bit about these three predictors and their relation to life expectancy simply by looking at the three simple equations.

1. Which predictor variable seems to be the best predictor of life expectancy _____? And why?

exercise $R^2 = 62.3\%$

2. Which predictor variable seems to be the worst predictor of life expectancy _____? And why?

wt control $R^2 = 29.1\%$

3. In answering the two questions above you probably (hopefully) selected "exercise" as the best predictor and "weight control" as the worst predictor, and you probably did so on the basis of the R^2 values..which is good. However, it might be instructive to note that all of the measures (R^2, s, and F) will indicate the same relationship. Fill in the table below:

	Exercise(#1)	Smoking(#2)	Weight Control(#3)
R^2	___	___	___
s	___	___	___
F	___	___	___

	EX	SMK	WC
R^2	62.3%	51.9%	29.1%
s	5.136	5.804	7.045
F	13.2	8.62	3.28

220

higher
exercise
$R^2 = 62.3\%$

low
exercise
s = 5.136

larger
exercise
F = 13.2

exercise

regression
total
R^2 = (explained/total)
R^2 = (290.47/560) = 51.86%

F = (MSEreg/MSEres)
F = (290.47/33.69)
F = 8.622

4. When examining values of R^2 the (higher/lower) the value of R^2 the better. Thus the "best" value of R^2 is found in the variable of _____ at R^2 equal to _____.

5. In contrast, when examining values of s, we would like to see s to be as _____ as possible. Thus the "best" value of s is found in the variable of _____ with s equal to _____.

6. When examining values of F, the (larger/smaller) the value of F, the better. Thus the "best" value of F is found in the variable of _____ with F equal to _____.

7. Hopefully you can see the consistency of these results. Smoking is closest in explanation to which variable?

Because your author is a good sport and a nice guy, you were given the values of R^2 and F. But you could have calculated those values from the analysis of variance table provided by the computer. Here are the ANOVA tables for each of the three equations:

Life Expectancy predicted by Smoking

ANALYSIS OF VARIANCE TABLE

DUE TO	DF	SS	MS=SS/DF
REGRESSION	1	290.47	290.47
RESIDUAL	8	269.53	33.69
TOTAL	9	560.00	

8. In looking at the SS, the explained variance is the same as the SS _____. And the total variance is the same as the SS _____. R^2 can be written as _____. Therefore the value of R^2 is equal to _____.

9. The value of F is equal to the mean square error for the regression divided by the mean square error of the residual (or error). Thus the value of F would be _____.

Life Expectancy predicted by Weight_Control

ANALYSIS OF VARIANCE TABLE

DUE TO	DF	SS	MS=SS/DF
REGRESSION	1	162.98	162.98
RESIDUAL	8	397.02	49.63
TOTAL	9	560.00	

10. The formula for R^2 is _____. The value of R^2 is _____.

R^2 = (explained/total)
R^2 = (162.98/560) = 29.10%

11. The formula for F is _____. The value for F is _____.

F = (MSEreg/MSEres)
F = (162.98/49.63) = 3.283

Life Expectancy predicted by Exercise

ANALYSIS OF VARIANCE TABLE

DUE TO	DF	SS	MS=SS/DF
REGRESSION	1	348.98	348.98
RESIDUAL	8	211.02	26.38
TOTAL	9	560.00	

12. Once again, the formula for R^2 is _____. The value of R^2 is _____.

R^2 = (explained/total)
R^2 = (348.98/560) =
R^2 = 62.32%

13. The formula for F is _____. The value for F is _____.

F = (MSR/MSE)
F = 348.98/26.38
F = 13.23

14. The total variance is the total of the variation between all of the original Y_i points and the average of the Y values (Ybar). For this reason, the TOTAL sum of squares is the same for all three lines. True or False

True

222

15. Yet analysis of the factors individually and independently of each other can create problems...and lead to some "conflicting" results. Let's say that a person is a real "do-nothing". He doesn't smoke, he doesn't overeat, and he doesn't exercise. What would be his predicted life expectancy?

In this case we have three answers:

From the <u>Smoking</u> equation:

73.3 years

$\hat{Y} = 73.3 - .406(X)$
Since X = 0, $\hat{Y} =$ _____

From the <u>Weight Control</u> equation:

74.2 years

$\hat{Y} = 74.2 - .44(X)$
Since X = 0, $\hat{Y} =$ _____

From the <u>Exercise</u> equation:

56.5 years

$\hat{Y} = 56.5 + .226(X)$
Since X = 0, $\hat{Y} =$ _____

Hard to say. Exercise is best fit, but X = 0 is unrealistically low, surely he would get some exercise, mowing the yard, taking out the trash, walking from his car to work.

16. We now have three equations with three different answers...which one is correct?

multiple

17. Obviously(?) we need to switch from analysis by simple regression to analysis by _____ regression.

Ergo, we will now use the computer to produce the multiple regression equation for the prediction of life expectancy when predicted by <u>Smoking</u>, <u>Weight Control</u>, and <u>Exercise</u>.

The Regression Equation:

Y = 64.9 - .255(SMK) - .093(WC) + .151(EXER)

ANALYSIS OF VARIANCE

DUE TO	DF	SS	MS=SS/DF
REGRESSION	3	450.31	150.10
RESIDUAL	6	109.69	18.28
TOTAL	9	560.00	

18. From the table above, what would be the value for R^2, the multiple correlation coefficient?

R^2 = explained/total
R^2 = 450.31/560.0
R^2 = 80.41%

19. From the table above, what would be the value for F?

F = MSEreg/MSEres
F = 150.10/18.28
F = 8.211

20. Compared with the best single equation from before (exercise) the value of R^2 has gone _____, the value of F has gone _____. (more about this later)

up
down

21. Now what would be our prediction for our "do-nothing"?

$\hat{Y}$ = 64.9 - .255(SMK) - .093(WC) + .151(EXER)
with SMK = 0, WC = 0, and EXER = 0
$\hat{Y}$ = _____.

64.9

22. Let's try another prediction. What would be our prediction for someone who smokes 10 cigarettes a day, is about 10 pounds overweight, and gets about 30 minutes of exercise a day?

From before our equation is:

$\hat{Y}$ = 64.9 - .255(SMK) - .093(WC) + .151(EXER)

$\hat{Y}$ = 64.9 - .255(10) - .093(10) + .151(30)
$\hat{Y}$ = _____

65.95

224

2.55
.93
4.53
1.05

-.255
weight control, exercise

-.093
smoking, exercise

+.151
smoking, weight control

No

normal distribution
constant
stat. independent

smaller

23. Notice how that in this example, some of his activities tended to cancel each other. He lost _____ years due to smoking. He lost _____ years for being ten pounds overweight. But he gained _____ years for exercising 30 minutes a day, for a net gain of _____.

24. Theoretically speaking, the value of b_1 from the regression equation (-.255) implies that for each cigarette which you smoke (each day) that reduces your life expectancy by _____ years, provided (and here is where the theoretical part comes), provided that _____ and _____ are held constant.

25. Likewise, the value of b_2 from the regression equation (-.093) implies that for each pound which you are overweight, that reduces your life expectancy by _____ years, provided that _____ and _____ are held constant.

26. Finally, the value of b_3 from the regression equation (+.151) implies that for each minute of exercise (per day) you increase your life expectancy by _____ years, provided that _____ and _____ are held constant.

27. Consider question #9: The only way that a change could be made in exercise while holding smoking and weight control constant would be if there were no relationships between either exercise and smoking, or between exercise and weight control. Is this realistic? Yes or No

28. There are several assumptions implicit in the use of the multiple regression model, especially with respect to the errors (residuals).
a. The errors follow a _____
b. The error is _____ irrespective of X
c. The errors are _____.

29. The residual standard deviation (also referred to as the standard deviation of the errors) provides a good measure of the closeness of the fit between the points and the line. Hence the _____ the value of s_e the better.

30. Because one of our assumptions had been that the distribution of errors was normally distributed, that means that the body of normal curve theory which we had introduced earlier can be used to compute confidence intervals for estimates involving regression lines. True or False	True
31. In the regression problem presented earlier we had computed a predicted life expectancy of 65.95 (when SMK = 10, WC = 10, and Exercise = 30 (problem 5)). If s = 4.276, use the Empirical Rule to give us the approximate 95% confidence interval.	Empirical Rule 2 std dev = approx. 95% 65.95 (+ or -) 8.552 57.398 to 74.502

<u>Hypothesis Testing and Confidence Intervals</u>	§ 15.2
1. It is possible for statistical analysis to "goof up" for a variety of reasons. Multiple regression is a very powerful tool, but sometimes, you can encounter a set of data which simply does not fit the regression model you have created. True or False	True

To save you the trouble of flipping back so many pages, here is a repeat of the results from the multiple regression analysis performed earlier:

The Regression Equation:

Y = 64.9 - .255(SMK) - .093(WC) + .151(EXER)

ANALYSIS OF VARIANCE

DUE TO	DF	SS	MS=SS/DF
REGRESSION	3	450.31	150.10
RESIDUAL	6	109.69	18.28
TOTAL	9	560.00	

226

Y

9
n-1

three
three

6
n - k - 1

explained
unexplained

109.69
6
18.28
4.27

all
at least one

True

2. The total variance has remained at 560 throughout the analysis of this problem. It was 560 with each of the three simple regression models, and it is still 560 with the multiple regression model. This is because the total variance is measuring the variance within the _____ variable (Yi-Ybar).

3. The total degrees of freedom is equal to _____. This is equal to _____.(give formula)

4. The regression degrees of freedom is equal to _____. This is because there are _____ predictor variables in the regression equation.

5. The residual degrees of freedom is equal to _____. The formula is _____.

6. The term SSregression tells us our _____ variance. The term SSresidual gives us our _____ variance.

7. Earlier (problem 14 from the last section) we had said that the value of Se was equal to 4.276. We can develop that same value from the residual sum of squares.
Residual Sum of Squares = _____
Residual Degrees of Freedom = _____
Mean Square Error Residual = _____
Square Root MSE = _____

8. In the test of significance for beta in simple regression we were testing whether the value of b was significantly greater than zero. In multiple regression, we are testing the null hypothesis that _____ of the β values are zero, versus the alternative hypothesis that _____ of the β values is significantly different from zero.

9. Continuing, thus it might be possible for one of the predictor variables to be quite valuable, whereas some of the others would not be of predictive value. But if at least one was of value, the equation might produce a significant F value. True or False

227

10. The degrees of freedom are equal to _____ (k) and _____ (n-k-1). The .05 table value is _____.

df = 3
6   F = 4.76

11. The actual value of F is equal to _____ / _____ (give formula). In this case F = _____.

MSR/MSE
150.10/18.28 = 8.211

The hypotheses are:
Ho: _____
Ha: _____

all βs equal to zero
(reg equation(group) no good)

at least one β stat sig
(reg equation (group) of value)

Based upon the actual value of F _____, as compared with the table value of F _____, we conclude _____.

8.21
4.76
there is a sig regression equation

12. Can we conclude that all three of the predictor variables have contributed significantly to the regression equation? Yes or No

No

13. We can test the individual b_i values by forming the t statistic, t = _____ (give formula).

b_i / s_{b_i}

14. This actual value of t is then compared with the table value of t where t has degrees of freedom equal to _____ (give formula). In this case the degrees of freedom would be _____, and the .05 two-tail cut-off value would be _____.

df = n-k-1
df = 6
t = 2.447

To perform these t tests you will need the standard deviations for each regression coefficient:

	COEFFICIENT(b)	STANDARD DEVIATION
Smoking	-.255	.114
Weight Control	-.093	.176
Exercise	.151	.065

228

2.24
No

-.53
No

+2.32
No, close but still no cigar.

15. What would be the t value for the b coefficient for smoking _____? Is this value statistically significant?

16. What would be the t value for the b coefficient for weight control _____? Is this value statistically significant?

17. What would be the t value for the b coefficient for exercise _____? Is this value statistically significant?

Hmmmm, this is most perplexing! The regression equation as a whole was statistically significant, but none of the individual values are significant. Let's add to the perplexity by looking back at the original **simple** regression equations which we computed at the beginning of this chapter. Shown below are those three regression equations, along with the standard deviations for the respective coefficients:

Life Expectancy predicted by Smoking

$$\hat{Y} = 73.3 - .406(SMK)$$

$$s_b = .1384$$

Life Expectancy predicted by Weight Control

$$\hat{Y} = 74.2 - .440(WC)$$

$$s_b = .2431$$

Life Expectancy predicted by Exercise

$$\hat{Y} = 56.5 + .226(EX)$$

$$s_b = .062$$

-2.93
8
2.306
Yes

18. What is the t value for the individual simple regression equation involving smoking as the predictor variable _____. If this is a student t with (n-2) degrees of freedom, the degrees of freedom would be _____, and the .05 two-tail cut-off value from the student t table would be _____. Is the coefficient of Smoking significant?

19. What is the t value for the individual simple regression equation which predicts life expectancy by weight control _____? Is the coefficient associated with weight control significant? | -1.81
No

20. What is the t value for the individual simple regression equation which predicts life expectancy by exercise _____? Is this coefficient statistically significant? | 3.64
Yes

Yes, most perplexing, indeed! Taken completely independently (simple regression), Smoking and Exercise were statistically significant. And taken as a group, the three variables of Smoking, Weight Control, and Exercise formed a statistically significant regression equation. But when the three variables were tested individually within the context of the multiple regression model, none of them were significant.

21. The reason that Smoking was significant in the simple regression model, but it was not significant in the multiple regression model is that that multiple regression model examines the increase in explanation after Weight Control and Exercise have already been included in the model. Some of the explanation which Smoking is providing is not unique, and it had already been accounted for by either(both) Weight Control or(and) Exercise. True or False | True

22. In all of the models, simple or multiple, Weight Control consistently provided the least explanation. Would it be appropriate to take our multiple regression model:

$\hat{Y} = 64.9 - .255(SMK) - .093(WC) + .151(EX)$

and simply drop the the Weight Control coefficient leaving the equation as:

$\hat{Y} = 64.9 - .255(SMK) \qquad + .151(EX)$ | No

(Yes or No)

230

True, as a matter of fact the reg equation for SMK and EX
$\hat{Y} = 62.8 - .26(SMK) + .168(EX)$

df = n-k-1
df = 6
t = 2.447

95% CI (SMK)
-.255 (+ or -) .278
-.533 to .023

95% CI (WC)
-.093 (+ or -) .431
-..523 to .338

95% CI (EX)
.151 (+ or -) .159
.008 to .310

§ 15.3

coefficient of determination
r^2
R^2

---

23. Should a term be dropped, you should recompute the regression equation using only two predictor variables. This will produce an entirely new equation with completely different values for b_0, b_1, and b_2. True or False

24. The confidence interval for the respective values of b_i is computed using the same values of the standard deviation of the coefficients, as well as the same t value. In this case df was equal to _____ which equals _____. The corresponding t value was _____.

To save you the trouble of flipping back, here are the regression coefficients and standard deviations which we had used previously:

	COEFFICIENT(b)	STANDARD DEVIATION
Smoking	-.255	.114
Weight Control	-.093	.176
Exercise	.151	.065

25. What would be the 95% confidence interval for the estimate of the true regression coefficient for smoking?

26. What would be the 95% confidence interval for the estimate of the true regression coefficient for weight control?

27. What would be the 95% confidence interval for the estimate of the true regression coefficient for exercise?

Determining the Predictive Ability

1. The percent of explained variance was explained by the term (give name) _____. The symbol for this term in simple regression was _____. The symbol for this term in multiple regression was _____.

2. The coefficient of determination can be (easily) determined from the ANOVA sum of squares table. The coefficient of determination is equal to _____.

SSR/SST

Once again I will provide you the ANOVA table from the multiple regression problem:

ANALYSIS OF VARIANCE

DUE TO	DF	SS	MS=SS/DF
REGRESSION	3	450.31	150.10
RESIDUAL	6	109.69	18.28
TOTAL	9	560.00	

3. Using the SS values from above, compute the value for the multiple coefficient of determination, R^2.

R^2 = SSR/SST
R^2 = 450.31/560.0 = 80.4%

4. Like the value of r^2 studied previously, the value of R^2 must be between _____ and _____. With 1.00 being _____ correlation (all) points falling on the line, and 0.00 being _____ correlation.

zero one
perfect
no

5. Previously we had computed the F statistic (giving a measure of the predictive strength of the entire regression equation by using the various sum of squares and mean squares. To refresh that procedure:
SS regression = _____
  divided by df(k) _____
  produces Mean Square Regression = _____

SSR = 450.31
df(k) = 3
MSR = 150.10

SS residual = _____
  divided by df(n-k-1) _____
  produces Mean Square Residual = _____

SSE = 109.69
df(n-k-1) = 6
MSE = 18.28

MSEregression/MSEresidual = F = _____

F = 150.10/18.28 = 8.211

6. Another method of computing F would be to use the formula involving R^2. This formula has the expression _____.
Compute the value for F using this formula. (If you use R^2 = .804 the value will not be identical due to rounding...but it will surely be close enough for our purposes.)

$F = (R^2/k)/((1-R^2)/(n-k-1))$
F = 8.204

b, mere association only...and don't be fooled by statistical shysters touting high, but meaningless correlation values.

increase

7. A high value of R^2 implies: (choose one)
   a. a true cause and effect relationship
   b. mere association, as one variable moved in one direction, the other variable (for what ever reason) also happened to move in that direction

8. As predictor variables are added to the equation, the value of R^2 must always _____, although the increase can be very minimal (of no significance).

In the previous question we touched upon two concepts:
One, that the value of R^2 must always increase as predictor variables are added,
Two, but the increase might not be significant (in fact, adding variables may decrease total, overall significance).

In this section we will deal with how one measures the amount and significance of the increase. In order to do that we need to compare a model with the predictor variable included vs. a model with the predictor variable not included.

The second predictor variable (Weight Control) has been the weakest predictor of the three. Let us examine two models, one with weight control included (complete model), and one with weight control omitted (reduced model). Here are the values for each of these models:

Complete Model:

$$\hat{Y} = 64.9 - .255(SMK) - .093(WC) + .151(EX)$$

$$R^2 = 80.4\%$$

Reduced Model:

$$\hat{Y} = 62.8 - .261(SMK) + .168(EX)$$

$$R^2 = 79.5\%$$

Just 'eyeballing' the numbers, it seems that Weight Control has added very, very little to the explanatory of the model...once

Smoking and Exercise have been included. (You may refer back to the beginning section where the discussion was made of simple regression. The simple regression equation involving weight control as a predictor variable explained 29.1% of the variance. But as can be seen from the equations above, most of that 29.1% could have been explained by the other variables (smoking and exercise). The unique contribution of weight control, after the effects of smoking and exercise have been included is only .9% (80.4-79.5).) Although our intuitive feeling is that this increase is very small, we can test the significance of that increase.

9. The formula for testing the significance of the increase in the value of R^2 is _____, where v1 = _____, and v2 = _____. Rc^2 = Correlation complete model
Rr^2 = Correlation reduced model

$$F = \frac{(Rc^2 - Rr^2)/v1}{(1 - Rc^2)/v2}$$

v1 = # pred C - # pred R
v2 = n - 1 - # pred C

10. Compute the actual value of F for the incremental or partial effect of Weight Control.

$$F = \frac{(.804 - .795)/1}{(1.0 - .804)/6}$$
F = .275

11. As usual, we need to compare the actual value of F with the value obtained from the table. What would be the .05 value of F? (Use same degrees of freedom as in computational portion of problem v1 = 1, v2 = 6.)

F = 5.99

12. Given a table value of F = 5.99, and an actual value of .275, what conclusion do you reach concerning the incremental value of the variable of weight control with respect to the regression equation?

weight control very insignificant as a predictor variable

13. Because we have measured the partial or incremental effect of these variables, the F value we computed is referred to as a _____ F statistic.

partial

14. Partial F statistics can be computed for any assortment of complete vs. reduced models. The complete model might have 6 predictors, and the reduced might have 5. Or the complete model might have 6 predictors and the reduced model only 1. True or False

True

$$F = \frac{(.804 - 0)/3}{(1-.804)/6}$$

$F = 8.204$

zero

$F = 5.387$

15. Or how about this one: Let the full model be the three variable multiple regression with which we have worked most of this chapter (SMK, WC, EX). In this case, R^2 was equal to .804. Let the reduced model be a model with zero predictors which would produce an R^2 value of zero. Use the partial F formula to compute the value of the F statistic for this situation.

16. Does this answer look familiar? It should. Look back at problem 5 from this section. The formula given at that time is a simplified version of the partial F formula for the special case when the reduced model has _____ predictors.

Since that was so much fun, let's try another permutation of our three predictor variables. This time let's compare a model with Smoking and Weight Control against the model with all three predictors.

Complete Model:

$\hat{Y} = 64.9 - .255(SMK) - .093(WC) + .151(EX)$

$R^2 = 80.4\%$

Reduced Model:

$\hat{Y} = 76.5 - .345(SMK) - .284(WC)$

$R^2 = 62.8\%$

17. Compute the partial F statistic for the incremental effect of Exercise after Smoking and Weight Control have already been included in the model.

no room...on to the next page

18. Are you ready for some real excitement? Look back at problem #9 and problem #16 from §15.3. At that time we computed t tests to measure the incremental effect of the variables after the other two variables had been included. Consider the following table:

Variable	Partial F Value	t value	t value squared
wt control	.275	.53	_____
exercise	5.387	2.32	_____

What do you find? The F value is equal to the t value _____. (allowing for differences due to rounding)   squared

19. Sometimes a set of data cannot be adequately modeled with a straight line. In such a situation, a _____ model is needed.   curvilinear

20. Actually, a model which exhibits a curvilinear relationship between the X and Y values can still be considered a "linear" regression, provided the values of _____ are still linear.   the β values (betas)

21. In the case of a quadratic equation (containing an X^2 term), X becomes your first "variable", and X^2 becomes your second "variable", with the problem continuing as a straight multiple regression situation. True or False   True

22. Tests of the overall significance of the regression equation, as well as tests for the appropriateness of the specific inclusion of the X^2 term can be handled in the same manner as the tests for individual variables was handled previously. True or False   True

23. When a change is made in the scaling of the independent variable, for instance the use of $1/X$ rather than X, or X^2 rather than X, such a change is referred to as a _____.   transformation

236

Very, very true. Extrapolate non-linear models only with the upmost of care.	24. When using any type of curvilinear regression, great care must be taken when extrapolating beyond the bounds of the actual data points. With curvilinear models it is easy to develop models that provide outstanding fit (the line fits the points) but once the line leaves the range of the observed data it can produce absolutely dreadful predictions. True or False
§ 15.4	The Problem of Multicollinearity
no (hopefully none, certainly very little)	1. Ideally, in a multiple regression situation you want to see a very strong relationship between each of the independent (predictor) variables and the dependent variable. But you also wish to see _____ relationship between the various independent variables and each other.
multicollinearity	2. When the various independent variables are correlated with each other, this is the problem of _____.

To check for the presence of multicollinearity in the life expectancy problem with which we have been working it is necessary to develop the correlation matrix showing the correlations between each of the variables.

CORRELATION MATRIX

	LIFE EXP	SMOKING	WT CONTROL	EXERCISE
LIFE EXP	1.00	-.72	-.54	.79
SMOKING	-.72	1.00	.31	-.44
WT CTRL	-.54	.31	1.00	-.53
EXERCISE	.79	.44	-.53	1.00

This is a correlation matrix in its "classic" form. As we will discuss, this matrix contains a number of redundant values. For that reason (redundancy), the correlation matrix presented by most computers will often look somewhat different.

3. The values down the main diagonal are all equal to _____. This is because the correlation between a variable and itself is _____.

| 1.00
| perfect (or 1.00)

4. The values on each side of the diagonal are mirror images of each other. This is because the (for instance) correlation of smoking with weight control value = _____) is the same as the correlation of weight control with smoking (value = _____).

.31

.31

5. Looking at the correlation of the independent variables with the dependent variable, which independent variable has the highest correlation with life expectancy _____? What is this correlation? What is the percentage of explained variance? (If this value seems vaguely familiar, it should. Go back to page 219 and look at the simple regression equation involving Life Expectancy predicted by Exercise and check the value of the coefficient of determination... they are the same.)

exercise
$r = .79$
$r^2 = .62$

Now we are ready to answer a question which we proposed earlier. Consider the contribution of the variable of weight control. Taken by itself (that is, life expectancy in a simple regression with weight control), weight control provides an r^2 value of 29.1%, implying that roughly 30% of the variation in life expectancy can be explained by the variation in weight control.

However, when we looked at the analysis of partials we found that to add weight control to the model which already contained exercise and smoking provided an increase in R^2 of less than one percent (.9%). Much of the variation which weight control was explaining could also be explained by smoking and exercise.

6. We have a measure of how much "overlap" in explanation to expect in the _____ coefficients found in the correlation matrix.

correlation

7. When you encounter the problem of multicollinearity the best (sometimes only) response that can usually be made is to simply _____ (or sometime combine) some of the factors which are highly correlated.

remove

238

dependent

8. When faced with the problem of multicollinearity it is generally advisable to select two variables that seem to be highly correlated, eliminate one of them, retaining the one which is most highly correlated with the _____ variable.

exercise
smoking

9. Looking at the correlation matrix. Which variable would you introduce first _____? Which variable would you introduce second _____?

True

10. Because the problem of multicollinearity is such a severe problem, and because the correlation matrix can be such a good guide as to the order in which the analysis should proceed, and because the correlation matrix is such an easy analysis to request (with most computer packages) computation of the correlation matrix is the ideal starting point for most analysis. True or False

---

§ 15.5-1

The Use of Dummy Variables

False

1. Dummy variables are used by students too stupid to understand the proper techniques. True or False

True

2. Dummy variables are used as a method of introducing qualitative (non-metric) variables into the analysis. True or False

two

3. Actually if you have three classifications (i.e. left handed, right handed, or ambidextrous) you should have only _____ dummy variables.

linear combination

4. You need "one less dummy variables than classes" because no mathematical solution will exist if one of the variables is a _____ _____ of the other variables.

zero or one

5. In a dummy variable, each subclassification is assigned a value of either _____ or _____

Stepwise Regression

§ 15.5-2

1. Stepwise regression is a technique that allows the computer to introduce variables into the model according to definite criteria. Rather than the user trying to decide which variable to introduce, the computer decides which variable to introduce. True or False.

True

2. It is called 'stepwise regression" because it either introduces or discards one variable at each iteration (or step). True or False

True

3. There are several types of "stepwise regression". They are named according to the manner in which the variables are introduced into the equation.

If the computer
a. starts with an "empty" model (no variables in the equation)
b. begins to add variables, starting with the variable with the highest coefficient of determination
c. continues to add variables, each time adding the variable which, when included with the variables already in the model makes the largest contribution to the value of R^2
d. and stops when no further additions will produce a significant increase in R^2;

this is called _____ regression.

forward

If the computer
a. starts with a "full" model (all variables in the equation)
b. begins to delete variables, starting with the variable with the lowest contribution to R^2
c. continues to delete variables, until the deletion causes a significant drop in R^2, the significant variable is replaced and the process is terminated;

this is called _____ regression.

backward

240

stepwise

If the computer
a. starts with an "empty" model
b. begins to add variables in terms of their predictive significance
c. but can also delete variables formerly in the model if the inclusion of subsequent variables (and the multicollinearity between those new variables and the previous variable) reduce the contribution of the former variable below the level of significance
d. with the process continuing until all variables of significant contribution are included

this is called _____ regression.

Shown are the results for the Stepwise regression for the Life Expectancy problem with which this chapter has been concerned.

The results of the stepwise regression analysis are shown below:

STEP	1	2
CONSTANT	56.48	62.84
Exercise	.226	.168
T-ratio	3.64	3.07
Smoking		-.26
T-ratio		-2.42
S	5.14	4.05
R-Squared	62.32	79.51

Hopefully some of these results look familiar (read down the STEP column)

STEP 1:

This is the simple regression equation for Life Expectancy predicted by Exercise (seen previously)

4. At this point Life Expectancy is being predicted by _____ only, and for that reason there is a hole in the chart

exercise

STEP 2:

5. At this point, exercise has been retained in the model, and the variable _____ has been added.(This model was also seen previously) | smoking

STEP 3:

6. Three variables were possible, but the stepwise regression only went through 2 steps (it only introduced two variables). The third variable (weight control) was not introduced because _____. | Weight Control did not add significantly to the regression equation.

7. Previously, in the section involving dummy variables we had given the rule that when forming a regression equation using dummy variables, you should have one less dummy variable than you have classifications. However, when using stepwise regression it is often advisable to include as many dummy variables as classifications since (choose one or both)
a. you don't know which variable it will want to include
b. the stepwise model will probably not include all of the dummy variables anyway. | both a. and b. could be reasons

8. Suppose that you put in as many dummy variables as you had classifications (categories), and the computer found all of them significant and attempted to place all of them into the model, what would happen? | Computer would come back with error message, unable to compute.

Examination of Residuals

15.5-3

1. Generally, all of the actual Y_i data points will not fall upon the line. The difference between the points and the line ($Y_i - \hat{Y}$) is known as the _____ or _____ term. | error or residual

2. In performing regression analysis, several assumptions are made concerning the distribution of these residuals:
a. _____
b. _____
c. _____

| a. normal, mean of zero
b. constant variance
c. errors are unrelated

242

plot or histogram

predictor

shotgun,
noise

autocorrelation

Durbin-Watson statistic

zero to four

positive

similar

negative

different

two

3. The easiest way to check for normality is with a _____ of the residuals.

4. Non-normality usually indicates that your model has overlooked possible additional _____ variables.

5. Equality of variances can also be checked most easily with a plot of the residuals, this time plotted against the predicted values of $\hat{Y}$. One hopes to observe no pattern, and certainly no consistent increase or decrease in the values. Such a desireable pattern is referred to as a _____ blast or _____.

6. When the residuals are related (correlated) with each other, this correlation is termed _____.

7. Autocorrelation is measured with the _____.

8. The Durbin-Watson statistic ranges in value from _____ to _____.

9. A value close to zero means that the residuals show strong _____ autocorrelation.

10. Positive autocorrelation occurs when the adjacent errors are quite _____ to each other.

11. A value close to four means that the residuals show strong _____ correlation.

12. Negative autocorrelation occurs when the adjacent residuals are quite _____ to each other.

13. The ideal value for the Durbin-Watson statistic is approximately _____.

Model Building - Interaction Effects

§ 15.6-1

1. Sometimes variables 'team-up' with each other in ways that produce effects that are far different from the effect of either variable considered independently. This is called _____ _____.

interaction effects

2. Let's consider the same model we have been investigating throughout this chapter...the prediction of Life Expectancy, but to simplify things, let's just have two variables, Exercise and Weight Control.

The model without interaction effects would be:
Y = WC ± EXER ± e, or more technically:
$\hat{Y} = \beta_0 + \beta_1 WC + \beta_2 EXER + e$

But we may find some significant interactions. Some folks, quite overweight, but eating very little (and not exercising at all). Other folks, eating voraciously, but quite slender, due to heavy exercise schedule.

So what would our model with the interaction effects look like?

Y = WC ± EXER ± (WC x EX) + e
or more technically:
$\hat{Y} = \beta_0 + \beta_1 WC + \beta_2 EXER + \beta_3 (WC \times EXER) + e$

3. If you graphed the two variables of WC and EXER, you would have two lines. If there was significant interaction between the two variables the lines would _____. If there was not any appreciable interaction between the two variables, then the lines would be _____.

intersect, or cross

parallel

Model Building - Quadratic Effects

§ 15.6-2

1. A quadratic model is one that in addition to the (linear) variable "X", also includes the value of _____.

X squared, or X^2

2. The use of the squared value of X, (X^2) will cause the model to be (Linear / Curvilinear) (choose one).

Curvilinear

3. A curvilinear model means that the situation is not being modeled by a _____ line.

straight

244

none

all

You have got to be kidding! If the computer is down, just forget it. Pack up your bags and take the rest of the day off.

Multiple regression requires tremendous amounts of number crunching and is usually performed using matrix algebra (which is why your textbook did not even show you any computational formulas).

4. A First-Order Model means that (none / all) of the interaction or quadratic terms are included.

5. A Second-Order Model is one that (none / all) of the interaction or quadratic terms are included.

6. If you are trying to compute a Second-Order Model with four variables and the computer is 'down', no problem, it is still easy to work out the math by hand. True or False

CHAPTER 16

Time Series Analysis and Index Numbers

CHAPTER OBJECTIVES

The previous chapter had dealt with regression analysis which can be conceptualized as a process of fitting a curve to a set of data. When the X-axis is time, that is, we are trying to model and predict the behavior of some variable of interest over time, such analysis is referred to as "time series analysis". Because so many business plans depend upon accurate forecasts, the study of time series is an important area of business statistics. In addition to simply performing time series regression the time series is also analyzed into its components of trend, seasonal and cyclical activity. In addition, index numbers with both simple and aggregate price indexes are discussed. By the end of this chapter you should be able to answer the following questions:

1. What is meant by "time series analysis"?

2. What are the four "components" of a time series?

3. How do you analyze the components of a time series?

4. How do you seasonalize and deseasonalize a set of time series data?

4. What are "index numbers", How are they computed? How are they used?

246

TIME SERIES ANALYSIS

§ 16.0 — A Look Back/Introduction

1. When linear regression is performed upon a set of data in which time is the independent or predictor variable, such analysis is called _____ _____.

time series

2. One advantage of this technique is that the analysis of (for example) sales volume is performed only upon the sales volume data (arranged over time). But one disadvantage is that although the sales may show definite patterns over time, no cause and effect relationship is shown, we have not linked the sales with a true predictor variable. True or False

True

3. Although predictions can be made "over time", time is not a true predictor variable. Time, itself, does not cause anything to happen. True or False

True

---

§ 16.1 — Components of Time Series

1. A time series represents a variable observed across _____.

time

2. There are four components (that is four, distinct types of movement) in a time series. The four are:
a. _____
b. _____
c. _____
d. _____

trend
cyclical
seasonal
irregular

3. The long term movement (either increase or decrease) is termed the _____ in the time series.

trend

4. If there seems to be no discernable pattern of increase or decrease, then the data is said to contain _____ _____.

no trend

5. If the change from year to year seems to be fairly constant, then the trend is _____.

linear

6. If the change from year to year is not constant, but seems to be consistently increasing or decreasing, then the trend is _____.

non-linear

It would probably be instructive to have a set of data with which to work, so consider the following figures involving the value of the dollar and the value of the peso over the years 1975 - 1986:

Year	Value for "t"	Dollar Value	Peso Value
1975	1	134	13
1976	2	149	15
1977	3	162	23
1978	4	170	23
1979	5	181	23
1980	6	195	23
1981	7	217	25
1982	8	247	70
1983	9	282	150
1984	10	304	200
1985	11	325	300
1986	12	344	400

Let's start by examining the relationship between the rate at which the dollar has inflated and time. (Note: you can handle time in one of several ways. You can leave the numbers in their original units (1975, 1976, etc.) or you can use a different scale (1, 2, 3, etc.). The regression equation will be the same (adjusted for the difference in scale) the value of b_1, the slope will be exactly the same (still going up by a year each time) but the value of b_0 (the y intercept) will be dramatically different.)

7. Plot the data points for the relationship between time and dollar index.

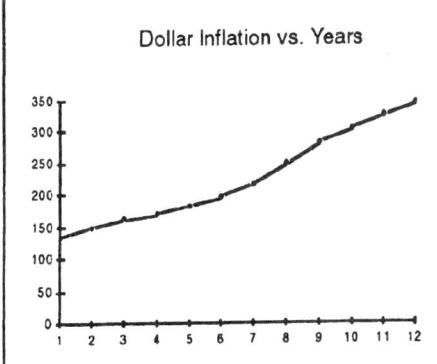

Dollar Inflation vs. Years

248

yes

$\hat{Y} = 97.0 + 19.8(X)$

r = .983
r² = 96.7%

Peso Inflation vs. Years

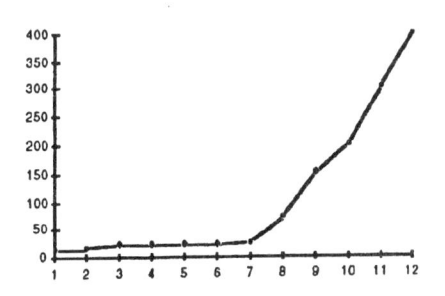

[plot showing values roughly flat from years 1-7, then rising steeply to ~400 by year 12]

Hmmmm....maybe, maybe not. Years 1-6 look linear, and years 7-12 look linear, but not 1-12.

$\hat{Y} = -95.5 + 30.9(t)$
Peso = -95.5 + 30.9(yrs)

r = .854
r² = 73.0%
As was visually apparent, the dollar inflation seemed much more constant (linear) than the peso inflation. Thus the fit of a straight line (measured by r²) was better for dollars than for pesos.

8. Does the plot look sufficiently linear to allow you to consider linear regression to be an adequate model?

9. Compute the regression equation for the relationship between time and dollar index.

10. As a measure of the strength of the relationship, compute the value of the correlation coefficient. What percent of the variance has been "explained"?

11. Plot the data points for the relationship between time and peso value.

12. Does this plot look sufficiently linear to allow you to consider linear regression to be an adequate model?

13. Compute the regression equation for the relationship between time and peso value.

14. As a measure of the strength of the relationship, compute the value of the correlation coefficient. What percent of the variance has been explained?

15. Just for fun (we are having fun, aren't we?) make a graph of the peso values versus time squared. Does this look any more linear?

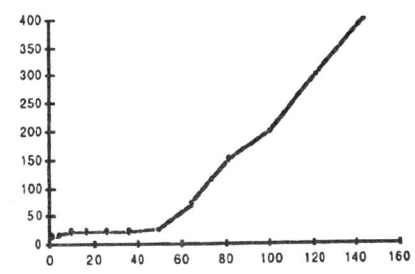

Peso Inflation vs. Years Squared

Yes, taken as a whole, years 1-12 look much more linear.

16. Compute the multiple regression equation for the prediction of peso value using "t" and "t-squared".

$\hat{Y} = 82.5 - 45.4(t) + 5.87(t^2)$
where Y = peso value
 t = years

17. As a measure of the strength of the relationship compute the value of the multiple correlation coefficient. What percent of the variance has been explained?

r = .987
r^2 = 97.5%

18. Periodic variation which occurs within a calendar year is referred to as _____ _____ or _____.

seasonal variation
seasonality

19. The key to the investigation of seasonality is that it must be within the year. Therefore annual data such as the peso and dollars example) could not show seasonality. True or False

True

20. Seasonal variation can also refer to periodic business fluctuations of shorter duration than the four "seasons" of the year. Periodic monthly fluctuations such as increased spending at the first of the month (after payday) and decreased spending at the end of the month (waiting for payday) can also be termed seasonal variation. True or False

True

21. The same techniques used to analyze seasonal variation can also be applied to weekly fluctuations, such as increases in certain activities throughout the weekend as opposed to during the workweek. True or False

True

cyclical

22. A more gradual, non-periodic (certainly no fixed period) of fluctuation generally attributable to the overall state of the economy is called _____ variation.

two to ten

23. Seasonal variation was confined to events happening within one calendar year. Cyclical variation usually ranges in length from _____ to _____ years.

peak to peak
trough to trough
zero point to zero point

24. The period of a cycle is measured in one of three ways:
a. from one _____ to the next _____
b. from one _____ to the next _____
c. from one _____ to the next _____

expansion
recession or depression

25. Cyclical peaks occur during times of economic _____. Cyclical troughs occur during times of economic _____.

irregular

26. After the effects of trend, seasonality and cyclical variation have been accounted for, the remaining variability in the data is termed _____ variation.

noise

27. Irregular variation can take one of two forms:
a. the natural, random scattering of the phenomena itself, sometimes referred to as _____
b. major, dramatic events (earthquakes, fires, floods) which produce sharp, temporary spikes in the data.

28. The "noise" factor varies from item to item within the economy. For the following categories, which item do you feel would have more "noise" (more random, unpredictable fluctuations)?

a. clothing
b. oil drilling supplies
c. audio tapes
d. auto sales

a. clothing vs. office supplies
b. oil drilling supplies vs. hospital supplies
c. potatoes vs. audio tapes
d. gasoline vs. auto sales
(and within categories as well)

aa. ladies' fashions
bb. Star Wars
cc. greeting cards
dd. accident

aa. clothing (ladies' clothes vs. men's business suits)
bb. childrens' toys (crayons vs. Star Wars action figures)
cc. paper goods (greeting cards vs. office paper)
dd. insurance (life insurance vs. accident insurance)

29. The second type of irregular variation, the dramatic event, will often produce a single extreme point on the graph (a point whose extremity can sometimes be easily explained). Such an extreme point is sometimes referred to as an _____.

outlier

30. When the cause of an outlier can be identified, is is often statistically appropriate to simply _____ that outlier from subsequent analysis.

omit, drop, eliminate

31. The time series model can be manipulated in two basic ways. If the four components are added together it is referred to the _____ _____.

additive structure

32. The notation for the additive structure is _____.

Y = T + S + C + I

33. If the four components of the time series analysis are multiplied together it is referred to as the _____ _____.

multiplicative structure

34. The notation for the multiplicative structure is _____.

Y = T x S x C x I

35. In the _____ structure, the value of a given component is not related to the values in the other components. Thus if the seasonal effect is +$200, then exactly that amount is added regardless of whether the trend is up or down, or whether the cycle is on an upswing or a downswing.

additive

36. In the _____ structure, the value of a given component is related to the values in the other components. Thus if the seasonal effect is +$200, then that amount is modified by the effect of the trend component, and by the cyclical component.

multiplicative

37. Because the components in the multiplicative structure do relate to each other, the multiplicative structure is generally thought to provide a more accurate model. True or False

True

252

§ 16.2

True

recoding the data

$\hat{Y} = 97.0 + 19.8(t)$
$\$ = 97.0 + 19.8(yrs)$

19.8 (dollars per year)

$\hat{Y} = -95.5 + 30.9(t)$
Peso $= -95.5 + 30.9(yrs)$

30.9 (pesos per year)

Measuring Trend: No Seasonality

1. Annual data will contain no seasonality. True or False

Let's review the data we had examined previously regarding the inflation trends of dollars and pesos:

Year	Value for "t"	Dollar Value	Peso Value
1975	1	134	13
1976	2	149	15
1977	3	162	23
1978	4	170	23
1979	5	181	23
1980	6	195	23
1981	7	217	25
1982	8	247	70
1983	9	282	150
1984	10	304	200
1985	11	325	300
1986	12	344	400

2. The years have been converted from 1975, 1976, etc. to 1, 2, 3, etc., this is called _____.

3. What was the linear trend line for the prediction of dollar index over time?

4. This implies that the dollar index is rising by _____ points each year. (It requires that many more dollars each year to buy the same item...the item that you could have bought for $325 in 1985 will cost you (approximately) $344 in 1986, etc.)

5. What was the linear trend line for the prediction of the peso index over time?

6. This implies that the peso index is rising by _____ points each year.

7. (Continuing from problem 6) The answer in problem 6 implied that the peso index is rising by 30.9 pesos per year. Yet the increases the last five times have been 45, 80, 50, 100, and 100. This discrepancy is due to the the fact that the value of 30.9 represents the _____ rate of increase over the 12 periods.

average

8. (Continuing) This increasing rate of increase also means that the data does not fit a _____ model.

linear

9. What is the quadratic solution to the peso prediction problem?

$\hat{Y} = 82.5 - 45.4(t) + 5.87(t^2)$

10. This equation implies that the peso index is rising by an average of approximately _____ points each year?

No answer!
  Increase in Y depends upon specific X value.

11. The process of extending a trend equation in order to make predictions of future values is called _____ or _____.

extrapolation or, more simply, forecasting

12. The CRUCIAL ASSUMPTION of statistical forecasting is the assumption that the data patterns observed in the past will continue in that same manner into the future. True or False

Very True! And this assumption is very critical and often not justified!

13. Forecasting or extrapolation is always risky, but it is especially dangerous when dealing with equations which are _____.

nonlinear

14. When dealing with nonlinear equations it is bet to confine one's analysis to _____ (predictions within the observed data range) and not attempt to make _____ (predictions outside the data range).

interpolation
extrapolation

Shown on the next page are predictions for pesos (using both t and t-squared, as well as predictions for the dollar index.

Predictions for Dollars and Pesos
Linear and Quadratic Equations

time	time sq	peso	dollar	(peso)(t)	(peso)(t²)	(dollars)(t)
1	1	13	134	-64.6	43.0	116.8
2	4	15	149	-33.7	15.2	136.6
3	9	23	162	-2.8	-0.9	156.4
4	16	23	170	28.1	-5.2	176.2
5	25	23	181	59.0	2.3	196.0
6	36	23	195	89.9	21.4	215.8
7	49	25	217	120.8	52.3	235.6
8	64	70	247	151.7	95.0	255.4
9	81	150	282	182.6	149.4	275.2
10	100	200	304	213.5	215.5	295.0
11	121	300	325	244.4	293.4	314.8
12	144	400	344	275.3	383.0	334.6
13				306.2	484.3	354.4
14				337.1	597.4	374.2
15				368.0	722.3	394.0
16				398.9	858.8	413.8
17				429.8	1007.1	433.6
18				460.7	1167.2	453.4
19				491.6	1339.0	473.2
20				522.5	1522.5	493.0
21				553.4	1717.8	512.8
22				584.3	1924.8	532.6

413.80

15. What would be the prediction for dollars in 1990?

553.4 vs. 1717.8

16. Notice how much more "aggressive" the quadratic equation is. Compare the prediction for pesos in 1995 using the linear equation vs. the prediction for pesos in 1995 using the quadratic equation.

17. (Continuing) In the problem above, we obtained two very different predictions (both of them obtained totally objectively and in a mathematically rigorous fashion). But one prediction is 553 and the other is 1717...which one are you to use?...which one is right?

(Answer: neither! Any forecast, like any estimate, cannot hope to be exactly correct. Just looking at the two predictions it seems that the 553 is too low and the 1717 is too high. One approach to this particular problem (the peso problem) might be to revise the data series. It seems obvious that the data before 1982 is quite different from the data after 1982. Therefore there would be some justification for simply truncating the data series at 1980 and using the data from 1981 through 1986.)

Year	Value for "t"	Dollar Value	Peso Value
1981	7	217	25
1982	8	247	70
1983	9	282	150
1984	10	304	200
1985	11	325	300
1986	12	344	400

18. The equation for the prediction of peso by time would now be _____?

$\hat{Y} = -70.7 + 74.7(t)$

19. This would imply an average increase in how many pesos per year?

74.7

20. What percent of the variance is explained by this equation?

$r^2 = 97.7\%$
(much better fit!)

Shown below are the predictions for the next ten years. Columns 5,6,7 are the predictions using all 12 years, columns 8,9,10 are the predictions using only the last 6 years. (The dollar values were also recomputed using the last six years.)

Predictions of Dollars and Pesos - Twelve Years vs. Six Years - Linear & Quadratic
(......All Twelve Years.....) (.....Last Six Years Only.....)

time	time sq	peso	dollar	peso x t	peso x t²	dollars x t	peso x t	peso x t²	dollars x t
1	1	13	134	-64.6	43.0	116.8			
2	4	15	149	-33.7	15.2	136.6			
3	9	23	162	-2.8	-0.9	156.4			
4	16	23	170	28.1	-5.2	176.2			
5	25	23	181	59.0	2.3	196.0			
6	36	23	195	89.9	21.4	215.8			
7	49	25	217	120.8	52.3	235.6	4.0	-12.5	222.5
8	64	70	247	151.7	95.0	255.4	78.7	-23.7	248.0
9	81	150	282	182.6	149.4	275.2	153.4	-22.3	273.5
10	100	200	304	213.5	215.5	295.0	228.1	-8.3	299.0
11	121	300	325	244.4	293.4	314.8	302.8	18.5	324.5
12	144	400	344	275.3	383.0	334.6	377.5	57.9	350.0
13				306.2	484.3	354.4	452.2	110.1	375.5
14				337.1	597.4	374.2	526.9	174.9	401.0
15				368.0	722.3	394.0	601.6	252.3	426.5
16				398.9	858.8	413.8	676.3	342.5	452.0
17				429.8	1007.1	433.6	751.0	445.3	477.5
18				460.7	1167.2	453.4	825.7	560.9	503.0
19				491.6	1339.0	473.2	900.4	689.1	528.5
20				522.5	1522.5	493.0	975.1	829.9	554.0
21				553.4	1717.8	512.8	1049.8	983.5	579.5
22				584.3	1924.8	532.6	1124.5	1149.7	605.0

256

$\hat{Y}$ (with t) = 1049.8
$\hat{Y}$ (with t²) = 983.5

linear

True, very, very true. No area of statistics is tempered with as much subjective judgment as the area of forecasting.

21. Now what would the prediction(s) be for the year 1995?

22. Since the r² value in problem 20 was almost 98%, this is a good indication that the data is much closer to a _____ relationship than previously, and for this reason the predictions of the simple regression in column 8 are very close to the quadratic predictions in column 9.

23. It is permissible to truncate data because the key tenant of time series forecasting is that the trends that are seen in the past will continue in the future. If the data series has obviously changed to the extent that the past is no longer typical of present conditions the past data should be eliminated. True or False

---

§ 16.3

Y = T x C x S x I

annual

Y = T x C x I

Y = T x C

cyclical

Measuring Cyclical Activity: No Seasonality

1. The full "multiplicative" time series model has the form of _____.

2. We are assuming in this section that we are dealing with a series of data that has no seasonality. An example of a data series without seasonality would be _____ data.

3. If the data series has no seasonality, the multiplicative time series model could be rewritten as _____.

4. Any analysis will be confounded by large amounts of noise or irregular variation...a data series in which there simply is no rhyme nor reason to what is happening. However, if we can assume that the noise is small enough to be discounted, the multiplicative model could be rewritten as _____.

5. The result of the equation in problem four (above) has implied that for the purposes of this analysis, any deviation from the trend line (either up or down) is attributable to _____ variation.

6. We can obtain an estimate of the magnitude of the cyclical component at any point by simply taking the ratio of the _____ value of Y, divided by the _____ value of Y.

$$\frac{\text{Actual}}{\text{Predicted}}$$

7. If the cycle is above the line, then the value of the cyclical component will be greater than _____. If the cycle is below the line, then the value of the cyclical component will be less than _____. When the cycle is crossing the line, the cyclical component will be exactly equal to _____.

1.00

1.00
1.00

8. Let's compute the cyclical component for the twelve time periods involved in the dollar inflation problem. Shown below is the data (and to show you what a good sport I am, I have included the predicted values from the trend equation).

Time	Actual Dollars	Predicted Dollars
1	$134	$116.80
2	149	136.60
3	162	156.40
4	170	176.20
5	181	196.00
6	195	215.80
7	217	235.60
8	247	255.40
9	282	275.20
10	304	295.00
11	325	314.80
12	344	334.60

1 = 1.15
2 = 1.09
3 = 1.04
4 = .96
5 = .92
6 = .90
7 = .92
8 = .97
9 = 1.02
10 = 1.03
11 = 1.03
12 = 1.03

9. Make a graph of these two sets of values, plotted on the same graph against time.

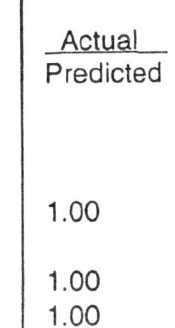

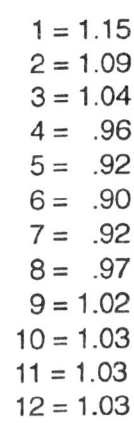

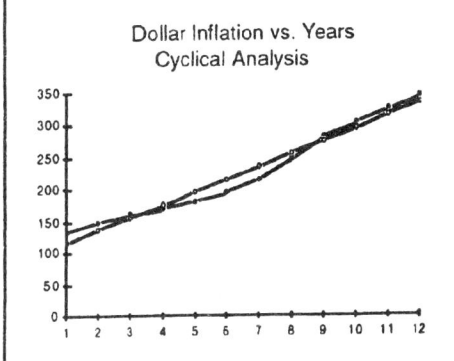

Dollar Inflation vs. Years
Cyclical Analysis

258

three and four eight and nine	10. The cycle shows "zero points" between periods _____ and _____ , as well as between periods _____ and _____.
zero point to zero point approximately 5 periods	11. In this example, the duration of a cycle is _____ periods.

§ 16.4	Types of Seasonal Variation
additive	1. In adjusting for seasonality, if we see the same increase each year, regardless of the value of Y, this is _____ seasonality.
multiplicative	2. In adjusting for seasonal variation, if we see that the value of the seasonal adjustment is related to (is proportional to) the value of Y, then we have a situation involving _____ seasonality.
Y = T + S	3. If we consider only trend and seasonality, the equation for additive seasonality is _____.
Y = T x S	4. If we consider only trend and seasonality, the equation for multiplicative seasonality is _____.
620 660	5. Generally speaking, the multiplicative model is preferred over the additive. If the seasonal effect was 20 when sales were 200, then the additive model would predict that the seasonal effect would be _____ when sales 600. On the other hand, if sales went to 600, the multiplicative model might suggest that the seasonal effect would be _____.

6. When using a multiplicative model, the following steps are followed when decomposing a time series containing the effects of all four components:
   a. _____
   b. _____
   c. _____
   d. _____

a. develop seasonal indices
b. deseasonalize. actual data
c. develop trend on deseas. data
d. develop cyclical indices

7. Usually, the cyclical component can be used for modeling, that is, for describing the effects of the cycle within the observed data series. However, the cyclical component cannot be used for prediction because the length and severity of future business cycles can not be predicted. True or False

True. If you can predict the business cycle, a fortune awaits you on Wall Street.

Measuring Seasonality

§ 16.5

1. Seasonality is present any time that there is a predictably recurrent, periodic pattern to the data set. The predictability of seasonality is what sets it apart from the unpredictability of cyclical fluctuation. True or False

True

2. In order to measure the seasonality of a set of data, we must compare the actual data values against values that have _____ seasonality.

no

3. To compute values for each time period that contain no seasonality we will utilize a technique known as _____ _____ averages.

centered moving average

Consider the data set of quarterly data provided below:
(no room, on to the next page)

259

These totals and averages are not centered

First total falls at quarter number 2.5.

Quarter	Total	Moving Average
2.5	19	4.75
3.5	20	5.00
4.5	21	5.25
5.5	22	5.50
6.5	24	6.00
7.5	26	6.50
8.5	28	7.00
9.5	27	6.75
10.5	31	7.75
11.5	30	7.50
12.5	31	7.75
13.5	31	7.75
14.5	32	8.00

Centered moving average

Quarter	Moving average
3	4.87
4	5.12
5	5.37
6	5.75
7	6.25
8	6.75
9	6.87
10	7.25
11	7.37
12	7.62
13	7.75
14	7.87

4. First compute the four quarter moving total, and the four quarter moving average.

Quarter	Sequential Quarter Number	Value
W	1	3
S	2	4
S	3	7
F	4	5
W	5	4
S	6	5
S	7	8
F	8	7
W	9	6
S	10	7
S	11	9
F	12	7
W	13	7
S	14	8
S	15	9
F	16	8

5. Although we have some very nice moving averages, these averages are not centered, they fall between the quarters. Therefore we need to center them (averaging the 2.5 and 3.5 moving averages to develop the 3.0 quarter moving average) Develop the centered moving averages for the following quarters:

3
4
5
6
7
8
9
10
11
12
13
14

6. The moving averages which we have created contain much less noise and consequently, are much smoother than the original time series (each quarter has been replaced by the average of four quarters...hence random ups and downs between quarters tend to cancel out). Because this has produced a smoother set of data, the process of forming moving averages is sometimes referred to as _____.

smoothing

7. Now we need to form the seasonal index for each quarter. This is done by forming the ratio of the actual value for that quarter divided by the centered moving average for that quarter. We would produce seasonal indices for the following quarters:

Quarter	Sequential Quarter Number
3	3
4	4
1	5
2	6
3	7
4	8
1	9
2	10
3	11
4	12
1	13
2	14

3 = 1.42 (7/4.87)
4 = .97 (5/5.12)

1 = .75
2 = .91
3 = 1.28
4 = 1.04

1 = .86
2 = .97
3 = 1.23
4 = .91

1 = .90
2 = 1.03

8. We now have three values for each quarter. Three methods are suggested for forming a measure of central tendency with respect to these values:
   a. _____
   b. _____
   c. _____

a. arithmetic. mean of all
b. median
c. discard high and low arithmetic mean of the rest

262

Q1= .84 (.75+.86+.90)
Q2= .97 (.91+.97+1.03)
Q3= 1.31 (1.42+1.28+1.23)
Q4= .97 (.97+1.04+.97)

4.09
.97799 = .978

  .82   (.84x.978)
  .95   (.97x.978)
1.28   (1.31x.978)
  .95   (.97x.978)

divide

---

9. The most common method for obtaining one summary statistic for the index for a given quarter is to simply take the arithmetic mean of those values. This is especially appropriate when the data series is rather short. Use that method to find the seasonal indices for the respective quarters.

Q1 _____
Q2 _____
Q3 _____
Q4 _____

10. However, we have a bit of a problem. The SUM of those four quarters is _____. We need to multiply each quarterly index by 4/SUM = _____. That will produce the following values for the quarterly indices:

Q1 = _____
Q2 = _____
Q3 = _____
Q4 = _____

11. To deseasonalize data we _____ the original data by the respective seasonal index.

Sorry about the blank space, but this problem needs more room, see you on the next page.

12. Compute the deseasonalized quarterly values for the original data set. (In case you have lost track of what is happening, here is that original data set.)

Quarter	Sequential Quarter Number	Value
W	1	3
S	2	4
S	3	7
F	4	5
W	5	4
S	6	5
S	7	8
F	8	7
W	9	6
S	10	7
S	11	9
F	12	7
W	13	7
S	14	8
S	15	9
F	16	8

Deseasonalized Data

Q1 = 3.66
Q2 = 4.21
Q3 = 5.47
Q4 = 5.26

Q5 = 4.87
Q6 = 5.15
Q7 = 6.25
Q8 = 7.37

Q9 = 7.31
Q10 = 7.37
Q11 = 7.03
Q12 = 7.37

Q13 = 8.54
Q14 = 8.25
Q15 = 7.03
Q16 = 8.42

Time Series Decomposition: S x T x C

§ 16.6

1. The four step process for decomposing a time series equation were:
a. develop the seasonal indices
b. deseasonalize the actual data
c. develop trend equation using deseasonalized data
d. develop cyclical indices using deseasonalized data

If we continue with the data from the problem above we are now ready for step _____.

c. develop trend equation using the deseasonalized data

2. Using the data from the previous problem, the trend equation will now be computed on the deseasonalized data (as follows):

Deseasonalized Data

Q1 = 3.66
Q2 = 4.21
Q3 = 5.47
Q4 = 5.26

Q5 = 4.87
Q6 = 5.15
Q7 = 6.25
Q8 = 7.37

Q9 = 7.31
Q10 = 7.37
Q11 = 7.03
Q12 = 7.37

Q13 = 8.54
Q14 = 8.25
Q15 = 7.03
Q16 = 8.42

The trend equation is _____.

$\hat{Y} = 3.98 + .292(Q)$

3. To compute the cyclical indices we now need the trend line prediction for each point. The indices for each quarter are found be dividing the actual value for that quarter by the _____ value for that quarter.

predicted

Once again, here are the actual deseasonalized values:

	Predicted	Cyclical.Index	
Q1	4.27	.86	Q1 = 3.66
Q2	4.56	.92	Q2 = 4.21
Q3	4.86	1.13	Q3 = 5.47
Q4	5.15	1.02	Q4 = 5.26
Q5	5.44	.88	Q5 = 4.87
Q6	5.73	.90	Q6 = 5.15
Q7	6.02	1.04	Q7 = 6.25
Q8	6.32	1.17	Q8 = 7.37
Q9	6.61	1.11	Q9 = 7.31
Q10	6.90	1.07	Q10 = 7.37
Q11	7.19	.98	Q11 = 7.03
Q12	7.48	.98	Q12 = 7.37

continued. . .

continued. . .

265

	Predicted	Cyclical.Index
Q13	7.78	1.10
Q14	8.07	1.02
Q15	8.36	.84
Q16	8.65	.97

Q13 = 8.54
Q14 = 8.25
Q15 = 7.03
Q16 = 8.42

4. The Cyclical indices as computed contain two components _____ and _____.

cyclical and irregular

5. In a continuing effort to eliminate the noise, it is suggested that the cyclical components be computed on _____ averages in the same manner that the seasonal indices had been computed on moving averages.

moving

6. The book suggests using a 3 period moving average. If an odd numbered period is used that would automatically provide a _____ average.

centered

7. Here are the cyclical indices, use them to compute the 3 period centered moving cyclical average

	Cyclical.Index
Q1	.86
Q2	.92
Q3	1.13
Q4	1.02
Q5	.88
Q6	.90
Q7	1.04
Q8	1.17
Q9	1.11
Q10	1.07
Q11	.98
Q12	.98
Q13	1.10
Q14	1.02
Q15	.84
Q16	.97

	Cyclical.Index	Cntr.Index
Q1	.86	
Q2	.92	.97
Q3	1.13	1.02
Q4	1.02	1.01
Q5	.88	.93
Q6	.90	.94
Q7	1.04	1.03
Q8	1.17	1.10
Q9	1.11	1.11
Q10	1.07	1.05
Q11	.98	1.01
Q12	.98	1.02
Q13	1.10	1.04
Q14	1.02	.99
Q15	.84	.95
Q16	.97	

266

$Y = T \times C \times S \times I$

	Irregular Index
Q1	
Q2 =	.95
Q3 =	1.10
Q4 =	1.01
Q5 =	.96
Q6 =	.98
Q7 =	1.00
Q8 =	1.06
Q9 =	.99
Q10 =	1.02
Q11 =	.97
Q12 =	.97
Q13 =	1.06
Q14 =	1.06
Q15 =	.89
Q16	

Q6:   5=5.73 x .94 x .95 x .98
Q9:   6=6.61 x 1.11 x .82 x .99
Q12: 7=7.48 x 1.02 x .95 x .97
Q15: 9=8.36 x .95 x 1.28 x .89

§ 16.7

index number

8. The general expression for the multiplicative model is _____.

9. The full multiplicative model is $Y = T \times S \times C \times I$. Since we have found the trend value, the seasonal index, and the cyclical index, we can simply divide the actual value by the product of those values to determine the irregular index for each quarter.

Compute the irregular component for each quarter.

10. Now armed with the trend, the cyclical, the seasonal, and the irregular, we can give the complete time series decomposition for any quarter. Give the full decomposition for Q6, Q9, Q12, and Q15:

Value = Trend x Cyclc x Seasn x Irreg
Q6: _____ = _____ x _____ x _____ x _____
Q9: _____ = _____ x _____ x _____ x _____
Q12: _____ = _____ x _____ x _____ x _____
Q15: _____ = _____ x _____ x _____ x _____

Index Numbers

1. A number (an index) which measures the change in a particular item (or group of items) between two time periods is an _____ _____.

2. An index number simply represents the ratio between the activity in the current year, as compared to the value of that same activity in one particular year against which all of the other years are compared. This "constant" year of comparison is referred to as the _____ year.

base

3. According to the dictionary, "base stresses the ignoble and may suggest greed, grossness, cowardice, cruelty and treachery...contemptible and ignoble". The base year is chosen because it was a particularly unhappy year. True or False

False. "Base" is also defined as "the origin or starting point".

4. The value of the base year index is always _____.

100

5. A set of index numbers determined from the same base year is called a _____ _____ _____.

time series index

6. The purpose of a set of time series index numbers is to measure the yearly values in _____ units.

constant

7. Index numbers can be fashioned for literally any set of values. One of the most popular uses for index numbers is the formation of price indices. Perhaps the best known of the prices indices is the CPI, or _____ _____ _____.

consumer price index

8. The Consumer Price Index is a composite index featuring the combined prices of over 400 items, generally used by most households. For this reason it is also referred to as the _____ of _____ index. You may also see the Consumer Price Index referred to by its initials, the _____. Many financial items, salaries, rents, transfer payments are adjusted using the CPI.

cost of living
CPI

9. An index that includes more than one item is called an _____ index.

aggregate

Consider the five item consumer price index shown below:

Consumer Price Index
(P = Price per unit, Q = Quantity of units per month)

	P 1975	Q 1975	P 1985	Q 1985
gasoline	.85	30	1.05	25
cigarettes	.60	10	.95	8
oranges	.50	12	.60	7
take-out hamburger	.75	8	1.20	12
dress shirt	5.00	1	10.00	1

10. If we simply took the total of the prices from 1975 and compared that with the total of the prices from 1985 we would have what is known as a _____ _____ price index.

simple aggregate

11. Compute the simple aggregate price index using 1975 as the base year.

179.2

12. The key assumption (and drawback) of the simple aggregate price index is the assumption that the purchase price of each item represents the total amount spent on that item, or in other words, the assumption that _____ amounts of each item are purchased.

equal

13. If the purchase price of the item is weighted according to the quantity of that item that is purchased, the resulting index is called a _____ _____ price index.

weighted aggregate

14. If we are to weight the prices by the quantity purchased we have several options.

a. If all of the prices are weighted by the base year quantities, the resulting index is termed a _____ index.

Laspeyres index

b. If all of the prices are weighted by the reference year quantities, the resulting index is termed a _____ index.

Paasche index

c. If the base year prices are weighted by the base year quantities and the reference year prices are weighted by the reference year quantities, the resulting index is termed a _____.

mess

(Such an index would give a measure of total household expenditures in the base year, versus total household expenditures in the reference year...which would measure both price changes as well as consumption shifts. The trouble with such an index (an expenditure index) is that it measures (incorporates) the changes in two phenomena at once. Once combined, there is no way to separate the two (at least by simply looking at the one index) hence we don't know which factor is causing which result.)

15. Compute the Laspeyres Index regarding the change in prices between 1975 and 1985.

Laspeyres index = 139.8

16. Compute the Paasche Index regarding the change in prices between 1975 and 1985.

Paasche index = 143.4

17. The Paasche Index (143.4) and the Laspeyres Index (139.8) are close to each other, but relatively far from the simple index (179.2). This is due to the disproportionately large impact of which item?

the shirt

CHAPTER 17

Quantitative Business Forecasting

CHAPTER OBJECTIVES

This chapter continues the work of the previous chapters as investigates additional methods of business forecasting. These procedures include the naive method, exponential smoothing (simple, Holt's and Winter's) and autoregressive models. Linear regression procedures using time series data are discussed including using dummy variables to capture additive seasonality and lagged independent variables. By the end of the chapter you should be able to answer the following questions:

1. What is the difference between forecasting using Time Series Methods, and forecasting using Multiple Linear Regression? What are the advantages and disadvantages of each technique?

2. What is exponential smoothing and how does it work? How would you select from the various exponential smoothing models?

3. What is meant by autoregressive forecasting?

4. What are lagged variables?

5. How are dummy variables used in forecasting?

6. How are residuals examined?

272

QUANTITATIVE BUSINESS FORECASTING

§ 17.0

A Look Back/Introduction

1. In previous chapters the technique of linear regression was introduced. In linear regression, the performance of some dependent (Y) variable is predicted by a single _____ (X) variable.

independent

2. The technique of multiple linear regression was also introduced in previous chapters. Whereas simple regression posits only one independent variable as a predictor of Y, multiple regression features _____ variables as predictors of Y.

two or more

3. In many respects, time series is very similar to linear regression (especially the determination of the trend component). In time series analysis the independent variable is always _____.

time

4. In the analysis of time series, the values are decomposed into four components: _____, _____, _____, and _____.

trend, seasonality, cyclical irregular

5. When you analyze a set of time series data, and you then proceed to forecast the future values by extending the patterns exhibited previously in the data, this is called _____.

extrapolation

§ 17.1

Methods of Forecasting

1. Forecasting can be broken into two main classes: forecasts based upon past data (numbers) and forecasts not based on objective data. These two approaches can be summarized as _____ vs. _____.

qualitative vs. quantitative

2. Although they may be quite accurate, any qualitative forecast is basically. . . a guess. True or False

Alas, very true.

3. One of the more famous qualitative methods uses a panel of experts which is polled in an iterative procedure until a consensus is reached. This is the _____ method.

Delphi

4. The "Delphi" method got its name in honor of a fraternity. The originator of the technique was in the Delta Pu Phi fraternity when he was in college. True or False.

False. Named after the Oracles at Delphi in ancient Greece.

5. All objective forecasts are based upon the assumption that _____.

the patterns shown in the past will continue into the future

The Naive Forecast

§ 17.2

1. The naive forecast simply states that the best estimate of tomorrow is _____.

today

2. The advantages of the naive forecast are:
   a. _____
   b. _____
   c. _____

a. easy
b. inexpensive
c. may predict better than more complex techniques if little trend or seasonality

3. Let's look at the time series data we had used previously concerning the price index of the dollar over the last 12 years:

Year	Value
1975	134
1976	149
1977	162
1978	170
1979	181
1980	195
1981	217
1982	247
1983	282
1984	304
1985	325
1986	344

Compute the naive forecast for each of these years and compute the residuals for those yearly forecasts.

Year	Value	Naive	Res
1975	134		
1976	149	134	15
1977	162	149	13
1978	170	162	8
1979	181	170	11
1980	195	181	14
1981	217	195	22
1982	247	217	30
1983	282	247	35
1984	304	282	22
1985	325	304	21
1986	344	325	19

274

better | 4. The smaller the value of the residuals, the better/worse the fit between the actual values and the estimated values.

---

§ 17.3

trend

$\hat{Y}$ = 97.0 + 19.8(yrs)

Year	Value	Trend	Res
1975	134		
1976	149	136.6	12.4
1977	162	156.4	5.6
1978	170	176.2	-6.2
1979	181	196.0	15.0
1980	195	215.8	-20.8
1981	217	235.6	-18.6
1982	247	255.4	-8.4
1983	282	275.2	6.6
1984	304	295.0	9.0
1985	325	314.8	10.2
1986	344	334.6	9.4

210
-15.6

trend

Projecting the Least Squares Trend Equation

1. Speaking honestly, the naive forecast from above suffers because the line exhibits a strong _____ component.

2. Using the same data from above, compute the trend equation, make predictions for each year, and compute the residuals for each yearly prediction. (Hint: we did most of that in the last chapter with this same data series.)

Year	Value
1975	134
1976	149
1977	162
1978	170
1979	181
1980	195
1981	217
1982	247
1983	282
1984	304
1985	325
1986	344

3. The magnitude of the residuals provides a good measure of the closeness of the predictors to the actual values. What is the total of the residuals when the naive method is used _____? What is the total of the residuals when the least squares trend equation is used _____? On the basis of these two values, which method has provided the best estimates _____?

Time Series with Trend and Seasonality

4. In the previous chapter we used seasonal indices to deseasonalize data. In that chapter we were primarily concerned with a multiplicative structure model, and therefore, to deseasonalize actual data we _____ the actual data by the appropriate seasonal index.

divide

5. In this chapter we are concerned with making predictions. Therefore we would take our trend line value (computed on the deseasonalized values) and _____ the trend line value by the appropriate seasonal index.

multiply

Shown below are the quarterly values used in the previous chapter:

Quarter	Value
1	3
2	4
3	7
4	5
5	4
6	5
7	8
8	7
9	6
10	7
11	9
12	7
13	7
14	8
15	9
16	8

The Seasonal Indices for the various quarters were:
Q1 = .82
Q2 = .95
Q3 = 1.28
Q4 = .95

The Value of the trend equation was $\hat{Y} = 3.98 + .292(t)$

275

276

Quarter	Trend Deseasonalized
17	8.94
18	9.24
19	9.53
20	9.82
21	10.11
22	10.40
23	10.70
24	10.99

6. Using the figures from the previous page (the values for the deseasonalized trend line) compute the quarterly predictions for the next 8 quarters (quarters 17 through 24).

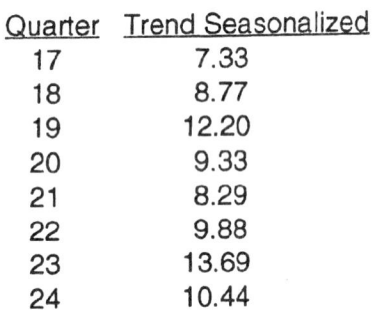

Quarter	Trend Seasonalized
17	7.33
18	8.77
19	12.20
20	9.33
21	8.29
22	9.88
23	13.69
24	10.44

7. Using the Seasonal indices for the various quarters (also provided on the previous page) seasonalize those eight quarterly predictions computed in question 11.

Trend Line and Seasonalized Values

8. Make a graph of these quarterly trend values, and the seasonally adjusted values.

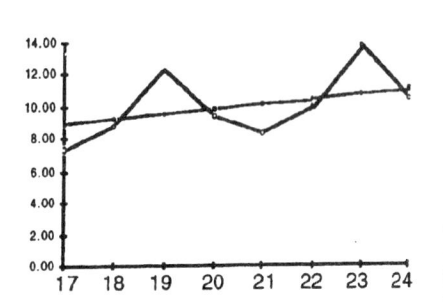

---

§ 17.4

Exponential Smoothing

1. In the previous chapter the technique of moving averages was used to provide a <u>smoothed</u> value. It was a smoothed forecast because by including values from several time periods the noise factor between periods tended to cancel, thus resulting in a _____ data series.

smoother

2. Simple exponential smoothing works quite well if there is little _____ in the data (the data series is stationary). | trend

3. In simple exponential smoothing, the value from the current time period is "smoothed" by combining it (in some manner) with the smoothed value from the _____ time period. | previous

4. The formula is _____. | $S_t = (A)Y_t + (1-A)S_{t-1}$

5. In this formula, A is the _____ _____. | smoothing constant

6. A is a percentage between _____ and _____. (A and (1-A) are very much like P and Q from the earlier chapters concerning probability.) | zero and one

7. In simplified form the exponential equation looks like this Smoothed Value = (%A)x present + (%1-A)x past.

The larger the value of A, the more weight the equation places on the _____. This would be desirable if the series is (stable/noisy (pick one)). | present value
stable

The smaller the value of A, the more weight the equation places on the _____. This would be desirable if the series is (stable/noisy (pick one)). | past values
noisy

8. Generally speaking, the larger the value of A, the better the exponential smoothing procedure will (track/smooth (pick one)). | track

The smaller the value of A, the better the exponential smoothing procedure will (track/smooth (pick one)). | smooth

Here is the data we have used previously regarding the price indices of the dollar over time.

Year	ES(.1)	ES(.5)	ES(.9)
1975	134.0	134.0	134.0
1976	135.5	141.5	147.5
1977	138.2	151.8	160.6
1978	141.3	160.9	169.1
1979	145.3	170.9	179.8
1980	150.3	183.0	193.5
1981	157.0	200.0	214.6
1982	165.9	223.5	243.8
1983	177.6	252.8	278.2
1984	190.2	278.4	301.4
1985	203.7	301.7	322.6
1986	217.7	322.8	341.9

A = .9

past
present

9. Use Exponential Smoothing to make yearly predictions. Let A = .1, .5, and .9

Year	Value
1975	134
1976	149
1977	162
1978	170
1979	181
1980	195
1981	217
1982	247
1983	282
1984	304
1985	325
1986	344

Look at the results from the exponential smoothing problem just completed, and compare them with the actual values.

Year	Actual	ES(.1)	ES(.5)	ES(.9)
1975	134	134.0	134.0	134.0
1976	149	135.5	141.5	147.5
1977	162	138.2	151.8	160.6
1978	170	141.3	160.9	169.1
1979	181	145.3	170.9	179.8
1980	195	150.3	183.0	193.5
1981	217	157.0	200.0	214.6
1982	247	165.9	223.5	243.8
1983	282	177.6	252.8	278.2
1984	304	190.2	278.4	301.4
1985	325	203.7	301.7	322.6
1986	344	217.7	322.8	341.9

10. Which value of A did the best job of tracking the decidedly upward trend evidenced by this series _____?

11. Notice how far the predicted values fell behind the actual values when the smoothing constant of .1 was used. This is because the exponential smoothing in that situation paid too much attention to the _____ values and not another attention to the _____ values.

12. (Continuing) Furthermore, because each "past" smoothed value is a function of the smoothed values that preceeded it, when the value of A is small, and the trend is noticeable, it continues to fall even further and further behind as it continues to smooth the more recent values according to the values of the past. As a matter of fact, each new smoothed value is affected by all of the past values. What we have is a weighted sum of all the previous values. The weight of each value decreases _____, which explains the source of the name.

exponentially

13. If the value of A is equal to 1.00, then exponential smoothing prediction is exactly the same as the _____, looking only at what happened in the very most recent period, with no concern with what happened previous to that.

naive

Linear Exponential Smoothing for Smoothing

§ 17.5

1. Simple Exponential Smoothing had a hard time keeping up with this data due to the strong _____.

trend

2. In order to properly account for the presence of trend in the data, the simple exponential smoothing model needs to contain a factor to handle the trend component. This is why Holt's linear exponential smoothing model is called the _____ parameter model. We now have two parameters, one to smooth the past data (as before), and a second parameter to attempt to incorporate the effect of the trend component.

two

3. In its simplest form, the model for the linear smoothing model is Y = (A)S + (B)b, where the value of the smoothed data (S) is modified by its smoothing constant _____, and the value of the trend part of the equation (b) is smoothed by its smoothing constant _____. And just as before, the value of these smoothing constants lies between _____ and _____. And as before, different coefficients can produce noticeably different results.

A
B
zero
one

280

slope

b

last

S(A=.1)	b(B=.3)	Yt
134	.00	
135.50	.45	134.0
138.56	1.23	135.95
142.81	2.14	139.79
148.55	3.22	144.95
156.09	4.52	151.77
166.25	6.21	160.61
179.91	8.44	172.46
197.72	11.25	188.36
218.48	14.10	208.97
241.82	16.88	232.58
267.23	19.44	258.70

4. (Reviewing) Let's go back a few chapters. In the simple linear regression equation (not linear exponential smoothing...just simple linear regression) we had an equation of the form Y = a + b(X). In this equation, a = the Y intercept, and b was referred to as the _____, and told us the average rate of change between each (sequential) unit of X. Thus if X increased by one unit, then the value of Y would increase by an amount equal to _____.

5. In linear exponential smoothing "b" again represents the change between units, but now it does not represent the average change between units, but instead it changes with each time period. In linear exponential smoothing, b is the difference between the smoothed value for this time period, and the smoothed value for _____ time period.

Here is the format for linear exponential smoothing.

Year	Actual	S(A=.1)	b(B=.3)	Yt
1975	134			
1976	149			
1977	162			
1978	170			
1979	181			
1980	195			
1981	217			
1982	247			
1983	282			
1984	304			
1985	325			
1986	344			

6. As mentioned in question #4, S 17.5, the selection of the values of A and B (the smoothing coefficients for the value of Y and for the slope respectively) can have a marked effect upon the results. Rework problem #5, S 17.5, but this time let A = .9 and B = .9. Once again the data and answer framework will be provided.

not enough room to get the whole year's data

Year	Actual	S(A=.9)	b(B=.9)	Yt	S(A=.9)	b(B=.9)	Yt
1975	134				134.00	.00	
1976	149				147.50	12.15	134.00
1977	162				161.77	14.05	159.65
1978	170				170.58	9.34	175.82
1979	181				180.89	10.21	179.92
1980	195				194.61	13.37	191.11
1981	217				216.10	20.68	207.98
1982	247				245.98	28.96	236.77
1983	282				281.29	34.68	274.94
1984	304				305.20	24.98	315.97
1985	325				325.52	20.79	330.18
1986	344				344.23	18.92	346.30

7. Like simple linear regression, the value of b (even though it was calculated in a different manner) gives us the ability to extrapolate the trend. If we use the linear exponential model to extrapolate to the next period only it is termed a _____ forecast. If the forecast is made "m" steps ahead it is known as a _____ forecast.

one-step ahead

m-step ahead

8. Use the values obtained in problems 35 and problems 36 to make forecasts for the next five years.

The problem would be set up as follows:

Year	Yt (A=.1,B=.3)	Yt (A=.9,B=.9)		Year	A.1,B.3	A.9,B.9
13				13	278.14	365.22
14				14	297.58	384.14
15				15	317.02	403.06
16				16	336.46	421.98
17				17	355.90	440.90

9. In these problems we simply let b=0 in the initial period, even though it starts at zero, it will soon begin to catch up to a more realistic value. However, another way to develop the starting values for b is to compute the _____ for the first few values and then use b, the regression coefficient as the value for the starting point.

regression equation

Exponential Smoothing for Trend and Seasonality | § 17.6

282

Winter's	1. If seasonal effects are also present, an extension of linear exponential smoothing known as _____ linear and seasonal exponential smoothing can be used.
smoothing	2. The Winter's method uses three parameters, that is three _____ constants.
smoothing the observations smoothing the trend smoothing the seasonality	3. The Winter's method provides smoothing constants for: _____ _____ _____

---

§ 17.7	Choosing the Appropriate Forecasting Model
False	1. There are a variety of forecasting methods, they all work equally well. True or False
False	2. Some methods **always** work better than other methods. True or False
True Remember, if you ever get a choice between smart and lucky, take lucky.	3. Sometimes, method A will work better than method B, sometimes method B will work better than A. It is almost more a matter of the data (the future) happening to match our predictions rather than our predictions brilliantly matching the future. True or False
naive	4. So, if you have two different methods, you will get two different predictions, and there is really no way of telling which one might turn out to be the better predictor. What you will probably do is to pick the one that seemed to do the better job during the most recent forecasting attempts...right? If you do that, you have actually used one of the first methods we discussed, the much-maligned _____ method. (Thinking of two predictions reminds me of the old "Chinese" proverb: "Man with one watch, know time; man with two watches, never sure.")

283

5. Previously we had used the concept of residual errors as a measure of the ability of the the model to track the data.

Three methods for measuring this residual error are suggested, the Mean Absolute Deviation (MAD), the Predictive Mean Square Error(MSE) and the Mean Absolute Percentage Error (MAPE).

Compute the Mean Absolute Deviation for the values computed in problems #5, S17.5 (A=.1,B=.3) and 36(A=.9,B=.9).
The format for the answers would be as follows:

Year	MAD(A=.1, B=.3)	MAD(A=.9,=B=.9)
1		
2		
3		
4		
5		
6		
7		
8		
9		
10		
11		
12		

MAD Values

A=.1, B.3	A=.9, B=.9
na	na
15.00	15.00
26.05	2.35
30.21	5.82
36.05	1.08
43.23	3.89
56.39	9.02
74.54	10.23
93.64	7.06
95.03	-11.97
92.42	-5.18
85.30	-2.30

6. The magnitude of these residuals is a good measure of the fit of the predictions to the actual values. What is the value of the mean absolute deviation for each of these approaches:

MAD(A=.1, B=.3) =
MAD(A=.9, B=.9) =

MAD(A=.1, B=.3) = 58.90
MAD(A=.9, B=.9) = 6.72

7. (Continuing) Looking just at the values of the MAD, what can we say about the relative tracking ability of the two approaches...that is, which set of coefficients did a better job of tracking the data _____ ?

A=.9, B=.9

No. At .9 and .9 it tracks, but does not provide much smoothing, and the whole point of exp. **smoothing,** is (obviously) **smoothing**.

PMSE Values

(A.1,B.3)	(A.9,B.9)
na	na
225.00	225.00
678.60	5.52
912.86	33.85
1299.91	1.16
1868.77	15.17
3179.83	81.39
5556.64	104.59
8769.23	49.89
9029.95	143.38
8541.26	26.82
7276.08	5.31

(A.1,B.3) = 4303.47
(A.9,B.9) = 62.92

False

large

8. (Continuing) Generally speaking, the higher the values of A and B, the better job the exponential equation will perform at tracking the data. Does this mean we should use high coefficients all of the time _____? Why not?

9. Compute the Predictive Mean Square Error for the values computed in problems 31(A=.1,B=.3) and 32(A=.9,B=.9). The format for the answers would be as follows:

Year PMSE(A.1,B.3) PMSE(A.9,B.9)
1
2
3
4
5
6
7
8
9
10
11
12

10. (Continuing) What is the value for each of the Predictive Mean Square Errors:

PMSE(A=.1, B=.3) =
PMSE(A=.9, B=.9) =

11. The predictive mean square error is a mean square error, just like the ones we studied in the analysis of variance sections, therefore we can perform an F test to determine the significance of these predictions. True or False

12. Both the Mean Average Deviation and the Predictive Mean Square Error will measure the degree to which the estimates fit the data, however, they treat the residuals differently. As a result, in certain situation, the MAD for one set of coefficients might be lower, only to find that the PMSE for that set of coefficients was higher than for the alternative coefficients. One property of the PMSE is that it accentuates the effect of _____ residuals. In other words, you might have a choice between one set of coefficients that produces many small residuals, but a few large ones too, versus a set of

coefficients that produces mostly medium sized (neither small nor large) residuals. As with so many things in forecasting, there is no right or wrong answer, it is simply a subjective choice between methods.

13. Different results can be obtained by selecting different values for the smoothing coefficients. True or False | True

14. (Continuing) Not only can different results be obtained by selecting different values for the smoothing coefficients, but success can sometimes be obtained by varying the coefficients at different times throughout the modeling process. Procedures for selecting different coefficients at different times are called _____ _____ procedures. | adaptive control

15. In the Mean Absolute Percentage Error (MAPE) method of examining the residuals, the error is expressed as a percentage of the actual value. This provides a way of expressing the error as a _____ value. | relative

16. Because the error has been expressed in relative terms, the MAPE method can be used to _____ the errors against different sets of data. | compare

17. Compute the Mean Absolute Percentage Errors for MAD values shown in problem #5, S17.7. (Hint: You will be comparing each of the two sets of MAD values against the actual values. Here are the MAD values from problem #5.)

MAD Values

A.1,B.3	A.9,B.9
na	na
15.00	15.00
26.05	2.35
30.21	-5.82
36.05	1.08
43.23	3.89
56.39	9.02
74.54	10.23
93.64	7.06
95.03	-11.97
92.42	-5.18
85.30	-2.30

MAPE Values

Qrt	A.1,B.3	A.9,B.9
1		
2	.10	.10
3	.16	.01
4	.18	.03
5	.20	.01
6	.22	.02
7	.26	.04
8	.30	.04
9	.33	.03
10	.31	.04
11	.28	.02
12	.25	.01
avg	.174	.054

286

A9, B9 You shouldn't be. These results are totally consistent with earlier techniques to examine the residuals.	18. When examined using the MAPE technique which set of coefficients has done the better job? Are you surprised at this finding?
§ 17.8	AutoRegressive Forecasting Techniques
	1. In regular, plain-vanilla, simple linear regression we posited some dependent variable as a function of a different (independent) variable (eg. Sales = advertising (sales is a function of advertising)). In time series analysis the dependent variable is seen as a function of time (eg. Sales = time). In autoregression, the dependent variable is seen as a function of the past values of _____ (eg. Sales = _____ past).
sales sales	
lagged	2. Autoregression is usually done by using multiple regression. The independent variables become 'older' as we move down the equation. $\hat{Y} = b_0 + b_1 Y(t-1) + b_2 Y(t-2) + b_3 Y(t-3)$. The independent variables are referred to as _____ variables since they lag behind the current time period.
the dollar values themselves	3. Here is the data for the dollar inflation problem with which we have been working. What would be the independent variables for a second order autoregression equation?. Fill in the data for that second order autoregression equation:

(Yt)	(Yt-1)	(Yt-2)	Year	Actual(Yt)	1st Order(Yt-1)	2nd Order(Yt-2)
134			1975	134		
149	134		1976	149		
162	149	134	1977	162		
170	162	149	1978	170		
181	170	162	1979	181		
195	181	170	1980	195		
217	195	181	1981	217		
247	217	195	1982	247		
282	247	217	1983	282		
304	282	247	1984	304		
325	304	282	1985	325		
344	325	304	1986	344		

4. Use multiple regression to find the autoregression equation for the data from the problem above.

$\hat{Y}=6.35+1.71(t-1)-.72(t-2)$

5. In addition to autoregressions, we can also find autocorrelations between the various lagged variables. The use of autocorrelations can help to uncover hidden periodicity in a data set. The dependent variable can be autocorrelated against a variety of lagged variables, when periodicity is uncovered that will show in a relatively (high/low (pick one)) value of r.

high

6 For the autoregression problem in question #3 (above) what would be the autocorrelation between:
Y(t) and Y(t-1) _____
Y(t) and Y(t-2) _____

.927
.834

7. If the data is not stationary, the nonstationarity can often be removed by taking a transformation. If the transformation is done by taking the difference between the independent variable and the various lagged variables it is called _____.

differencing

8. The nonstationarity can be removed by continuing to take differences until the autocorrelations of the new (the one figured on the differences) drops to nearly _____.

zero

9. The technique of differences can also be used to make seasonality more obvious. True or False

True

10. To illustrate how the technique of first differences can make seasonality more apparent here is the "seasonality" data with which we have been working. Find the first and second differences for this data set.

once again, not enough room, alas!

288

Value	First	Second
3		
4	-1	
7	-3	2
5	2	-5
4	1	1
5	-1	2
8	-3	2
7	1	-4
6	1	0
7	-1	2
9	-2	1
7	2	-4
7	0	2
8	-1	1
9	-1	0
8	1	-2

Quarter	Value	First Diff.	Second Diff.
1	3		
2	4		
3	7		
4	5		
5	4		
6	5		
7	8		
8	7		
9	6		
10	7		
11	9		
12	7		
13	7		
14	8		
15	9		
16	8		

Actual Values vs. First Differences

Data by Quarters

the first differences

11. Make a sketch of the original data versus the first differences. Which shows the seasonality most dramatically?

---

§ 17.9

dummy

additive

The Other Side: Linear Regression Using Times Series

1. Time series can also be performed within the multiple regression format. Seasonality and other elements can be introduced either directly or through the use of _____ variables.

2. Previously seasonality has been incorporated using a multiplicative structure model. When dummy variables are used to capture seasonality, it means that an _____ structure model is now being used.

3. If we were to once again examine the "seasonal" data set (last presented in problem #10, S17.8 we could model the seasonal variation using dummy variables, one for each quarter. Show the structure of this situation (that is, how you would code the variables):

Quarter	Value	Q1	Q2	Q3	Q4
1	3				
2	4				
3	7				
4	5				
5	4				
6	5				
7	8				
8	7				
9	6				
10	7				
11	9				
12	7				
13	7				
14	8				
15	9				
16	8				

Dummy Variables

Quarter	Q1	Q2	Q3	Q4
1	1	0	0	
2	0	1	0	
3	0	0	1	
4	0	0	0	
5	1	0	0	
6	0	1	0	
7	0	0	1	
8	0	0	0	
9	1	0	0	
10	0	1	0	
11	0	0	1	
12	0	0	0	
13	1	0	0	
14	0	1	0	
15	0	0	1	
16	0	0	0	

4. In the coding exercise from above, if you used Q4 as the base quarter you would have coded a "1" for Q1 (and its multiples), a "1" for Q2 (and its multiples) and a "1" for Q3 (and its multiples). Everything else would be zero. In addition, Q4 and its multiples would also be all _____.

zeros

5. Let's do a bit of forecasting of our own. The seasonal indices which we computed originally were:

Q1 = .82
Q2 = .95
Q3 = 1.28
Q4 = .95

The multiple regression additive model will obviously produce different values than these, but they should be in the same ballpark. Thus in comparison with Q4, the b(Q) coefficient for:

Q1 large negative

Q1 should be   a. large negative
                b. small negative
                c. near zero
                d. small positive
                e. large positive
(large and small relative to the other coefficients)

Q2 near zero

Q2 should be   a. large negative
                b. small negative
                c. near zero
                d. small positive
                e. large positive

Q3 large positive

Q3 should be   a. large negative
                b. small negative
                c. near zero
                d. small positive
                e. large positive

Q4 as base quarter
  bo = 4.00
  bt = .275
  bQ1 = -.925
  bQ2 = -.200
  bQ3 = 1.77
  bQ4 = base

6. If we compute the multiple regression solution for that equation we find the following results:
bo = _____
b(trend) = _____
b(Q1) = _____
b(Q2) = _____
b(Q3) = _____
b(Q4) = _____

7. Let's try the same dummy variable routine, only now make the first quarter the base quarter. What would be the structure of the dummy variables?

Quarter	Value	Q1	Q2	Q3	Q4
1	3				
2	4				
3	7				
4	5				
5	4				
6	5				
7	8				
8	7				
9	6				
10	7				
11	9				
12	7				
13	7				
14	8				
15	9				
16	8				

Dummy Variables

Quarter	Q1	Q2	Q3	Q4
1		0	0	0
2		1	0	0
3		0	1	0
4		0	0	1
5		0	0	0
6		1	0	0
7		0	1	0
8		0	0	1
9		0	0	0
10		1	0	0
11		0	1	0
12		0	0	1
13		0	0	0
14		1	0	0
15		0	1	0
16		0	0	1

8. If we compute the multiple regression solution for that equation we find the following results:

b_0 = _____
b(trend) = _____
b(Q1) = _____
b(Q2) = _____
b(Q3) = _____
b(Q4) = _____

Q1 as base quarter
b_0 = 3.08
bt = .275
bQ1 = base
bQ2 = .725
bQ3 = 2.70
bQ4 = .925

9. Since Q1 was the lowest quarter, all of the coefficients were _____.

higher

Q2 as base quarter

Quarter	Q1	Q2	Q3	Q4
1	1		0	0
2	0		0	0
3	0		1	0
4	0		0	1
5	1		0	0
6	0		0	0
7	0		1	0
8	0		0	1
9	1		0	0
10	0		0	0
11	0		1	0
12	0		0	1
13	1		0	0
14	0		0	0
15	0		1	0
16	0		0	1

Q2 as base quarter
bo = 3.80
btr = .275
bQ1 = -.725
bQ2 = base
bQ3 = 1.98
bQ4 = .200

10. That was so much fun, let's try another one. This time let Q2 be the base quarter.

Quarter	Value	Q1	Q2	Q3	Q4
1	3				
2	4				
3	7				
4	5				
5	4				
6	5				
7	8				
8	7				
9	6				
10	7				
11	9				
12	7				
13	7				
14	8				
15	9				
16	8				

11. If we compute the multiple regression solution for that equation we find the following results:

bo = _____
b(trend) = _____
b(Q1) = _____
b(Q2) = _____
b(Q3) = _____
b(Q4) = _____

12. Hey! We are on a roll! Now try it with Q3 as the base quarter.

(next page)

293

Quarter	Value	Dummy Variables Q1 Q2 Q3 Q4
1	3	
2	4	
3	7	
4	5	
5	4	
6	5	
7	8	
8	7	
9	6	
10	7	
11	9	
12	7	
13	7	
14	8	
15	9	
16	8	

Q3 as base quarter

Quarter	Q1	Q2	Q3	Q4
1	1	0		0
2	0	1		0
3	0	0		0
4	0	0		1
5	1	0		0
6	0	1		0
7	0	0		0
8	0	0		1
9	1	0		0
10	0	1		0
11	0	0		0
12	0	0		1
13	1	0		0
14	0	1		0
15	0	0		0
16	0	0		1

13. If we compute the multiple regression solution for that equation we find the following results:

bo = _____
b(trend) = _____
b(Q1) = _____
b(Q2) = _____
b(Q3) = _____
b(Q4) = _____

Q3 as base quarter
bo   = 5.78
btr   = .275
bQ1   = -2.70
bQ2   = -1.98
bQ3   = base
bQ4   = -1.77

14. Since Q3 was the quarter with the highest seasonal index, each of the coefficients for the other quarters was (higher/lower).

lower

Because each of these multiple regression runs was marking the strength of the quarters relative to each other, noticeable similarities can be observed.

15. What value did each of the multiple regressions find for the b coefficient for the trend equation _____?

b(trend) = .275

16. Other similarities are also apparent:
When Q4 is the base, the value for Q3 is _____.
When Q3 is the base, the value for Q4 is _____.
When Q1 is the base, the value for Q2 is _____.
When Q2 is the base, the value for Q1 is _____.

+1.77
-1.77
+.725
-.725

lagged	17. Sometimes economic events have a definite relationship to each other, but it is not a concurrent relationship...one activity tends to lag behind the other activity. For instance, the actual construction of a building lags many months, even years behind the application for the building permit (although the building permit remains a good indicator of what is coming). Sometimes you may wish to "line-up" variables, not with current time period activity, but with the activity several periods behind. The use of a variable in such a manner is called a _____ variable.
§ 17.10	AutoCorrelation and the Durbin-Watson Statistic
autocorrelation	1. One problem with autoregression is that the independent variables are not independent of each other. When the independent variables are not independent of each other (whether it occurred in an autoregression analysis or not) the variables are said to be _____.
Durbin-Watson	2. Testing for autocorrelation is done with the use of the _____ statistic.
zero four	3. The value of the Durbin-Watson statistic ranges between _____ and _____.
positive too close	4. A value close to zero indicates (positive / negative) autocorrelation. This means that the values of the residuals are (too close/too far) from each other.
negative too far	5. A value close to four indicates (positive/ negative) autocorrelation. This means that the values of the residuals are (too close/too far) from each other.
two	6. The ideal value for the Durbin-Watson statistic is _____.

7. The table of Critical Values of the Durbin-Watson statistic is concerned with testing for positive autocorrelation. You may recall in hypothesis testing, we had two choices, reject and fail to reject. Of these two choices, fail to reject was pretty inconclusive result. But the Durbin-Watson test gets even more inconclusive than that.
*If the value is sufficiently low you can reject.
*If the value is sufficiently near 2.00 you can fail to reject.
*But if the value is in the midrange, you can't do either of those!

The value of "k" represents the _____ in the regression equation.

number of predictors

8. For the multiple regression analysis involving the dummy variables and the prediction of the seasonal indices, k would be equal to _____, and n would be equal to _____. The .05 Durbin-Watson statistic gives the following upper and lower limits: _____ and _____.

4
16

74 <=> 1.93

9. The multiple regression analysis provided a value of the Durbin-Watson statistic of 1.34. What would be our conclusion?

Alas, our rather weak conclusion, is no conclusion...can't even fail to reject.

CHAPTER 18

Decision Making Under Uncertainty

CHAPTER OBJECTIVES

The objective of this chapter is to introduce the topic of how to mathematically approach a decision which must be made under conditions of uncertainty. Although no amount of analysis can remove the element of uncertainty, at least it can be treated in an objective and analytical manner. This involves structuring a decision problem into various actions under consideration and states of nature describing the uncertain future, as well as the use of utility values. Decision trees and the use of posterior or revised probabilities is also discussed. By the end of the chapter you should be able to:

1. Define a decision problem in terms of actions and states of nature.

2. Compute profit tables, incorporate subjective probabilities, compute expected profits and losses and conduce sensitivity analysis.

3. Make decisions using Minimax, Maximax, and Largest Expected Value criterions.

4. Compute revised probabilities using decision trees and Bayes' Theorem as well as compute the expected value of perfect information (EVPI) and the value of sample information (EVSI).

298

DECISION MAKING UNDER UNCERTAINTY

§ 18.0

A Look Back/Introduction

1. We have already looked at decision making when we performed statistical tests of hypotheses. In these tests we would decide to either _____ or _____ the null hypothesis.

reject, fail to reject

2. These tests looked only at the _____ (related to probability) aspects of the decision making, those tests did not look at the dollar values of the situations.

probabalistic

§ 18.1

Defining the Decision Problem

1. Decision problems are generally defined along two dimensions. One dimension represents the choices you can make and is referred to as _____. The other dimension represents the things that can happen to you, the fates or outcomes that possibly await your choices. These are referred to as the _____.

actions

states of nature

2. It is assumed that only one of the states of nature will occur, that is to say, the states are mutually _____.

exclusive

3. A table which shows the expected profit (or loss) that is associated with each action and its interaction with each state of nature is called a _____ _____.

payoff table

4. In most payoff tables, the optimal course of action will change depending upon which state of nature actually occurs. True or False

True

Consider the following situation: A student club is brewing coffee. It costs them $2.00 for each pot of coffee that they brew. They sell each pot of coffee for $3.00. Assume that they have the potential to brew up to four pots of coffee, and that the students (depending largely upon the day of the week and the weather) will buy from one to four pots. Fill in the pay-off table

PAYOFF TABLE

Actions	States of Nature 1	2	3	4		1	2	3	4
Make One						1.00	1.00	1.00	1.00
Make Two						-1.00	2.00	2.00	2.00
Make Three						-3.00	.00	3.00	3.00
Make Four						-5.00	-2.00	1.00	4.00

5. Suppose that you were able to estimate demand using the weather report and you "knew" that the demand would be for 2 pots of coffee. What would be your optimal action _____?

make two

6. What action could provide us with the largest possible gain _____? Since this is the largest possible gain, why do we not select this option every time?

make four
also largest loss

Decision Strategies

§ 18.2

1. The first step towards performing the Minimax strategy is to create the opportunity loss table. This is done by subtracting the values in each state of nature from the _____ value for that state of nature.

largest

(next page)

300

	1	2	3	4
	.00	1.00	2.00	3.00
	2.00	.00	1.00	2.00
	4.00	2.00	.00	1.00
	6.00	4.00	2.00	.00

3.00
2.00
4.00
6.00

$2.00
two

false

make one

largest

OPPORTUNITY LOSS TABLE

States of Nature

Actions	1	2	3	4
Make One				
Make Two				
Make Three				
Make Four				

2. (Continuing with the Minimax Solution) Now that the table of losses has been constructed, the table is searched to find the largest value (which is an opportunity loss) in each row. Thus the losses would be:
Make One =
Make Two =
Make Three =
Make Four =

3. Now we select the minimum of these maximum losses. The minimum opportunity loss would be _____, which suggests that we should make _____ pots.

4. An opportunity loss is just like any other kind of loss, you incurred a negative balance and now you have to pay back a debt. True or False

5. Actually, the action which would incur the possibility of the least real loss would be to _____.

6. The Maximax strategy simply takes the action which has the possibility of the _____ payoff.

7. In this case the largest possible profit would be _____ which would suggest that they make _____ pots.

$4.00
four pots

8. The Minimax is a (conservative/risky (pick one)) strategy.

conservative

9. The Maximax is a (conservative/risky (pick one)) strategy.

risky

10. The strategic approach to decision making is to attempt to incorporate the probability of the various events occurring. That is, to make specific statements about the probabilities of the various states of nature. Two ways were suggested for determining these probabilities:
   a. _____
   b. _____

empirical
subjective

11. A "subjective probability" is actually just a fancy name for a plain, old _____.

guess

Using the expected payoff method, we multiply the cell values in the payoff table times the expected probabilities (states of nature probabilities). This gives the expected value for each cell. The expected value for each action is determined by summing the values for the various states of nature. Compute the expected value payoff table.

Suppose that the weather report predicted warm weather for the day (thus depressing coffee sales):

Thus the Probabilities for the states of Nature would be:
  sell 1 = .50
  sell 2 = .30
  sell 3 = .20
  sell 4 = .00

(next page)

	1	2	3	4
	.50	.30	.20	.00
	.50	.60	.40	.00
	-1.50	.00	.60	.00
	-2.50	-.60	.20	.00

$ 1.00 Make One Pot
$ .50
$ -.90
$-2.90

	1	2	3	4
	.00	.20	.30	.50
	.00	.40	.60	1.00
	.00	.00	.90	1.50
	00	-.40	.30	2.00

EXPECTED PAYOFF TABLE (Warm Weather)

States of Nature

Actions	1(.50)	2(.30)	3(.20)	4(.00)
Make One				
Make Two				
Make Three				
Make Four				

12. What would be the expected value for each of the various actions, and state the optimal decision.

Make One   =
Make Two   =
Make Three =
Make Four =

Suppose they now expect cold weather (probabilities reversed):

EXPECTED PAYOFF TABLE (Cold Weather)

States of Nature

Actions	1(.00)	2(.20)	3(.30)	4(.50)
Make One				
Make Two				
Make Three				
Make Four				

13. Continuing the cold weather problem, what would be the expected value for each of the various actions, and state the optimal decision.

Make One = $ 1.00
Make Two = $ 2.00
Make Three = $ 2.40   Make 3 pots
Make Four = $ 1.90

And finally, suppose that you really have no idea what the weather will be, so you select a value of .25 for each of the four states of nature. Compute the expected pay-off table.

EXPECTED PAYOFF TABLE (Unknown Weather)

Actions	1(.25)	2(.25)	3(.25)	4(.25)		1	2	3	4
Make One						.25	.25	.25	.25
Make Two						-.25	.50	.50	.50
Make Three						-.75	.00	.75	.75
Make Four						-1.25	-.50	.25	1.00

14. Continuing with the problem of the unknown weather, what would be the expected value for each of the various actions, and state the optimal decision.

Make One = $ 1.00
Make Two = $ 1.25   Make 2 Pots
Make Three = $ .75
Make Four = $ -.50

15. So, we can see that the analysis is very sensitive to the probabilities that are selected. If we use the cold weather probabilities we would decide to _____. If we use the warm weather probabilities we would decide to _____. If we go with the "weather unknown" probabilities we would decide to _____.

Make 3
Make 1

Make 2

304

Any of these expected value payoff tables could be converted to opportunity loss tables simply by taking the largest value for each state of nature and subtracting the other values under that state of nature from that largest value.

OPPORTUNITY LOSS
EXPECTED PAYOFF TABLE (Unknown Weather)

		States of Nature		
Actions	1(.25)	2(.25)	3(.25)	4(.25)
Make One				
Make Two				
Make Three				
Make Four				

	1	2	3	4
	.00	.25	.50	.75
	.50	.00	.25	.50
	1.00	.50	.00	.25
	1.50	1.00	.50	.00

16. For each action, we must now find the maximum opportunity loss:
Make One   =
Make Two   =
Make Three =
Make Four =

.75
.50
1.00
1.50

17. Since the Minimax strategy takes the minimum of the maximum opportunity losses, the minimax strategy would be to _____.

Make 2 pots

18. Another strategy sometimes used is the Maximin strategy. The maximin strategy examines the minimum payoff for each action and selects the action having the maximum of these minimum payoffs. Returning to the table used in problem 20 (expected value, uncertain weather) what would be the minimum gain for each of these actions:
Make One   =
Make Two   =
Make Three =
Make Four =

.25
-.25
-.75
-1.25

19. Using the Maximin strategy our decision would be to _____. | Make 1 pot

20. Both Minimax and Maximin are very (conservative/ risky) strategies which are more concerned with avoiding a loss than they are with making a gain. | conservative

---

Sensitivity Analysis

21. As we have already seen (especially problem 21,) the selection of values for the various states of nature can decidedly influence the action that is selected.

Sensitivity analysis is the deliberate examination and manipulation of these probabilities to determine how "sensitive" the decision is to a change in the probabilities.

One problem with alternative scenarios is that with even a limited number of states of nature (ie 4) you an quickly run into dozens...even thousands of possible scenarios.

Suppose that our coffee merchant was still trying to decide whether to make one pot of coffee or four, but now he is in a miserable climate where it is either very hot (sell 1) or very cold (see 4), and nothing in between. Develop the expected payoff tables for the following ranges of values (you fill in the actions columns).

States of Nature		Actions			
S1	S2	Make 1	Make 2	Make 3	Make 4
.9	.1				
.8	.2				
.7	.3				
.6	.4				
.5	.5				
.4	.6				
.3	.7				
.2	.8				
.1	.9				

	1	2	3	4
.9/.1	1.00	-.70	-2.40	-4.10
.8/.2	1.00	-.40	-1.80	-3.20
.7/.3	1.00	-.10	-1.20	-2.30
.6/.4	1.00	.20	-.60	-1.40
.5/.5	1.00	.50	.00	-.50
.4/.6	1.00	.80	.60	.40
.3/.7	1.00	1.10	1.20	1.30
.2/.8	1.00	1.40	1.80	2.20
.1/.9	1.00	1.70	2.40	3.10

306

hot
six out of nine
three out of nine
none of the nine

risk

$\mu_i = p_i x_i$

$\sigma^2 = \Sigma x^2 p - \mu^2$

.00
1.69
6.12
11.25

22. Looking at the "Actions" table you have created several things seem apparent. If S1 represents the hot and S2 represents the cold, the actions seem to be more heavily skewed toward favoring the _____. Make 1 won _____ out of 9 times, Make 4 won _____ out of 9 times, Make 2 and Make 3 were the suggested action _____.

23. In addition to varying in expected value, the different actions often vary in terms of the amount of risk that they incur. The greater the variance in an action, the greater the _____.

24. Thus the expected payoff for a given action is _____ (give formula).
And the risk associated with that action is _____ (give formula).

25. Compute the variances for each action in the expected payoff table - unknown weather (originally presented in problem 13, § 18.2).
Make One =
Make Two =
Make Three =
Make Four =

26. Actually, the computation of the variance is an expenditure of more statistical firepower than might have been required to perform this risk analysis. Here is the original payoff table:

PAYOFF TABLE

Actions	States of Nature			
	1	2	3	4
Make One	$1.00	$1.00	$1.00	$1.00
Make Two	-$1.00	$2.00	$2.00	$2.00
Make Three	-$3.00	.00	$3.00	$3.00
Make Four	-$5.00	-$2.00	$1.00	$4.00

Just 'eyeballing' the actions, what would be the ranges for each of these actions?
  Make One   =
  Make Two   =
  Make Three =
  Make Four   =

1 to 1	= 0
-1 to 2	= 3
-3 to 3	= 6
-5 to 4	= 9

27. On the basis of these ranges, which action is the most risky _____? the least risky _____?

risky? make 4
safe? make 1
obvious, huh?

28. Although the examination of the variance may seem simplistic, it can point to good combinations of payoff and risk. Looking at the variances, the action to make _____ (pots) shows the best combination of risk and payoff.

two

29. An action is said to be dominated if for every state of nature, there is another action which has a larger payoff for each and everyone of those states. True or False.

true

30. Another way to describe what has happened in the case of a dominated action is to say that the particular action in question is _____, because it will never be 'admitted' to the group of 'best' actions.

inadmissible

31. Looking at the payoff table (warm weather) why did we not remove column four (customers buy four) since that whole column was zero, and obviously dominated by column three (#11, § 18.2)?

"Dominated" is concerned with the removal of actions, not states of nature...you have the choice of carrying an umbrella or not, you don't have the option of choosing whether it will rain or not.

32. Let's look at that table from #11 § 18.2, the warm weather payoff table.

308

PAYOFF TABLE - Warm Weather

	States of Nature			
Actions	1(.50)	2(.30)	3(.20)	4(.00)
Make One	$1.00	$1.00	$1.00	$1.00
Make Two	-$1.00	$2.00	$2.00	$2.00
Make Three	-$3.00	.00	$3.00	$3.00
Make Four	-$5.00	-$2.00	$1.00	$4.00

If you had perfect information, that means that you would know (in advance) what the state of nature would be:
Customers will buy one, so you would _____ for a profit of _____, or
Customers will buy two, so you would _____ for a profit of _____.

Make one
$1.00
Make two
$2.00

33. The values associated with operating under perfect information will usually be found around the diagonal of the payoff matrix (they will be precisely down the diagonal if the payoff features a matching number of states of nature and actions). The expected value under certainty is found by taking each optimal action times its probability of occurrence. Thus:
$1.00 x .50 = _____
$2.00 x .30 = _____
$3.00 x .20 = _____
TOTAL   = _____

.50
.50
.60
1.70

34. The expected value of perfect information is the value under certainty (from problem #33) minus the best we could do under uncertainty (from problem #13, § 18.2). In this case _____ minus _____ equals _____. In other words, even on "warm weather" days there is noticeable differences in consumption. If someone could offer you a better (perfect) forecast, you could pay up to _____ for this forecast. But of course their information will probably be less than perfect, hence you should pay even less than the theoretical upper limit of 70 cents.

$1.70-1.00 = .70

70 cents

The Concept of Utility

§ 18.3

1. We have investigated payoff matrices strictly from the standpoint of payoff. And we have investigated matrices strictly from the standpoint of risk. In an effort to measure both the payoff and and risk we use the concept of _____ values.

utility

2. Previously we have introduced the use of subjective information in the selection of the states of nature probabilities. We again must use subjective information in the formation of the utility table. Rather than "hard" data, the utility table simply represents your _____ toward the various events.

preference

3. The formation of the utility starts with the arbitrary assignment of end values for the largest and smallest values in the payoff table. Although it is the relative values of the utilities that matters, the book suggests using a utility value of _____ for the smallest value, and a utility value of _____ for the largest value.

0(zero)
100

Consider the problem of our coffee merchant who is operating in the face of uncertain weather. Should he gamble, or should he play it safe? The expected value is one way to approach the problem, but what about his intrinsic attitude toward risk? Here is the original payoff table:

PAYOFF TABLE - Uncertain Weather

Actions	States of Nature			
	1(.25)	2(.25)	3(.25)	4(.25)
Make One	$1.00	$1.00	$1.00	$1.00
Make Two	-$1.00	$2.00	$2.00	$2.00
Make Three	-$3.00	.00	$3.00	$3.00
Make Four	-$5.00	-$2.00	$1.00	$4.00

310

-$5.00
$4.00

4. The utility value of zero would be given to what value _____? The utility value of 100 would be given to what value _____?

5. Utility values must be provided for you since they are (theoretically) totally subjective values:
-5.00 = 0
-3.00 = 5
-2.00 = 10
-1.00 = 15
 .00 = 25
1.00 = 40
2.00 = 55
3.00 = 70
4.00 = 100

If this seems confusing (especially the negative numbers) add 5.00 to all of the numbers. That would produce the following:
 .00 = 0
2.00 = 5
3.00 = 10
4.00 = 15
5.00 = 25
6.00 = 40
7.00 = 55
8.00 = 70
9.00 = 100

6. Make a graph of the utility curve for this situation.

Based upon the information and the graph, is this person a (risk taker/risk averter)?

Utility Curve

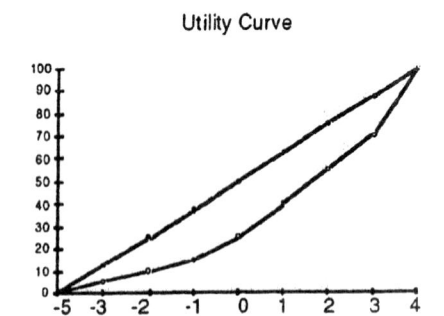

risk taker

Shown is the utility table, with the utilities substituted for the payoffs.

UTILITY TABLE - Uncertain Weather

Actions	States of Nature			
	1(.25)	2(.25)	3(.25)	4(.25)
Make One	40	40	40	40
Make Two	15	55	55	55
Make Three	5	25	70	70
Make Four	0	10	40	100

7. Compute the expected utility for each action:
Make One   =
Make Two   =
Make Three =
Make Four =

Utility Values
40.0
45.0, therefore, Make Two
42.5
37.5

Suppose that the utilities had been as follows:
-5.00 =   0
-3.00 = 30
-2.00 = 50
-1.00 = 65
 .00 = 75
1.00 = 85
2.00 = 90
3.00 = 95
4.00 = 100

312

Utility Curve

risk averter

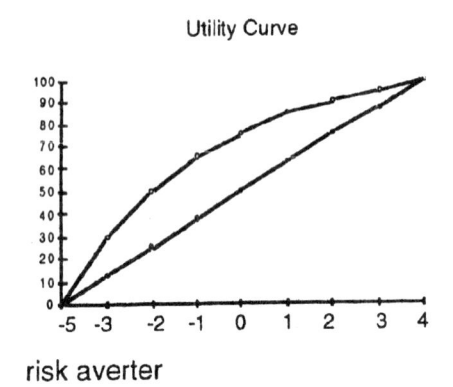

8. Make a graph of the utility curve for these revised utility values.

Based upon the information and the graph, is this person a (risk taker/risk averter)?

Shown is the utility table, with the utilities substituted for the payoffs.

UTILITY TABLE - Uncertain Weather

Actions	1(.25)	2(.25)	3(.25)	4(.25)
Make One	85	85	85	85
Make Two	65	90	90	90
Make Three	30	75	95	95
Make Four	0	50	85	100

States of Nature

9. Compute the expected utility for each action:
Make One =
Make Two =
Make Three =
Make Four =

85.00, therefore, Make One
83.75
73.75
58.75

Decision Trees and Bayes' Rule   § 18.4

1. A schematic representation of a sequence of decisions is referred to as a _____ diagram.

    decision tree

2. In a decision tree, situations that represent a decision are represented by a _____, and situations that are strictly the result of chance are represented by a _____.

    box
    circle

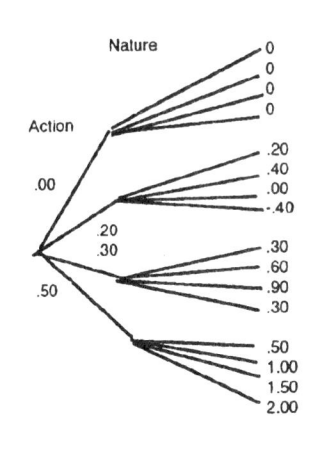

3. Structure the coffee problem as a decision tree. (For a change, use the cold weather state of nature probabilities.)

4. A method for computing revised or posterior probabilities was originated by the English clergyman _____.

    Thomas Bayes

5. The formula for Bayes' Theorem is P(A|B) = _____.

    $$P(A|B) = \frac{P(A)P(B|A)}{P(B)}$$

6. Looking back at the various tables we see the following facts regarding the possibility of selling four pots of coffee given various weather conditions
P(sell four|warm weather) = .00
P(sell four|uncertain weather) = .25
P(sell four|cold weather) = .50

Now suppose that an empirical study of the weather on a certain day documents the following probabilities:
P(warm weather) = .40
P(uncertain weather) = .40
P(cold weather) = .20

314

.20

$\dfrac{.10}{.20} = .50$

Bayes' Theorem is designed to answer the following question: We have sold four pots of coffee, what is the probability that it was a cold day? The prior probability of a cold day was _____. However, we now can construct the following chart:

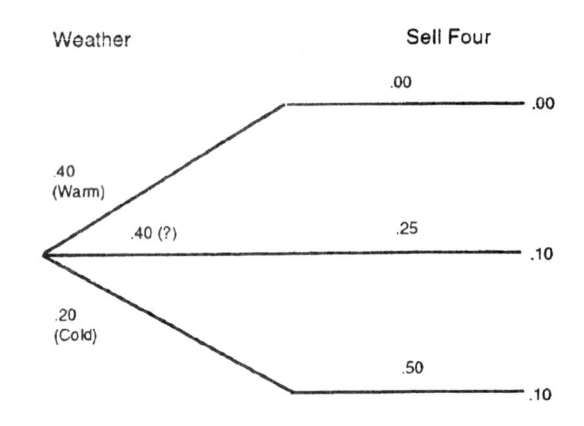

```
Weather                    Sell Four
                      .00
            ──────────────────── .00
      .40
     (Warm)
            .40 (?)    .25
     ──────────────────── .10
      .20
     (Cold)
                      .50
            ──────────────────── .10
```

Using the tree diagram, what is the revised probability that it was a cold day?

Previously we were given the following prior probabilities regarding the expected sales when the weather is uncertain:
P(sell one) = .25
P(sell two) = .25
P(sell three) = .25
P(sell four) = .25

We now contract with an expensive marketing consultant who presents the following "track record" of his predictions on uncertain weather days:

Consultant Predicted	Actually Occurred			
	1	2	3	4
Sell 1	.70	.20	.10	.00
Sell 2	.10	.60	.10	.10
Sell 3	.10	.20	.50	.20
Sell 4	.10	.10	.20	.60

Suppose that the weather is uncertain, but the consultant is predicting that three pots will be sold.

7. Now we need to revise our state of nature probabilities on the basis of this new information.
P(sell 1) =
P(sell 2) =
P(sell 3) =
P(sell 4) =

revised probabilities
P(sell 1) = .11
P(sell 2) = .22
P(sell 3) = .55
P(sell 4) = .22

What is needed is a new payoff table using these revised probabilities.

EXPECTED PAYOFF TABLE (Unknown Weather)

Actions	**States of Nature** Revised Probabilities				1	2	3	4
	1(.11)	2(.22)	3(.55)	4(.22)				
Make One					.11	.22	.55	.22
Make Two					-.11	.44	1.10	.44
Make Three					-.33	.00	1.65	.66
Make Four					-.55	-.44	.55	.88

8. Now what would be the expected values for each of the actions?
Make One =
Make Two =
Make Three =
Make Four =

1.10
1.87
1.98 Make Three pots
 .44

316

1.00
1.25 former decision
 .75
-.50

make two, now make three

| 9. Find the expected values from the original analysis, we had:
Make One   =
Make Two   =
Make Three =
Make Four =

10. This would imply that we should observe a shift in strategy from making _____ to making _____.

CHAPTER 19

Nonparametric Statistics

CHAPTER OBJECTIVES

In the course of this study, a variety of statistical methods have been presented. As frequently mentioned, however, many of these techniques rely upon certain assumptions regarding the population. This chapter presents methods called nonparametric tests which do not rely upon such assumptions. These tests include the runs test for randomness, the Mann-Whitney test for two independent groups, the Kruskal-Wallis test for more than two groups, the Wilcoxon and Friedman tests for paired or dependent samples, and the Spearman rank-order correlation. By the end of this chapter you should be able to answer the following questions:

1. What is meant by nonparametric statistics? Why are nonparametric tests necessary?

2. What is the "Runs Test"? How is it used?

3. What is the "Mann-Whitney U Test? How is it used?

4. What is the "Wilcoxon Signed Rank Test"? How is it used?

5. What is the "Kruskal-Wallis Test"? How is it used?

6. What is the "Friedman Test"? How is it used?

6. What is "Spearman Rank Correlation"? How is it used?

318 NONPARAMETRIC STATISTICS

§ 19.0 A Look Back/Introduction

1. Many of the tests of hypothesis with which we have dealt in this study of statistics have been concerned with the value of a parameter (such as the population mean or variance). Hence these tests are referred to as _____ tests.

parametric

2. A serious problem with many of these parametric tests is that they rely upon certain assumptions regarding the 'parent' population. One of the most common assumptions is the assumption of _____.

normality

3. Many times, the nonparametric test will not deal with a data set in its original units. Rather it will compare each item with the other items and _____ each item based upon its position relative to the other items.

rank

4. Ranked data is (nominal/ordinal/interval/ratio) in strength.

ordinal

5. As suggested from the problem above, since most nonparametric tests work with ordinal data, that means that nonparametric tests do not require data of the same strength that the parametric tests require. Most parametric tests require that the data be _____ data.

ratio

6. The disadvantage of using data which has been converted from its original units of measure to its rankings is that (as ordinal data) you are using a _____ form of data.

weaker

§ 19.1 The Runs Test

1. One of the key assumptions in many statistical tests is the notion of randomness. Randomness means that there is no readily apparent pattern to the numbers or errors. True or False

True

2. Numbers or errors should 'oscillate' back and forth, but not on a predictable basis. Both too much oscillation and too little oscillation are undesirable. True or False

True

SMALL SAMPLES

1. Professor Blowhard claims that his early upbringing as a farmboy has never left him...that he still likes to "get up with the cows", that his rising is independent of the days. You think that he is bluffing, so you hide in the bushes outside his house to see what time he comes into breakfast each morning. You record the following times (AM): 6:45, 6:37. 6:41, 6:24, 6:52, 7:48, 8:02. This comes out to an average morning breakfast appearance of _____. (Remember, you are averaging 60 minute hours, scale is not 100.) Use the symbols of E (for early) and L (for late) to mark the runs for this situation _____.

7:01

E E E E E L L

2. (Continuing) How many runs do we see in this sequence _____?

2

3. What is the value of n1 _____? What is the value of n2 _____? What is the probability of seeing only two runs _____?

$n_1 = 2$
$n_2 = 5$
$P(2\ runs) = .095$

4. What is your conclusion about Professor Blowhard?

Looks like he is sleeping in on the weekend. Waking is determined by work schedule, not by internal rhythms.

LARGE SAMPLES

1. Suspicions aroused, you now wish to monitor Professor Blowhard in the classroom. The question is: does he keep the students for the full period, or does he let them go early. Class begins on Wednesday and you keep records for the semester. The following results are found: (F = full class, S = short class)

F S F F S F F S F F S F F S F F S F F S F F S F F S F F
S F F S F F S F F S F F

320

14
29
29

19.89
2.83
Z = 3.2
therefore, stat. sig. diff - not a random sequence, short classes only on Friday

Of the total of 43 class periods, n1(S) = _____, and n2(F) = _____. The number of runs in this series is _____.

2. (Continuing) The expected number of runs is _____. The standard deviation for the number of runs is _____. The Z value is _____. What is your conclusion about Professor Blowhard.

3. Autocorrelation can be a major problem with many types of analysis. The runs test can provide a means of examining the residuals that result from a regression equation.

Here are the results from the "naive" trend predictions from #3, § 17.2, along with the residuals from those predictions:

Year	Value	Naive	Residual
1975	134		
1976	149	134	15
1977	162	149	13
1978	170	162	8
1979	181	170	11
1980	195	181	14
1981	217	195	22
1982	247	217	30
1983	282	247	35
1984	304	282	22
1985	325	304	21
1986	344	325	19

Can't do it!
No runs at all!

Analyze these residuals using the runs test. What is your conclusion?

4. (Continuing) That was a bit sneaky, and that model was (as mentioned at the time) simply not adequate to keep up with the rapidly climbing trend. Later, from #2, § 17.3 another attempt was made to make predictions, but this time a regression trend line was incorporated. That analysis produced the following set of predictions and residuals:

Year	Value	Trend	Residual
1975	134		
1976	149	136.6	12.4
1977	162	156.4	5.6
1978	170	176.2	-6.2
1979	181	196.0	15.0
1980	195	215.8	-20.8
1981	217	235.6	-18.6
1982	247	255.4	-8.4
1983	282	275.2	6.6
1984	304	295.0	9.0
1985	325	314.8	10.2
1986	344	334.6	9.4

Analyze the residuals using the runs test. In this situation n1 = _____, n2 = _____, and there are _____ runs. The probability associated with 5 runs is _____. Our conclusion would be:

n1 = 4
n2 = 7
5 runs
P(5 runs) = .333
no stat. sig. diff.
residuals seem acceptable

5. The runs test for autocorrelation of the residuals is the nonparametric version of which parametric test?

Durbin-Watson

6. Assuming that all of the assumptions have been met for each test, which test would be preferable (the runs test or the Durbin Watson test)? Why?

Durbin-Watson is more powerful, it uses more of the data.

Nonparametric Tests of Central Tendency

§ 19.2

1. One of the main assumptions of most statistical tests is that the populations are normal. One of the advantages of nonparametric tests is that the shape of the underlying distribution is of no concern. True or False

True

2. Another advantage to the nonparametric tests is that they do not require that the data be as "strong" as with the parametric tests. Most parametric tests require that the data be at least interval. Many nonparametric tests can work with ordinal, or even nominal data. True or False

True

322

dependent or paired

3. Sometimes samples are collected in such a way that the items from one sample are related (or matched) with the items from the other sample. When the samples are matched in some way they are said to be _____ or _____.

independent

4. When the two samples are not related, they are said to be _____.

independent

5. The Mann-Whitney U Test is a nonparametric test designed for situations involving _____ samples.

paired

6. The Wilcoxon Signed Rank Test is a nonparametric test designed for situations involving _____ samples.

THE MANN-WHITNEY U TEST

medians

1. The Mann-Whitney U test can be used to test for significant difference between two means, or two _____.

rankings

2. Like many nonparametric tests, the Mann-Whitney U test does not work with the data in its original form, but rather it converts the data to a set of _____, and then works with these rankings.

average

3. When ranking a set of data, if two (or more) items "tie" for a given spot, then each item is assigned the _____ of those spots.

3.5   ((3+4)/2=3.5)

4. (Continuing) For instance, if 1st place had been taken, and 2nd place had been taken, and then two items had tied for 3rd place, then these two items would each be assigned the value of _____.

6.0   ((5+6+7)/3=6.0)

5. (Continuing) In problem four, we have now assigned values to four items. Suppose that three items now tie for that 5th spot. Each of the three would be assigned the value of _____.

Mann-Whitney U test for SMALL Samples

Consider this list of students and their grades on the first exam (their names have obviously been shortened to preserve anonymity).

Student	Grade
Ch	92
Co	90
Ja	95
Jo	85
Le	85
Li	85
Lu	86
Mo	95
Pu	83
Ra	88
Ro	75
Sa	95
Sm	87
So	75
St	84
Ta	84
Th	78
Wi	50

Just glancing over the list, the instructor has suspicions that the first half of the list did better than the second half.

Divide the group in half (Ch-Pu) vs. (Ra-Wi) and test for significant difference using the Mann-Whitney U test.

1. For the problem of the grade distribution just presented, what would be the ranks for each half (Ch-Pu) and (Ra-Wi)?

Rank Ch-Pu	Rank Ra-Wi
2	
2	
	2
4	
5	
	6
	7
8	
10	
10	
10	
	12.5
	12.5
14	
	15
	16.5
	16.5
	18

324
T1 = 65
T2 = 106

U1 = 61
U2 = 20

N1 = 9
N2 = 9
U = 20
p = .0217
stat sig diff
 reject null, is a diff

- -

normally

True

2. What would be the values for T1 and T2?

3. What would be the values for U1 and U2?

4. In obtaining the value from the tables, what is the value of n1 _____? What is the value of n2 _____? What is the value of U _____? What is the distribution value from the table _____? What is your conclusion?

- -

Mann-Whitney Test for LARGE Samples

1. In the Mann-Whitney test for large samples, a statistic is produced that is approximately _____ distributed.

2. In order to use the normal curve (the Z values from the table in the back of the book) we need to know only three things:
   a. the distribution is normally distributed
   b. the mean
   c. the standard deviation
True or False

(Due to space, the problem begins on the next page.)

Consider the Quiz One results from these two classes:

Class One	Class Two		Rank Class One	Rank C. Two
74	30			1
48	60			2
51	56		4	
64	48			4
68	51			4
40	44			7.50
39	35		7.50	
42	79			7.50
40	38			7.50
66	72		10.50	
53	68			10.50
53	60		12	
56	62		13	
45	33		14.50	
34	52			14.50
40	62			16
34	74			18.00
18	50			18.00
41	87			18.00
36	52			20.50
41	29			20.50
21	42			22.50
53	49		22.50	
55	64			24.50
36	58		24.50	
72	63		26	
50	72		27.50	
44	62			27.50
39	72		30.00	
58	50		30.00	
31	24		30.00	
54	74			33.00
50	48			33.00
52	54		33.00	
44			35.50	
48				35.50
67				39.00
42			39.00	
50			39.00	
39				39.00
49			39.00	
32				42.50
			42.50	
			45.50	
				45.50
				45.50

1. Determine the rankings for each group:

(Rankings Continued)

325

326

45.50	
48	
	50.00
50.00	
50.00	
53.00	
	53.00
53.00	
55.50	
55.50	
58.00	
58.00	
58.00	
61.00	
61.00	
61.00	
	63
64.50	
64.50	
	66
67.50	
67.50	
	69
70	
71	
	72
	73
	74
75	
76	

$n_1 = 42$
$n_2 = 34$

2. What are the values for n1 and n2?

$T_1 = 1849$
$T_2 = 1077$

3. What are the values for T1 and T2?

$U = 714$
$\sigma = 95.72$

4. What is the value for U, and for the standard deviation of U?

$U_1 = 482$
$Z = -2.42$

5. What is the value for U1, and what is the Z value associated with this value of U1?

6. What is the value for U2, and what is the Z value associated with this value of U2? (Note the Z values better be the same, just with opposite sign.)

U2 = 1077
Z = +2.42

7. What is your conclusion based upon these Z values?

statistically significant difference
groups are different

Wilcoxon Signed Rank Test for Paired Samples

1. The Mann-Whitney test assumes independent samples, but the Wilcoxon test is designed to work with _____ samples.

dependent, matched, paired

2. Whereas the Mann-Whitney test just looked at the values of the ranks, because we are dealing with matched pairs, the Wilcoxon test is concerned with the _____ between the ranks.

difference

3. If a pair of observations shows no (zero) difference, then that pair of observations is simply _____ from the sample.

deleted

Consider these scores from the same students:

Test One	Test Two
90	93
74	71
85	93
69	79
95	84
75	63
87	73
70	87
65	93

Differences
-3
3
-8
-10
11
12
14
-17
-18

4. We can test for significant difference using the Wilcoxon signed rank test. Compute the differences and the ranks for each test.

Rank One	Rank Two
1.5	
	1.5
3	
4	
	5
	6
	7
8	
9	

327

T+ = 25.5
T- = 19.5
Total (T+,T-) = 45

n = 9
(9x10)/2 = 45, it checks

T = 6
T(minimum) = 19.5
no stat sig diff

normal

Rank One	Rank Two
1	
	2
---	---
	4
4	
4	
	6.5
6.5	
	8.5
8.5	
10	
	11
12	
13	
	14.5
---	---
14.5	
16	
17	
	18

5. What are the values of T+ and T- ? (Note: depending upon which test you subtracted from which, your T+ and T- values may be reversed from the answer in this study guide...it makes no difference in the conclusion.) What is the total of T+ plus T-?

6. What is the value of n _____? To check, what should be the total of the sum of the ranks (((n)(n+1))/2)

7. What is the .05 critical value for T(minimum) _____? What is the minimum of T+ and T-? What is our conclusion?

8. In performing the Wilcoxon test upon large samples the level of significance can be determined using the _____ curve.

9. Consider these matched pairs of scores from 20 students: Determine the differences between the pairs and form the rankings for each quiz.

Quiz One	Quiz Two
75	76
75	73
86	86
88	85
75	78
80	83
70	66
75	79
85	80
70	75
70	76
79	72
75	83
80	90
75	60
70	70
75	90
75	93
73	95
80	55

10. Originally there were 20 students in the sample. But what is the useable sample size _____?	18
11. What are the values for T+ and T-? What is the total of T+ plus T-?	T+ = 106.5 T- = 64.5 Total (T+,T-) = 171
12. What is the value of n _____? To check, what should be the total of the sum of the ranks?	n = 18 (18x19)/2 = 171, it checks
13. What is the expected value of U_T? What is the standard deviation?	U_T = 85.5 σ = 22.96
14. What is the Z value using U_T versus T+?	Z = +.914
15. What is the Z value using U_T versus T-?	Z = -.914
16. What is our conclusion based upon these Z values?	no stat sig diff

The Kruskal-Wallis Test

§ 19.3

1. Remembering back to the parametric tests discussed earlier in the book we could use the Z and t tests to test for significant differences between (only two, two or more) means.	only two means
2. (Continuing) We could use analysis of variance to test for significant differences between (only two, two or more) means.	two or more means
3. With respect to nonparametric tests, the Mann-Whitney U test can be used to test for significant differences between (only two, more than two) means.	only two means
4. With respect to nonparametric tests, the Kruskal-Wallis test can be used to test for significant differences between (only two, more than two) means.	two or more means

Let's try the Kruskal-Wallis test on the data we had used previously in the analysis of variance chapter. This problem is #7 from § 11.2. We will need the ranks for the three groups

Rank G1	Rank G2	Rank G3	Group One	Group Two	Group Three
2.5	9	12.5	10	6	3
4	7	11	9	7	4
1	7	10	11	7	5
2.5	5	14	10	8	2
	7	15		7	1
		12.5			3

$T(G1) = 10$
$T(G2) = 35$
$T(G3) = 75$
Total = 120

5. What are the sums from the ranks from the various groups? What is the total of the ranks?

$n = 15$
$(15 \times 16)/2 = 120$

6. What is the value of n _____? To check, what should be the total of the sum of the ranks?

$df = (3-1) = 2$
chi-square value = 5.99

7. The Kruskal-Wallis statistic is tested using the chi-square test. What is the value which is used for the degrees of freedom _____? What is the critical value for the chi-square test (let alpha equal .05)?

KW = 12.35
statistically significant difference
same conclusion as parametric

8. What is the value of the Kruskal-Wallis statistic? What is our conclusion? How does this compare with the parametric result seen earlier?

Now let's try another problem from that parametric section. This was problem #8, § 11.2.

Rank Ty	Rank Hn	Rank Ns	Toyota	Honda	Nissan
3.5	10	7	6	3	5
3.5	12	7	6	1	5
9	1	3.5	4	7	6
3.5	11		6	2	
	7			5	

9. What are the sums from the ranks for the various groups? What is the total of the ranks?	T(G1) = 19.5 T(G2) = 41 T(G3) = 17.5 Total = 78
10. What is the value of n? To check, what should be the total of the sum of the ranks?	n = 12 (12 x 13)/2 = 78
11. The Kruskal-Wallis statistic is tested using the chi-square test. What is the value which is used for the degrees of freedom _____? What is the critical value for the chi-square test (let alpha equal .05)?	df = 2 chi-square = 5.99
12. What is the value of the Kruskal-Wallis statistic? What is our conclusion? How does this compare with the parametric result seen earlier?	KW = 2.03 no stat sig diff same result as parametric
13. In the last two example problems, the Kruskal-Wallis nonparametric test reached the same conclusion that the parametric analysis of variance had reached. Assuming that the data fits the parametric assumptions which test would be preferable? Why?	Choose parametric test, parametric test is stat. more powerful, makes fuller use of the data.
14. (Continuing) What if you did not know whether all of the assumptions had been met...which test should you choose? Why?	Choose nonparametric if you have serious reservations about assumptions
15. Let's try one a bit longer than those last two. Given three groups tested on the same quiz, form the rankings for the groups.	

(next page)

332

Rank G1	Rank G2	Rank G3	Group One	Group Two	Group Three
21.5	28.5	4	76	60	95
17.5	11.5	4	80	85	95
14	31.5	11.5	83	55	85
7	28.5	10	90	60	86
20	28.5	13	78	60	84
4	33	15	95	45	82
19	34.5	4	79	40	95
17.5	23.5	16	80	75	81
26	28.5	8	71	60	89
25	36	23.5	72	15	75
21.5	34.5	4	76	40	95
1	31.5	9	96	55	88

T(G1) = 194
T(G2) = 350
T(G3) = 122
Total = 666

16. What are the sums from the ranks for the various groups? What is the total of the ranks?

n = 36
(36x37)/2 = 666
Revelation 13:18

17. What is the value of n? To check, what should be the total of the sum of the ranks? Hmmm, 666, suspicious sounding number, where is it found?

df = 2
chi-square = 5.99

18. The Kruskal-Wallis statistic is tested using the chi-square test. What is the value which is used for the degrees of freedom _____? What is the critical value for the chi-square test (let alpha equal .05)?

KW = 20.4
stat. sig. diff.

19. What is the value of the Kruskal-Wallis statistic? What is our conclusion?

The Friedman Test

1. The Friedman Test is designed as the nonparametric equivalent of the parametric randomized block design. True or False

True

1. data not normal
2. data ordinal (non-metric)

2. Two situations which would suggest the use of the nonparametric Friedman are :

3. Back in chapter 11 (ANOVA) we worked a problem (#4, § 11.4) where seven people evaluated three different brands of beer. Here is the data from that problem.

Person	Budweiser	Miller	Shiner
1	4	4	5
2	3	4	5
3	2	1	2
4	3	2	2
5	4	3	4
6	5	5	4
7	4	4	5

The Friedman statistic follows an approximate _____ distribution with _____ degrees of freedom.

chi-square
df = k-1 = (3-1) = 2
if alpha = .05, chi-square value from table = 5.99

If we wish to work this same problem using the Friedman test, the first thing which must be done is to convert the scores for each person (each rater's evaluations) into a ranking score.

Person	Budweiser	Miller	Shiner
1	2.5	2.5	1
2	3	2	1
3	1.5	3	1.5
4	1	2.5	2.5
5	2.5	1	2.5
6	1.5	1.5	3
7	2.5	2.5	1
Totals	14.5	15.0	12.5

Friedman statistic:
b = 7
k = 3
FR = 84.5 - 84 = .5

Conclusion:
.5 is much less than 5.99 therefore, no stat. sig. diff
There is not a sig diff between the brands of beer (this is the same conclusion we had reached when this problem was worked previously in Chapter 11.)

Spearman Rank Correlation

§ 19.4

The Spearman Rank Correlation coefficient is designed to compute a measure of correlation (association) between variables which consist only of ranked data.

In problem 12, S 14.1, the correlation coefficient was computed to be .3475. For the data (repeated below) compute the Spearman Rank Order coefficient.

X	Y
3	12
4	13
6	11
4	15
7	16
8	13
9	15

Rank X	Rank Y	d	d^2
1	2	1	1
2.5	3.5	1	1
4	1	3	9
2.5	5.5	3	9
5	7	2	4
6	3.5	2.5	6.25
7	5.5	1.5	2.25
			32.50

n = 7

d^2 = 32.5

1. What is the value of n?

2. What is the value of d^2?

r_s = 1 - (.568) = .432
(compare r_p = .3475)

3. What is the value of the Spearman Correlation Coefficient?

Spearman cutoff = .714
not stat sig

4. What is the .05 cutoff for the Spearman correlation coefficient? What is our conclusion?

Treated as ratio data, a Pearson product-moment correlation coefficient of .87 was computed for the relationship between Study Time and GPA. Here is a repeat of that data set.

Study	GPA
2.4	3.9
1.7	3.5
2.6	3.4
2.1	3.2
1.3	3.1
1.4	2.8
1.6	2.5
1.5	2.1
.5	1.8
.1	1.4

Rank X	Rank Y	d	d^2
9	10	1	1
7	9	2	4
10	8	2	4
8	7	1	1
3	6	3	9
4	5	1	1
6	4	2	4
5	3	2	4
2	2	0	0
1	1	0	0
			18

n = 10

5. What is the value of n?

6. Continuing...what is the value of d^2? | $d^2 = 28$

7. What is the value of the Spearman correlation coefficient? | $1 - (.169) = .831$
(compare $r_p = .87$)

8. What is the .05 cutoff for the Spearman correlation coefficient? What is our conclusion? | .564
Statistically significant correlation between Study and GPA...Aren't you glad you have been studying? It all was worthwhile after all. Good Luck and God Bless.